Unlocking
The Zohar

LAITMAN
KABBALAH PUBLISHERS

Michael Laitman

UNLOCKING THE ZOHAR

ISBN 978-1-897448-59-5
Library of Congress Control Number: 2011903649

Copy Editor: C. Gerus

Associate Editors: N. Burnot, D. Rudder, G. Shadmon, D. Aharoni,
A. Sofer, L. Gur, L. Navon, M. Admoni, A. Ohayon, D. Nahari, M. Visel,
P. Yahod Netanel, S. Mimon, T. Yichia

Zohar for All Editors: B. Girtz, M. Cohen, A. Cherniavsky, T. Yfhar,
H. Rozenwasser, L. Vigdor, L. Peles Chen, A. Mula, L. Shema Pinhas,
M. Yichia, D. Akerman, N. Doyev, Y. Wolfman, G. Baumfeld, M. Sinklair,
S. Havani, H. Levi, G. Izhakov, K. Gabay, T. Refaeli, N. Levi, N. Hassid,
A. Rozenwasser, Y. Gruver, B. Farjoon, M. Bar, V. Dvash

Translation: C. Ratz

Cover and Layout Design: Studio Yaniv, B. Khovov

Executive Editor: O. Levi

Publishing and Post Production: Uri Laitman

FIRST EDITION: DECEMBER 2011
FIRST PRINTING 2011

CONTENTS

FOREWORD

"And the wise shall shine as the brightness of the firma-ment"...They are the ones who exert in this brightness, called The Book of Zohar.

The Book of Zohar,
Behaalotcha [When You Raise], Item 88

*T*he Book of Zohar contains a very special force that can bring us to perfect, utter bliss. It is thrilling, exciting, and mesmerizing to the point that those who read it crave never to stop reading. For those delving into it, *The Zohar* is a source of energy and vitality. With *The Zohar*, we can begin a new life and bond with the good and pleasurable that exists in the world.

Unlocking the Zohar is the introductory volume in a series of books titled *Zohar for All*, which is a reader-friendly edition of *The Book of Zohar*. To make the best of the series, it is recommended to first read this book, which will usher the reader into the right approach when reading *The Zohar*, thus maximizing the benefits of engaging in it.

No prior knowledge is required when reading this book. Part 1 explains the essence of the wisdom of *The Zohar*, the reasons for its concealment for so many years, and how it can benefit us today. Part 2 talks about the way we perceive reality and the plan of Creation, and finally, how we will unlock *The Zohar* together to hopefully decode its secret.

As a special treat for the curious among the readers, Appendix 3 contains selected excerpts from *Zohar for All*. After reading this book, you will be able to feel the power of *The Zohar* and enjoy its benefits.

The Zohar is to be concealed ... until the arrival of the last generation at the end of days, and then it will appear.

Rav Isaiah Horowitz (the Holy Shlah)

THE GREATNESS OF THE BOOK OF ZOHAR

One who has never seen the light of *The Book of Zohar* has never seen light in his life.

Rabbi Tzvi Hirsh Eichenstein of Ziditshov[1]

The prohibition from Above to refrain from open study of the wisdom of truth was for a limited period, until the end of 1490. Thereafter, it is considered the last generation, in which the prohibition was lifted and permission has been granted to engage in *The Book of Zohar*. And since the year 1540, it has been a great *Mitzva* (commandment) for the masses to study, old and young.

Abraham Ben Mordechai Azulai[2]

And because Israel are destined to taste from the tree of life, which is *The Book of Zohar*, through it, they will be delivered from exile with mercy.

The Book of Zohar, *Nasso* [Take], Item 90

Now the time requires accelerated acquisition of the inner Torah. *The Book of Zohar* breaks new paths, makes a highway in the desert. *The Zohar* and all its yield are ready to open the doors of redemption.

The Rav Raiah Kook[3]

The livelihood of the person of Israel depends on *The Book of Zohar*.

Rav Yitzhak Yehuda Yehiel Safrin of Komarno[4]

I

The Wisdom of
The Zohar

TIME TO ACT

The whole of the wisdom of Kabbalah is only to know the guidance of the Higher Will, why It has created all these creatures, what It wants with them, and what the end of all the cycles of the world will be.

Ramchal, *Pitchei Hochma* (*Doors of Wisdom*), Door no. 30

*T*he Zohar is THE book of the wisdom of Kabbalah, the wisdom of truth. It is surfacing today to lead us forward to a higher dimension. Yet, what is so special about *The Zohar* and about the Kabbalah? Why is this wisdom taking center stage specifically for those living today?

Humanity is ever developing. In ancient times, people's needs were very basic: food, shelter, and procreation. These are natural desires, as well as existential needs. In time, greater needs and greater desires have arisen in us: for wealth, domination, respect, and knowledge.

Throughout history, we have been trying to satisfy the needs that emerged in us. We have been trying to find within these changes happiness, love, and a good life. Today, we see that this chase was futile. While each generation is more advanced materialistically, each also suffers more. The ubiquitous use of drugs and antidepressants as an escape are symptoms of our generation's internal emptiness.

At each given moment, the media is presenting us with more and more temptations, which we then rush to satisfy. It may be a new piece of clothing, a car, a house, a better job, an academic title, a trip overseas, or even a good restaurant. But each time we obtain something, the pleasure dissipates shortly afterwards and we are left wondering, "What's next?" Then the chase begins anew.

For how long? Today, more and more people are asking this question. And not only, "For how long?" but also, "Why?"

Why are our lives unfolding as they are? Why are we in a constant race, never actually finding any rest? Why does everything become dull and tasteless once we have obtained it? And in general, if this is what life is about and there is nothing we can do about it, why do we need it anyway?

There has never been such a state where questions about the purpose and meaning of life have arisen in so many people. In the past, we simply didn't ask. We lived because we were born. But today, such questions that suddenly arise within us leave us restless, prodding us forward, and after years of searching we come to the wisdom of Kabbalah, the wisdom that teaches us how to receive much more from life.

Previously, we had no need for Kabbalah, hence its concealment. But today, our need for it is the primary reason for its appearance in our generation.

The second reason is the special situation we are in today. The development of technology and media has turned the world into a small village in which we are completely interdependent. Yet, at the same time, our egos and our hatred of one another are increasing.

It is becoming barely possible for us to tolerate others, beginning on the most personal level, where each member of a family needs a personal room, a personal car, and virtually a personal home. People find it very difficult to maintain relationships, and divorce rates are soaring. The family unit is falling apart the world over.

We are living together, cramped on a tiny planet, antagonistic towards each other and unable to get along. The amount of weapons of mass destruction accumulated worldwide have brought us to a perilous state where everything around us is unstable and unpredictable. It is safe to say that we have lost our ability to govern the world.

Looking forward, if we continue on our present path, it is unclear how we will survive. What kind of world are we leaving for our children? Today's generation is the first in which people have stopped believing that their children will have a better life than their own!

With all this in the background, *The Book of Zohar* and the other sources of Kabbalah are appearing. They explain that the situation we now face has long been predicted.

The first time such a state occurred was thousands of years ago in ancient Babylon. The Biblical story about the Tower of Babel described people gathered in one place, wishing to build a tower whose top reached the sky. This was an expression of the great egoism that appeared among them, and the hatred combined with interdependence. It was precisely in that place and in that state that the wisdom of Kabbalah appeared.

The wisdom offers a very simple thing. It says that in addition to the reality we currently sense, there is another, more expansive reality, a higher one. From this higher reality, forces extend to our world and govern it. The development we have achieved over the generations was intended to bring us into recognizing the forces that operate on us and govern us.

When we discover this higher reality, we will understand that our development over thousands of years has taken place only to bring us to acquire and experience a more expansive sensation of reality. Thus, we will not remain in the confined state in which we live and die, live and die. Instead, we will know life in its eternal, broad, and boundless form.

Man was made to raise the heavens

Rabbi Menahem Mendel of Kotzk

In ancient Babylon, it was Abraham the Patriarch, a resident of Ur of the Chaldeans, who discovered that humankind's program of development was prodding it toward discovering a new reality. Abraham realized that in the end, the material evolution of man on earth would exhaust itself, and humanity would discover that something beyond satisfying corporeal desires was required, and that without it, life on earth would be futile and meaningless.

Abraham discovered that at the end of the material evolution begins the spiritual evolution. Once he himself exhausted the desires we all possess, a new desire appeared in him—to understand the purpose of his life.

In Kabbalah, all of one's earthly desires are regarded as "the heart," while the desire to discover the meaning of life is described as "the point in the heart." The point in the heart is a desire that awakens in our hearts and pulls us "upward." That new desire led Abraham to discover the complete reality, the spiritual reality.

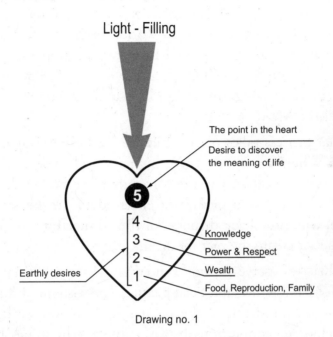

Drawing no. 1

Abraham's wisdom is called "the wisdom of Kabbalah," and it describes the network of Nature's forces and how we can study the program by which they affect us. The wisdom of Kabbalah describes rules, forces, and work formulae of the upper worlds.

Kabbalah explains how reality began to expand from the world of *Ein Sof* [infinity], through the worlds of *Adam Kadmon* [ancient man], *Atzilut* [Emanation], *Beria* [Creation], *Yetzira* [Formation], and *Assiya* [Action], down to our world. It speaks of how souls come

Drawing no. 2

down and "dress" in bodies in this world, and how we can cause our souls to rise from here back to the world of *Ein Sof*.

Abraham was the first Kabbalist to teach people how to discover the soul and gradually experience a higher world through it. There are five higher worlds, each with five degrees, each of which are then divided into five additional degrees. If we multiply 5x5x5, we will arrive at the 125 degrees by which we ascend in our feeling, understanding, and attainment until we discover the whole of reality.

That process takes place while we are here in our material bodies. When we achieve these higher worlds, reality becomes much broader and we feel the forces that operate on the world we are in. It is like a picture of embroidery. In the front is a picture, while the back displays all the connections among the threads that create the picture on the front.

When we observe our world and what is happening in it, we are merely observing the superficial picture. The wisdom of Kabbalah helps us see the depth of the picture. This is how we begin to understand the connections between things—why things happen and how we can affect one element through another element.

In other words, we not only see the image of this world, but we also begin to see the operating system. Only then can we control our lives and our fates, and arrive at the perfect state.

The wisdom of Kabbalah explains that our lives are built in such a way that troubles of all kinds present themselves before us, leaving us no other alternative but to know the operating system. If we do not achieve the higher dimension, discover the forces that affect us, and

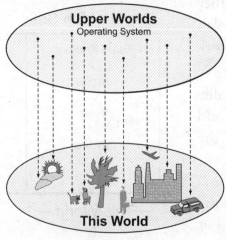

Drawing no. 3

begin to manage our lives through them, we will not be able to cope in life. This is why this wisdom is manifesting itself—so we can know the upper worlds.

Kabbalah explains everything that has happened in human history: why we have developed one way and not another, and why all the wars and changes we have undergone took place. It also relates to the future and describes how we can evolve from this point on.

There are two paths before us:

1. To escape from the bad—to evolve through a negative force that prods us from behind, as we have been doing throughout history: We would discover that something was missing and that we had no other choice but to exit the negative state and make a change.

2. To be drawn toward the good—to evolve through a positive force that pulls us forward. This is what Kabbalah offers us: to evolve by discovering the good life and then understand how to achieve it through a wondrous adventure.

The sages of the Kabbalah have predicted our state in advance. They knew that without the Kabbalah we would not be abele to survive. They pointed to the end of the 20th century as the time when its wisdom would appear to all. They explained that if we did not shift from negative advancement to positive, we would be goaded into it mercilessly.*

---

* Kabbalists refer to the two paths toward knowing the upper worlds as the "path of Torah" [path of light] and the "path of suffering." In his "Writings of the Last Generation," Baal HaSulam explains it in the following way: "There are two ways to discover the completeness: the path of Torah and the path of suffering. Hence, the Creator eventuated and gave humanity technology, until they have invented the atom and the hydrogen bombs. If the total ruin that they are destined to bring is still not evident to the world, they can wait for a third world war, or a fourth one and so on. The bombs will do their thing and the relics after the ruin will have no other choice but to take upon themselves this work ... If you take the path of Torah, all will be well. And if you do not, then you will tread the path of suffering."

For more on this topic, see Baal HaSulam's "Introduction to The Book of Zohar" (item 16), "Introduction to the book, The Tree of Life" (item 7), and the essay, "The Peace."

But we are faced with problems not only on the social level, but also on the ecological level, including volcanic eruptions, earthquakes, tsunamis, hurricanes, fires, intense heat waves, and cold spells. All these will come only to compel us to continue our development. Nature is shaking us up through a negative force so we will take the positive force into our hands.

To advance, we must first discover the forces that come down to here and affect us. We must learn how to penetrate Nature's higher system if we are to govern these forces. Even when we wish to develop technologies to improve our lives, we must first study Nature and discover which hidden laws exist in it and how it governs. But because Kabbalah speaks of even higher forces, more concealed, the process of discovering them is far more complex. It is truly a fascinating process, and we will expand on it in the next chapter.

> This wisdom is no more and no less than a sequence of roots, which hang down by way of cause and consequence, by fixed, determined rules, interweaving to a single, exalted goal described as "The revelation of His Godliness to His creatures in this world."
>
> Baal HaSulam, "The Essence of the Wisdom of Kabbalah"

Since Abraham's time some 3,800 years ago, until approximately 2,000 years ago, the wisdom of Kabbalah was known only to the people of Israel. Since the ruin of the Temple approximately 2,000 years ago, through our generation, Kabbalah has been hidden from the public and has been secretly passed on from generation to generation among Kabbalists.

During the period when Kabbalah was concealed, various stigmas were attributed to it. It was considered mysticism, witchcraft, magic, etc., but no one knew what it was really about, hence the false notions. Also, the thriving present-day industry that uses the name "Kabbalah" to market services and products has nothing whatsoever to do with the actual essence of the wisdom of Kabbalah.

But the time of concealment has ended. Today, the original wisdom of Kabbalah is resurfacing for all people, regardless of age, sex, religion or race. Kabbalah is a higher science. It does not belong to any religion or faith, nor does it pose any boundaries or limitations to one who wishes to study it. Any person who wishes to understand the world he or she lives in, to know the soul, to know one's fate and to learn how to govern it is welcome to study Kabbalah.

"If my people heeded me ... they would delve in the study of *The Book of Zohar* ... with nine-year-old infants,"[5] said Kabbalist Rabbi Yitzhak Yehuda of Komarno as early as the 19th century. Following him, other Kabbalists recommended teaching this knowledge to children from a young age, giving them an explanation of the world that surrounds them, the connections among its parts, and the forces that affect it. Through such education grows a confident human being connected to the source of abundance, feeling in control of one's life. Such a person knows how to best use these forces, and understands that life is unlimited.

The holy *Zohar* connects to *Ein Sof* [infinity].

Rabbi Moshe Israel Bar Elijahu, *The Residue of Israel*[6]

The Book of Zohar is the seminal book of Kabbalah. It was written precisely when Kabbalah shifted from being an open doctrine to becoming a hidden one. The authors of *The Zohar* knew that the world would need this book thousands of years later, hence they concealed it immediately after writing it.

The *Book of Zohar* was actually written for this generation, to deliver us from a state of "spiritual exile," the inability to perceive the upper force and the expansiveness of reality. If we wish to improve our situation, we must make *The Book of Zohar* the keynote book of our world, since *The Zohar* is more than a book, it is a means to connect us to the upper force.

When we learn how to read *The Zohar* correctly, we will discover that it is a means of receiving abundance, and we will see how, with its help, everything changes. Gradually, we will begin to feel that another force is present, a higher and good one, engulfing us, and the air is "imbued" with that force.

In conclusion: Nature has brought us to a special point in human development, a step before a new degree of existence. We are about to make a qualitative leap to the spiritual degree, and this is why the springboard—the wisdom of Kabbalah and primarily *The Book of Zohar*—is appearing before us.

In the depths of the human soul, the voice of the Lord is ever calling. The commotion of life may daze the soul so it does not hear that calling voice for the majority of one's life, but it can never uproot the basis, the root, and the essence of that voice, which is indeed the very heart of human life ... Even in those who strain to escape it and to silence it, the fleeing and the silencing only further disclose the inherent connection of the soul to that mighty voice, which never ceases to hum and to crave in their hearts, too. Indeed, all efforts to escape it and all tactics to silence it are in vain.

Rav Raiah Kook, *Treasures of the Raiah*, p 113

A HIDDEN TREASURE

The greatest Kabbalist of our time was Rav Yehuda Ashlag (1884-1954). Thanks to his work, *The Book of Zohar* began to become known. Rav Ashlag is known as Baal HaSulam [Hebrew: Owner of the Ladder] for his *Sulam* [Ladder] commentary on *The Book of Zohar*. In his latter years, Baal HaSulam wrote what is known as "Writings of the Last Generation," which begin with the following words:

"There is an allegory about friends who were lost in the desert, hungry and thirsty. One of them had found a settlement filled abundantly with every delight. He remembered his poor brothers, but he had already drawn far off from them and did not know their place. What did he do? He began to shout out loud and blow the horn; perhaps his poor hungry friends would hear his voice, approach and come to that abundant settlement filled with every delight.

"So is the matter before us: we have been lost in the terrible desert along with all mankind, and now we have found a great, abundant treasure, namely the books of Kabbalah in the treasure.

... "Now, distinguished readers, this book lies here before you in a closet. It states explicitly all the wisdom of statesmanship and the behavior of private and public life that will exist at the end of days, meaning the books of Kabbalah...

"Open these books and you will find all the good comportment that will appear and the end of days, and you will find within them the good lesson by which to arrange mundane matters today, as well."

2

NATURE AND US

It is best for us to accept the words of Kabbalist, that HaTeva [the nature] is equal [in Gematria] to Elokim [God].

Baal HaSulam, "The Peace"

*T*he Book of Zohar explains that we exist in a single, vast system, called "Nature" or *Elokim* [God], yet we sense only a fraction of that system, a fraction called "this world."

The purpose of our existence is to rise above the boundaries of this world and feel the entirety of the system known as "Nature," the upper force. When we achieve this degree, we will be filled with abundance, infinite pleasure and light, with sublime perception and understanding, a sense of balance, wholeness, and harmony as they exist in the overall Nature.

To understand what we must do to arrive at all this bounty, *The Zohar* recommends that we examine Nature's conduct from a slightly broader angle than usual.

Our world is a closed world. We exist in a single, general system whose every part is interconnected. We cannot consider ourselves above Nature and omnipotent; it is a sure way of destroying ourselves. We also cannot escape Nature because we are an integral part of it. Hence, we must study the general law of Nature and go hand in hand with it.

Our urge to evolve is wonderful, but we must do it in the right way, towards a healthy connection between us and the rest of Creation in a way that does not violate the harmony and the overall balance of Nature. This, in fact, is the basis of the wisdom of Kabbalah.

Observing Nature teaches us that all living organisms are built on the basis of caring for others. Cells in an organism connect to each other by mutual giving for the purpose of sustaining the whole organism. Each cell in the body receives what it needs for its existence and spends the rest of its efforts caring for the entirety of the organism. An inconsiderate cell that does not take its environment into consideration and harnesses it for its own good is a cancerous cell. Such a selfish act eventually leads to the death of the entire organism.

At the levels of inanimate, vegetative, and animate, the specific acts for the good of the general and finds its completeness in that. Without such harmonious activity, existence would not be possible. The only exception is human society. Why? Because unlike the other degrees, where Nature's law enforces balance and harmony, Nature has given human beings free choice, a place for their conscious participation in the overall harmony of Nature.

If we take part in the system incorrectly, the corruption we inflict reflects on us and we experience it as suffering. Thus, gradually, over thousands of generations, Nature is leading us to understand that we must study its overall law and eventually act accordingly.

The problem is that we do not feel Nature's comprehensive force affecting us—the force of love and giving—also known as the "Creator." However, today science is advancing toward discovering that Nature has a "mind," "emotion," and the power of great wisdom that sustains and governs everything. And yet, our egos do not wish us to see it.

The current state of the world proves that such blindness and unawareness of Nature's system cannot last. Baal HaSulam wrote about it in the 1930s: "Now it is vitally important for us to examine Nature's commandments, to know what it demands of us, lest it would mercilessly punish us" (Baal HaSulam, "The Peace").

DISCOVERING NATURE'S OVERALL LAW

The will to receive is the whole substance of Creation from beginning to end.

Baal HaSulam, "Preface to the Wisdom of Kabbalah," Item 1

When we want to be impressed by something, whether emotionally, intellectually, or otherwise, we must be on the same "wavelength" with it and thus possess the same quality. For example, to detect radio waves, the receiver must produce the same wavelength, and only then can we detect the wave on the outside.

Nature's overall force is a "desire to give," to bestow, to impart abundance. Conversely, our nature is one of "desire to receive delight and pleasure," a desire to enjoy for ourselves alone. Our nature is self-centered; it is how we were made, as Kabbalah tells us. In other words, we are in contrast with the upper force, opposite from it, and hence we cannot sense it.

Is there anything we *can* do to sense it? We cannot destroy our nature and our will to receive, nor do we need to. We should continue with our lives as usual, and at the same time acquire new tools of perception.

But where can we find such an instrument that will supplement us with the new nature—to give—in addition to our original nature—to receive? Here, the wisdom of Kabbalah comes to our aid. At the moment, we are receivers. We absorb. And if we do give something to someone, it is only after we have calculated that it is worthwhile for us to do so. Our nature prevents us from giving without receiving something in return. It simply denies us the energy to perform an act that does not yield profit.

We are willing to give $50 if we receive $100 in return. We might also give $80 in return for $100. But if we try to give $101 in return for $100 it is impossible. This modus operandi is true not only with money or an act toward others, but for *anything*, as Baal HaSulam explained it:

It is well known to researchers of Nature that one cannot perform even the slightest movement without motivation, without somehow benefiting oneself. When, for example, one moves one's hand from the chair to the table, it is because one thinks that by putting the hand on the table will be more enjoyable. If he did not think so, he would leave his hand on the chair for the rest of his life without moving it at all. It is all the more so with greater efforts.

Baal HaSulam, "The Peace"

Even people who assist other people more than most, such as volunteers at hospitals or elsewhere, do it only because, at the end of the day, it gives *them* pleasure.

Baal HaSulam explains that within humanity, there are always up to ten percent "natural born altruists." Such people respond to others a little differently than most. They sympathize with others and feel their pain as though it were their own, and this feeling compels them to try to help others. Naturally, this altruistic inclination rests on a self-centered basis that requires correction, too, but it is hidden from the eye, as studies in behavioral genetics demonstrate.*

Man's very essence is only to receive for oneself. By nature, we are unable to do even the smallest thing to benefit others. Instead, when we give to others, we are compelled to expect that in the end, we will receive a worthwhile reward.

Baal HaSulam, "A Speech for the Completion of The Zohar"

To begin to understand how the wisdom of Kabbalah assists us in sensing the upper force, consider a growing child. There is nothing more natural than the process of maturing, hence this comparison will accompany us throughout the book.

When a baby is born, it begins to hear, to see, and to react. It learns and develops from examples that we present to it.

If we left the baby to grow in the woods, it would imitate the animals and grow like an animal. With the exception of a few instincts and reflexes, everything about us comes from learning.

Can we learn the upper system in the same way if we do not feel it? How can we be like that baby, or even a drop of semen that only wishes to be born into a new quality called "giving"?

In other words, a human infant evolves out of a drop of corporeal semen. It learns from examples and eventually becomes

---

* Changing certain gene sequences affects a person's ability to be good to others, Prof. Ebstein and a team of researchers in behavioral genetics discovered. The researchers assume that there is an immediate reward for altruistic behavior in the form of a chemical called "dopamine," released in the benefactor's brain and prompting a pleasant feeling.

M. R. Bachner, I. Gritsenko, L. Nemanov, A. H. Zohar, C. Dina & R. P. Ebstein, "Dopaminergic Polymorphisms Associated with Self-Report Measures of Human Altruism: A Fresh Phenotype for the Dopamine D4 Receptor", *Molecular Psychiatry* 10(4), April 2005, pp. 333—335.

a grownup. And now, a drop of spiritual seed, called "the point in the heart," appears in that person, a new desire—to know what he or she is living for, to reach what exists beyond life, the force that affects us and operates us. In corporeal growth, the ego develops and the quality of reception for oneself becomes improved. In the process of spiritual growth, the quality of *giving* develops in us.

So what do we need in order to commence the process? We need examples—spiritual teachers. This is why *The Book of Zohar* was written. Just as children stare with eyes wide open and jaws dropped, craving to devour the world and learn all about it, we should approach *The Book of Zohar*, which provides us with examples of the quality of giving.

The more we learn how to give, the more we will resemble Nature's comprehensive power, the power of love and giving. In Kabbalah terminology, it is called "equivalence of form," which is a gradual process that leads to our sensing Nature's overall force to the extent that we become similar to it.

THE ZOHAR—A BOOK OF MANY LAYERS

Studying The Zohar builds worlds.

Rabbi Shalom Ben Moshe Buzzaglo, *The King's Throne*[7]

Ten Kabbalists, headed by Rabbi Shimon Bar Yochai (Rashbi), joined together at the highest spiritual degree. From their union, they wrote *The Zohar* for us. *The Zohar* is not merely a book. It is a closed system, from our level to the highest level of reality. It is a system designed to launch us into experiencing unbounded existence, both in understanding and feeling the whole of Nature.

The book is built in a very special way. It speaks of things that seemingly happen in our world: stories about people, animals, trees and flowers, mountains and hills. However, in truth, it tells us about the soul and the higher forces.

Thousands of years after the writing of *The Zohar*, the greatest Kabbalist of the 20th century, Baal HaSulam, wrote the *Sulam* [Ladder] commentary on *The Zohar*, where he explained *The Zohar* in the language of Kabbalah. The language of Kabbalah helps us put the pieces together and understand what is really being said in *The Zohar*.

When you read *The Zohar* with the *Sulam* commentary, even without first understanding how everything unfolds, *The Zohar* begins to change our perception into an opposite perception. It changes our attitude toward the world. *The Zohar* provides examples that connect us to our next state, a more evolved state in giving.

It is similar to the way we rear our children. We continue to show them examples of a slightly more advanced state in order to develop them. Thus, we gradually bring them to more evolved states. *The Zohar* affects us similarly, unveiling the next degree that awaits us.

The world we currently experience is the lowest and worst state that exists in reality. We have been deliberately brought down to it through 125 degrees from the highest state of the overall power of reality.

In our initial state, our current one, the next degree is right before us: me+1. Then comes the next degree: me+2, then me+3, and so forth. There are 125 before us, each containing a piece of information that defines the way we should be. In the language of Kabbalah, this piece is called *Reshimo* [recollection]. We will elaborate on it further in the book because it has a crucial impact on our lives.

The connection between our current selves and the self of our next degree is formed using *The Book of Zohar*. Just like a parent, *The Zohar* elevates us from one world to another. A "world" means the current state we are in, and a "higher world" or "upper world" means our higher state.

It is important to understand that in the course of our spiritual development, we do not "vanish" from this world. We do not stop working or functioning as usual. Rather, a sensation of the force that actually operates in reality is added to our lives. We come to a state where the whole of reality appears as a single entity, a single system. We feel that there is one force operating here—eternal, whole, beyond time, space, and motion. This is what *The Book of Zohar* helps us to discover.

All the conducts of Creation, in its every corner, inlet, and outlet, are completely prearranged for the purpose of nurturing the human species from its midst, to improve its qualities until we can sense Godliness as one feels one's friend.

Baal HaSulam "The Essence of Religion and Its Purpose"

LETTERS AND WORDS

Let us now approach the first reading of *The Book of Zohar*. The excerpt below is taken from the portion *VaYikra* [The Lord Called], and discusses letters.

"Ask for a letter from the Lord your God; ask either in the depth, or raise it above. What is the difference between the first generations and the last generations? The first generations knew and observed the high wisdom; they knew how to put together the letters that Moses was given in Sinai. ...And we know that in the upper letters that extend from *Bina*, and in the lower letters that extend from *Malchut*, it is wise to conduct actions in this world."[8]

Where do letters come from? They come from the upper force. I must demand of the upper force to give me letters.

What are "letters"? Letters are forms by which I turn my substance—the will to receive, the ego—into being similar to the upper force—the power of love and giving. Each letter is a new form of giving that I have built within me, and in which I am somewhat similar to the upper force.

I must put the letters that I receive together into "words," which are spiritual operations of transforming from one form to another, from the form of one letter to the form of another letter. When I perform such actions, it is as though I am "speaking" with the upper force, and it is speaking with me. Thus, we have a common language.

When such a "conversation" between me and the upper force takes place and I become capable of "listening" to its words, I become its partner and I acquire all of the high wisdom. This is how Baal HaSulam explains it in his essay, "The Teaching of the Kabbalah and Its Essence."

3
THE ZOHAR RETURNS TO ALL

When Israel come out of exile ... the world will know
the sublime and precious wisdom that they have never
known before.

The Book of Zohar, VaYera [The Lord Appeared], Items 157-158.

Anything that people need spreads naturally in the world. But when it comes to *The Zohar* and the Kabbalah, matters are not that straightforward.

The disclosure of the writings of Kabbalah has been accompanied by intriguing stories. *The Book of Zohar* has undergone many hardships, and only a small portion of the original manuscript remains today. The writings of the Ari [Rav Isaac Luria, author of *The Tree of Life*], were dug out of his grave only three generations after his demise. Indeed, there is a special integration of revealed and concealed, and painful labor pangs when it comes to expanding the wisdom of Kabbalah.

Baal HaSulam made great efforts to publish his interpretation on *The Zohar*, the *Sulam* [Ladder] commentary, and wrote as much as 20 hours a day. When he fell asleep on his desk, it was hard to pull the pen out of his hand because his fingers were cramped around it.

For lack of funds to print the manuscripts, he had to wait until he could find the resources. And once he found them, he arranged the lead letters in the printing press by himself, although he was already ill and very weak. Yet, volume by volume, his life's work was completed.

Still, people were afraid to open *The Zohar* and preferred to stay clear of it. As early as 1933, Baal HaSulam began to disseminate the wisdom of Kabbalah in an effort to prevent the looming holocaust. "Time to Act" was the title of his opening essay in the first tract that he printed—out of fifty that he had planned to publish. However, his work was frowned upon by certain orthodox circles, and within a few weeks they managed to apprehend the printing of the tracts to prevent the expansion of the wisdom.

In 1940, Baal HaSulam published a paper, *The Nation*, in which he called upon the Israeli nation to unite. His wish was to establish a by-weekly paper, but the paper initiative, too, was thwarted after the publication of the first issue.

In the 1950s, Baal HaSulam described the situation with a mixture of great sadness and hopes for the future:

> *I have already conveyed the rudiments of my perception in 1933. I have also spoken to the leaders of the generation, but at the time, my words were not accepted, though I was screaming like a banshee, warning about the destruction of the world. Alas, it made no impression. Now, however, after the atom and hydrogen bombs, I think that the world will believe me that the end of the world is coming rapidly, and Israel will be the first*

nation to burn, as in the previous war. Thus, today it is good to awaken the world to accept the only remedy, and they will live and exist.

Baal HaSulam, "Writings of the Last Generation," Part 1, Section 2

The question that arises out of all that is "Why does everything that concerns the disclosure of the wisdom of Kabbalah happens in such an odd way and evokes so much resistance?" After all, it is a wisdom that discusses human psychology, our inner makeup, family values, education and culture, conducts of Nature and the foundation of Creation. Don't we need this information?

Whatever the case may be, within each of us is a special feeling, a kind of internal recoil from *The Book of Zohar* and the wisdom of Kabbalah, which originates in our very nature. What separates Kabbalah from any other teaching is the issue of correction. Kabbalah talks about how we should correct ourselves, change our attitude toward ourselves and toward those around us, so it is only natural that our egos wince at that dictate.

The sages of Kabbalah certainly knew all that, which is why they hid the wisdom for millennia until the moment was ripe and people would really need it. They themselves were the ones who stirred the public away from it, declaring strict limitations on studying it: age 40 or above, men only, married, and only after having been filled with all the other parts of the Torah. The sages also spread rumors that Kabbalah could make you lose your sanity!

In previous generations, the desire to discover the spiritual world still did not awaken in the hearts of most people; hence, the wisdom of Kabbalah was kept hidden. However, if the desire did awaken in anyone, the wisdom was opened to that person. The Ari [Isaac Luria], Chaim Vital, the Baal Shem Tov, the Vilna Gaon, the Ramchal, Rabbi Nachman of Breslov, and many others studied and taught the wisdom of Kabbalah long before they reached the age of 40. In our generation, this desire is awakening in millions of people the world over, hence the wisdom is being shared openly with the public.

As we mentioned earlier, the process of revealing and concealing the wisdom is not new. It actually began over 5,770 years ago. This is when the first human discovered the spiritual world. Many generations of humans lived before his time, but he was the first in whom the desire for what lies beyond the boundaries of this world appeared. His name was Adam, from the words *Adame la Elyon* [I will be like the most high],[9] and he was the first Kabbalist, the first person to ascend in qualities and discover the upper force.

> *Adam ha Rishon [The First Man] was the first to receive a sequence of sufficient knowledge by which to understand and to successfully maximize everything he saw and attained with his eyes. And this understanding is called "the wisdom of truth."*
>
> Baal HaSulam, "The Teaching of the Kabbalah and Its Essence"

The day that Adam began to discover the upper force is called "the day of the creation of the world." On that day, humanity first touched the spiritual world. This is why Adam's existence is the point from which the Hebrew count of years begins.

According to Nature's plan, the whole of humanity will discover the upper force within 6,000 years.[10] During those years, the human ego is to gradually grow and bring humanity to the realization that it must be corrected, as well as to the ability to understand the correction method and to implement it.

The first Kabbalah book, *Angel Raziel*—meaning the "hidden force," the force of Nature, which governs us but is hidden from us—is attributed to Adam. According to Kabbalah, angels are not winged heavenly entities, but forces acting in Nature.

Adam did not rush to the announce his discoveries to the world. For ten generations, the knowledge was quietly passed on from Kabbalist to Kabbalist until the generation of Noah. From there it was passed on through ten more generations until the generation of Abraham.

During the twenty generations that had passed between Adam and Abraham, conditions had changed. In Abraham's time, humanity was centered in Babylon and lived as a big family, as it is written, "And the whole earth was of one language and of one speech."[11] People sensed each other, lived in harmony among themselves and with Nature, until the first substantial burst of the ego occurred. In the Bible, it is described as the story of the tower of Babel:

Nimrod said to his people, "Let us build us a great city and dwell within it, lest we become scattered across the earth like the first ones, and let us build a great tower within it, rising upward to the heaven ... and let us make us a great name in the land..."

> They built it high ... those who would bring up the bricks came from its eastern side, and those who would come down, would come down from its western side. And if a person fell and died, they would not mind him. But if a brick fell, they would sit and cry and say, "When will another rise in its stead."
>
> Chapters of Rabbi Eliezar, Chapter 24

The tower of Babel symbolizes the tower of human egoism. Nimrod, who leads the building of the tower, symbolizes the desire to rebel, to disobey Nature's comprehensive law of balance and giving.

Because he wished to understand what was happening to his people, Abraham began to look into the nature of Creation. He discovered that the leap in egoism was not coincidental, but a preordained move in Nature's development plan. Abraham found that the ego did not intensify to separate people, but to make them unite at a higher level and discover the upper force that was causing this shift. He tried to prevent the destruction and to explain to people how to rise above the hatred and the separation.

> Abraham, son of Terach, went by and saw them building the city and the tower ... but they loathed his words ... They wished to speak each other's language but they did not know each other's language. What did they do? They each took his sword and fought one another to death. Indeed, half the world died there by the sword.
>
> *Chapters of Rabbi Eliezar*, Chapter 24

Yet, Abraham did not give up. He continued to circulate the wisdom he had discovered with all his might because he knew that among his contemporaries were people who were already ripe for development. This is how Maimonides describes it:

> At forty years of age, Abraham came to know his Maker. ...He was calling out, wandering from town to town and from kingdom to kingdom ... Finally, tens of thousands assembled around him, and they are the people of the house of Abraham. ...This continued and expanded in the children of Jacob and in those accompanying them, and a nation that knows the Lord was made in the world.
>
> Maimonides, *Mishneh Torah (Repetition of the Torah)*,
> Idolatry Rules, Chapter 1, 11-16

The Book of Creation, attributed to Abraham, explains the system that governs reality. The book speaks not only of a single, comprehensive force, but about its entire system and subsystems, about primary and secondary forces through which that single force affects us.

The Book of Creation describes the 32 paths towards affecting the whole of reality—how these systems work, and how they cascade in hierarchy from degree to degree until they reach us and operate on us.

Abraham and his wife, Sarah, made great efforts to explain and circulate this new information. They gathered around them people who felt as they did—that this life was given to us only so that during it, we will reach a higher dimension of existence. In so doing, we can attain spirituality and wholeness and exist forever at the "human" degree, similar to the upper force.

To those who were still not ready to perceive the wisdom of Kabbalah, Abraham gave "gifts," as it is written, "But to the sons of his concubines, Abraham gave gifts, and sent them ... to the land of the east".[12] Those gifts are the foundations of all the belief systems that people would follow for millennia until they ripen and grow.

The group of Kabbalists, Abraham's successors, used the correction method that it learned from him over several generations until another burst of egoism took place. Then, a need arose to disclose the correction method at a higher level, over the new ego. That new method was given to the group of Kabbalists by Moses, the great Kabbalist who lived at that time. Moses led them to the exodus from the exile in Egypt—out of the domination of the new ego—and taught them how to exist "as one man in one heart" (RASHI, Exodus, Chapter 19), as parts of a single organism.

Because of its size, the group was now named "a people." Its name, "Israel," points to the desire within them to reach *Yashar El* [straight to God], directly to the upper force, through attainment of Its quality of love and giving.

Moses' correction method is called "the Torah," and is an adaptation of Abraham's method to Moses' generation. The Torah is not a history book or an ethics book, as it is often treated today. Rather, it is a method, a guide, a manual for correcting the ego.

"Torah"* comes from the word *Horaa* [instruction] and *Ohr* [light]. Kabbalah uses the term "light" in two ways: 1) as a force that corrects a person, as it is written, "The Light in it reforms him."[13] 2) as the pleasure that fills a person who has corrected the ego.

The group of Kabbalists continued to evolve, correcting all the egoistic desires that appeared in them using Moses' method. The light that they received into the corrected desires was called "The House of Holiness" [The Temple]. That is, their corrected desires formed "a house" filled with "holiness"—the quality of love and giving.

Children were born and raised by the correction method and reached spiritual attainment, too. The education of the nation was a spiritual one, and there was not a child who did not know the spiritual laws.

> *They checked from Dan to Beer Sheba ... and did not find a baby boy or a baby girl, a man or a woman who were not proficient in laws of impurity and purity.*
>
> Babylonian Talmud, Sanhedrin 97b

The wisdom of Kabbalah explains that the term, *Tuma'a* [impurity], refers to the egoism in a person, and the term, *Tahara* [purity], refers to the power of love and giving. Thus, the people lived in sensation of the upper force, in bonding and brotherly love until the ego leaped once more to a new degree, causing the loss of that sensation. The act of detaching from the sensation of the upper force was called "the ruin of the Temple," and the domination of the new ego was called "the exile in Babylon."

---

* "Torah means the light that is clothed in the Torah. That is, what our sages said, 'I have created the evil inclination; I have created the spice of Torah,' refers to the light in it, since the light in the Torah reforms him" (Baal HaSulam, *Shamati* [*I Heard*], Article No. 6). "The Torah is the only spice to annul and subdue the evil inclination" (Baal HaSulam, "The Teaching of the Kabbalah and Its Essence). "the Torah is Simple Light that expands from His Essence, whose sublimity is endless" (Baal HaSulam, "Introduction to The Mouth of a Sage"). "The word 'Torah' comes from the word Horaa [instruction]" (Baal HaSulam, Letter No. 11).

The return from the exile in Babylon and the construction of the Second Temple symbolized the correction of the ego that caused the ruin of the First Temple. This time, however, the nation was divided into two: Some succeeded in correcting the ego, but others whose intensity of egoism was greater could not. Gradually the ego intensified even among those who succeeded in correcting it, eventually causing the entire nation to lose its ability to sense the upper force.

Thus, everyone went into a concealment of spirituality. The domination of the ego this time was called "the ruin of the Second Temple," and this was the beginning of the last exile.

The ruin of the quality of love and giving, and the eruption of unfounded hatred, made the entire people lose the sensation of the upper force. Yet, what actually happened to Israel in that ruin was a fall from brotherly love to unfounded hatred. From a life of harmony and the sensing of the upper world, Israel has declined into the narrowest, most turbid sensation in reality, otherwise known as "this world."

Ever since, for nearly 2,000 years, Israel has been living in a state of total oblivion to the fact that there is something far better.

And yet, in each generation, there were a chosen few Kabbalists who continued to sense the Creator. In hiding, far from the public eye, which was unaware of their engagement, the Kabbalists continued to develop the correction method for human nature to match humanity's growing egoism. Their role was to prepare the method for the time when the whole of humanity would need it—our time.

* * *

Throughout history, the wisdom of Kabbalah has reached beyond just the people of Israel. Thinkers from around the world have always come to study with the Kabbalists. In his essay, "The

Wisdom of Kabbalah and Philosophy," Baal HaSulam explains that philosophy originated in contact between students of the prophets and the first philosophers. The philosophers took fragments of the concepts of Kabbalah, and without correcting themselves developed different theories out of them.

Johannes Reuchlin (1455-1522), a German humanist, political counselor to the Chancellor, and an expert in ancient languages and traditions, was affiliated with the heads of the Platonic Academia. In his book, *De Arte Cabbalistica*, he describes the process we just mentioned:

"My teacher, Pythagoras, who is the father of philosophy, did not receive those teachings from the Greeks. Rather he received them from the Jews. ...And he was the first to convert the name 'Kabbalah,' unknown to the Greeks, into the Greek name 'philosophy.'"

"Pythagoras' philosophy emanated from the infinite sea of the Kabbalah."

"The Kabbalah does not let us spend our lives on the ground, but rather raises our intellect to the highest goal of understanding."[14]

Let us return to those people who could not perceive Abraham's notion in ancient Babylon. When they departed Babel, they scattered across the globe as seventy nations and developed materially.

Alone, they would never have been able to perceive the notion of the spiritual. Yet, if they could not perceive it, it would contradict the purpose of Creation: to bring all the people to the level of the Creator. Hence, the contact point between Israel and the rest of the nations had to be recreated.

That process unfolded by intensifying the ego within Israel, after which the people declined from their degree and scattered among the nations. The idea was to mingle the souls of Israel with the souls of the nations of the world, to "sow" seeds of spirituality within the other nations.

How was this done? The people of Israel sank into egoism and corporeality similar to the other nations, so now there was common ground between them. However, we must keep in mind that within the souls of Israel, the spiritual seed had already been sown. While they were in exile, Israel avoided physically assimilating with other nations; yet internally, the mingling did indeed occur.

Thus, the desired spiritual result was achieved and sparks of the souls of Israel now permeate the nations, allowing them to join Israel in the process of general correction. In total, Israel experienced four exiles in which such mingling between Israel and other nations occurred.

Prior to the exit to the last exile, in the 2nd century CE, *The Book of Zohar* was written by Rabbi Shimon Bar Yochai (Rashbi) and his group of students. It was written in Aramaic and contains depictions of all the states that humanity is destined to experience until the end of the general correction.

Although *The Zohar* was written prior to the departure of Israel into exile, *The Zohar* states that the book will be discovered only at the end of the spiritual exile and in fact, facilitate its end. It also states that toward the end of the 6,000 year period of the correction of human nature, the book will be revealed to the whole of humanity: "At that time, it will be revealed to all."[15]

Immediately after its completion, *The Book of Zohar* was concealed. In the 16th century, some 1,400 years later, the Ari appeared in Zephath.* The Ari used a scientific, systematic approach to detail the correction method that *The Zohar* presents through intimations and allegories. The writings of the Ari include descriptions of the structure of the upper world, and explain how one should enter that realm of reality.

---

* A town in the upper Galilee, Israel, known for the Kabbalists that lived in it around the Ari's time.

However, because during the Ari's time the ego had not yet been revealed in its full intensity, very few could understand his words. A more developed ego yields a keener perception, and there were few such egos at that time.

Following the Ari, Kabbalists craved that the wisdom of Kabbalah be known, as is evident from their words:

> The wisdom of Kabbalah makes the fool wise. Also, one who did not see the light of this wisdom has never seen lights in his life, for then he will understand and learn the meaning of His uniqueness, blessed be He, and the meaning of His governance ... and all who retire from it, retire from the spiritual, eternal life.
>
> Rav Isaiah Ben Abraham HeLevi Horowitz (the Holy Shlah), "First Article," p 30

> Redemption depends primarily on the study of Kabbalah
>
> The Gaon, Rabbi Eliyahu of Vilna (GRA)[16]

> Rabbi Shimon Bar-Yochai so cried over it, and called upon those who engage in the literal Torah that they are asleep ...Indeed, this the fruit of the exile, that Israel have forgotten this path and remained asleep, immersed in their slumber, not paying attention to it... And we are here in the dark, as the dead, verily as blind searching the wall. It is unbecoming for the upright to walk on this path, but on the contrary to open blind eyes.
>
> Rav Moshe Chaim Luzzato (Ramchal)[17]

> The study of The Book of Zohar is higher than any other study
>
> Rabbi Yosef David Azulai, HaChida[18]

> The language of The Zohar is good for the soul ... young and old are there, each according to one's understanding and the root of one's soul.
>
> Rav Tzvi Hirsh Ben Yaakov Horowitz, Upright Conducts, Item 5

Yet, despite the yearning of these great Kabbalists to circulate the wisdom of Kabbalah, they had to be discreet, to reveal, yet to conceal. The generation was not fully ripe. Only today are people gradually beginning to rid themselves of the stigmas and realize that Kabbalah is not mysticism, magic, charms, magic cures, or blessings for a good life in this world.

The emptiness and the gap that has appeared in our generation toward corporeal life and the cravings for something new and fulfilling have brought us to a point where we are finally able to understand the value of Kabbalah. Here lies a method that elevates one to another level of existence—the level of the upper force. That ripeness proves that our souls have awakened, that they have reached an entirely new level of development. This degree allows for, or better put, *necessitates* the revelation of the wisdom of Kabbalah to the entire world.

If we examine matters from the perspective of Nature's program of development, the approaching end of the allotted time for correction has brought human egoism to its final degree. Humanity has come into a comprehensive, existential crisis and deadlock. From this state, the need for a method to correct the ego becomes clear, and many people wish to perceive what in the past was perceived by only a few.

This is the reason why the correction method is being exposed today in full. Baal HaSulam interpreted *The Book of Zohar* and the writings of the Ari so that each of us could connect to them. This is why he said, "I am glad that I have been born in such a generation when it is already permitted to publicize the wisdom of truth. And should you ask, 'How do I know that it is permitted?' I will reply that I have been given permission to disclose."[19] And also, "My being rewarded with the manner of disclosing the wisdom is because of my generation."[20]

We are in a generation that is standing at the very threshold of redemption, if we only know how to spread the wisdom of the hidden to the masses. ... And the dissemination of the wisdom in the masses is called "a Shofar" [special horn]. Like the Shofar, whose voice travels a great distance, the echo of the wisdom will spread all over the world.

Baal HaSulam "Messiah's *Shofar*"

↙ Point in the heart?

It is important to remember that the "Jewish" nation was not formed on a racial or a national basis. Jews today are incarnations of the same souls that gathered around Abraham in ancient Babylon to realize the spiritual idea of "Love thy friend as thyself," which leads to the discovery of the Creator.

Kabbalists explain that initially, the correction method was offered to every nation, for "The purpose of Creation lies on the shoulders of the whole of the human race, black, white or yellow, without any essential difference" (Baal HaSulam, "The Arvut" [Mutual Guarantee], Item 23). However, at the time, not a single nation was willing to take it because humanity still did not need it. This is why the method was given to the people of Israel, "By which the sparks of purity would shine upon the whole of the human race the world over ... to such an extent that they can understand the pleasantness and tranquility that are found in ... love of others" ("The Arvut" [Mutual Guarantee], Item 24).

The Jews must begin to reuse the wisdom of Kabbalah to shift from unfounded hatred to brotherly love, return to their spiritual roots, and to bring the light to the world—to be "a light to the nations."[21]

By that, the two paths that parted ways in ancient Babylon—the people of Israel and the rest of humanity—will come together and the thought of Creation will be complemented: all creations will unite with the upper force, the power of love and giving.

Now the days are near when all will know and recognize that the salvation of Israel and the salvation of the entire world depend only on the appearance of the wisdom of the hidden Light of the internality of the secrets of Torah in a clear language.

Rav Raiah Kook, Letters 1, Item 92

The study of *The Zohar* and the wisdom of Kabbalah connect people from all over the globe, regardless of race, sex, nationality or religion. This wisdom bridges over mentalities, character, age, and socioeconomic differences. From all over the world, tens of thousands of people gather each year in many different places in the world for conventions of Kabbalah studies. There is hardly a country in the world without a representative. In these conventions, everyone bonds with brotherly love for the purpose of discovering the Creator, proving *de facto* the truth in the words of the prophets and Kabbalists of all generations.

When the Children of Israel [those who aspire Yashar El (straight to God)] are complemented with the complete knowledge, the fountains of intelligence and knowledge shall flow ... and water all the nations of the world.

Baal HaSulam, "Introduction to the Book Panim Meirot uMasbirot," Item 4

THE ALLEGORY ABOUT
THE KING AND THE QUEEN

In all of Israel's exiles, He set a time and an end to all of them. And in all of them, Israel return to the Creator, and the virgin of Israel, *Malchut*, returns to her place at the set time. But now, in the last exile, it is not so. She will not return as in the other exiles. This verse teaches, "She has fallen; she will not rise again—the virgin of Israel," and it does not say, "She has fallen and I will not raise her again."

It is like a king who was angry with the queen and expelled her from her palace for a certain period of time. When that time was through, the queen would immediately come and return before the king. This was so once, twice, and thrice. But on the last time, she became remote from the king's palace and the king expelled her from his palace for a long time. The king said, "This time is not as like the other times, when she came before me. Instead, I and all my household will go and seek her."

When he reached her, he saw that she was lying in the dust. Who saw the glory of the queen at that time, and the king's requests of her? Finally, the king held her in his arms, raised her, and brought her to his palace. And he swore to her that he would never part from her again and will never be far from her.

It is similar with the Creator: every time the assembly of Israel were in exile, she would come and return before the King. But now, in this exile, it is not so. Rather, the Creator will hold her by the hand and will raise her, appease her, and bring her back to His palace.

Zohar for All, VaYikra [The Lord Called], Items 78-81

In all the previous exiles, Israel wished to come out of exile and return to its native land. They wished to return to the spiritual degree that was held while still in exile. Today, however, everything is ready for redemption, yet Israel has no desire to rise.

Why is it so? In the last exile, there was such intense egoism in Israel that they had neither a way nor a will to come out of it. Like the queen, Israel now lies in the dust, immersed in corporeality as though hypnotized, living like zombies. In truth, the world is filled with light. If Israel only opened its eyes a little, they and the world would discover it. But for now, dust fills their eyes.

In the spiritual sense, the word "exile" is an advanced state, a moment before redemption, when one feels that all that's needed is the revelation of the upper force. This feeling can generally be described as such: "I may have everything in the corporeal sense, but I feel that it is all worthless, that I am completely dissatisfied. Why? I haven't a clue but it is what I feel. I have a home, I make a good living, I can afford to travel, to enjoy myself, I have friends, yet something is missing."

In previous generations, people lived far worse than we do. Compared to them, our lives are lives of kings, yet they are tasteless. The emptiness experienced today is leading us to discover what lies behind the verse, "Taste and see that the Lord is good," which Kabbalists offer to us as the remedy.

We must discover the upper force that creates us, that takes us through this process, and that is now pulling us back to it through the question, "What am I living for?" This question is really like a door handle. If we open that door we will discover heaven.

In truth, the King has already come to the Queen, *The Book of Zohar* has already been revealed, the King is here and He already wishes to raise the Queen out of the dust. All that is needed now is getting the Queen's attention.

4

A LADDER TO THE ZOHAR

To understand the words of the Holy Zohar, one should first ... be cleaned of self love. ...Otherwise, there are Klipot that hide and block the truth in the words of the Holy Zohar.

Baal HaSulam, *Shamati* [*I Heard*], Article No. 89[22]

The story of *The Book of Zohar* begins some 1,800 years ago in a tiny, dimly lit cave in Peki'in, in the Western Galilee, Israel, where Rashbi and his son, Rabbi Elazar, hid from the Roman emperor. For thirteen years they prepared themselves for the writing of the book that would change the face of history.

The years passed and Rabbi Shimon and his son completed the correction that they had to complete and came out of the cave. Eight other Kabbalists joined Rabbi Shimon and his son and together they studied and wrote *The Book of Zohar*.

This is how I am arranging you: Rabbi Aba will write, Rabbi Elazar will learn verbally, and the rest of the friends will speak in their hearts.

The Book of Zohar, Haazinu [Give Ear], Idra Zuta, Item 27

Among Rashbi's students was Rabbi Aba, a Kabbalist with a special gift. He was the only one who knew how to write the words of his teacher in such a way that they would be both revealed and concealed. *The Book of Zohar* refers to that gift as "Disclosing in secret."*

Legend has it that the manuscript of *The Zohar* was hidden in a cave near Zephath, and after a few centuries was discovered by Arabs living in the area, who were delighted to find paper— which was a rare commodity in those days. When one of the Kabbalists of Zephath bought some fish in the market, he was astounded to discover the contents of the text of *The Zohar* on the wrapping paper of the fish. As soon as he discovered it, he bought all the "wrapping paper" that was still available and compiled the pieces into a book.

The Book of Zohar that we have today is only a small part of the original because much of it was never retrieved. The pieces that were found and compiled into *The Book of Zohar* that we have today were passed on secretly among Kabbalists from generation to generation until early in the 14ᵗʰ century. At that time, the widow of Rabbi Moshe De Leon inherited the manuscript from her husband. "He probably told her nothing of the prohibition to disclose, and she, by chance, put it up for sale."[23]

---

* And we also find in *The Book of Zohar*, that Rashbi (Rabbi Shimon Bar-Yochai) instructed Rabbi Aba to write the secrets, because he knew how to reveal with intimation. ...For each secret that Rashbi disclosed in the wisdom, he would cry and say, "Woe if I tell; woe if I do not tell." ...This means that he was in distress from both angles: if he did not reveal the secrets of the Torah, the secrets would be lost from the true sages... And if he did reveal the secrets, unworthy people would fail in them for they would not understand the root of the matters and would eat unripe fruit.

Hence, Rashbi chose Rabbi Aba to write because of his wisdom in allegories, arranging matters in such a way that it would be sufficiently revealed to those worthy of understanding them, and hidden and blocked from those unworthy of understanding them. This is why he said that Rabbi Aba knew how to disclose in secret. In other words, although he revealed, it still remained a secret to the unworthy. (Baal HaSulam, "General Preface," Item 1.)

Some mistakenly attribute the writing of *The Zohar* to Rabbi Moshe De Leon himself, but the Kabbalists explain that this is a mistake: "All those who know the ins and outs of the holy *Book of Zohar*, that is, who understand what is written in it, unanimously agree that the holy *Book of Zohar* was written by the Godly Tanna (sage) Rabbi Shimon Bar Yochai. Only some of those who are far from this wisdom doubt this pedigree and tend to say, relying on fabricated tales of opponents of this wisdom, that its author is the Kabbalist Rabbi Moshe De Leon, or others of his time" (Baal HaSulam, "Introduction to The Book of Zohar," Item 59).

Since then, *The Book of Zohar* has been present, but only in our generation is it truly being revealed, thanks to Baal HaSulam's commentary. Baal HaSulam explains that the generation of the authors of *The Zohar* was the only generation in which the desired wholeness had been attained, that is, all 125 spiritual degrees. And because our generation should achieve the same perfection, it has been given the chance to unlock *The Zohar*.

> Prior to the days of the Messiah, it is impossible to be granted all 125 degrees. ...An exception is Rashbi and his generation, the authors of *The Zohar*, who were granted all 125 degrees in completeness, even though it was prior to the days of the Messiah. It was said about him and his disciples: "A sage is preferable to a prophet." Hence, we often find in *The Zohar* that there will be none like the generation of Rashbi until the generation of the Messiah King. This is why his composition made such a great impact in the world, since the secrets of the Torah in it occupy the level of all 125 degrees.
>
> Hence, it is said in *The Zohar* that *The Book of Zohar* will be revealed only at the End of Days, the days of the Messiah. ...And since *The Zohar* appeared in our generation, it is a clear proof that we are already in the days of the Messiah, at the outset of that generation upon which it was said, "For the earth shall be full of the knowledge of the Lord."

Baal HaSulam, "A Speech for the Completion of The Zohar"

THE SULAM [LADDER]
COMMENTARY

And I have named that commentary *The Sulam* (The Ladder) to show that the purpose of my commentary is as the role of any ladder: if you have an attic filled abundantly, then all you need is a ladder to reach it. And then, all the bounty in the world will be in your hands.

Baal HaSulam, "Introduction to The Book of Zohar," Item 58

There is no point opening *The Book of Zohar* without the *Sulam* commentary. Other commentaries have been written on *The Zohar*, but the *Sulam* commentary is the only one that is complete. The *Sulam*, as its name (Ladder) implies, is the only one that can lead us to perfection because Baal HaSulam attained all 125 degrees from which the authors of *The Zohar* wrote the book. He connected to them and interpreted *The Zohar* for us from that level.

The *Sulam* commentary adapts *The Zohar* to the souls that are appearing in the world today. Thus, our souls can face the Zohar, the brightness, the upper light, so that it reforms us and brings our souls back to bonding, a bonding in which the Creator appears.

The *Sulam* helps us build ourselves in the "middle line" so that our form is best suited to the form in which the upper light comes to us[*] so we may receive it.

The middle line is the formula by which we should properly combine the two forces that exist in Nature: the Creator's force—giving, abundance, light—and the creature's (humans') force—the

---

[*] In the language of Kabbalah, the form in which the light comes to us is called "association of the quality of mercy in judgment." For more details, see "Preface to The Book of Zohar," Items 36-38 by Baal HaSulam.

will to receive. Building the middle line is our whole world, and this is where our free choice lies.

Baal HaSulam directs our vision, our approach, and our sensations so that the words of *The Zohar* will pass through us in the middle line, the golden path.

The language of *The Zohar* is filled with seemingly corporeal allegories, which the *Sulam* commentary interprets.* The *Sulam* helps us perceive *The Zohar* more elaborately so that we feel that the text is close to us.

Baal HaSulam also translated *The Zohar* from Aramaic into Hebrew, divided *The Zohar* into paragraphs and essays, and added interpretations, introductions, and introductory explanations.** All that is left for us to do is to climb the rungs of the ladder from our world to the world of *Ein Sof*.

---

* And the books of Kabbalah and *The Zohar* are filled with corporeal parables. Therefore, people are afraid lest they will lose more than they will gain ... And this is what prompted me to compose a sufficient interpretation to the writings of the Ari, and now to the Holy *Zohar*. And I have completely removed that concern, for I have evidently explained and proven the spiritual meaning of everything, that it is abstract and devoid of any corporeal image, above space and above time, as the readers will see, to allow the whole of Israel to study *The Book of Zohar* and be warmed by its sacred Light. (Baal HaSulam, "Introduction to The Book of Zohar," Item 58)

** All the interpretations of *The Book of Zohar* before ours did not clarify as much as ten percent of the difficult places in *The Zohar*. And in the little they did clarify, their words are almost as abstruse as the words of *The Zohar* itself. But in our generation we have been rewarded with the *Sulam* (Ladder) commentary, which is a complete interpretation of all the words of *The Zohar*. Moreover, not only does it not leave an unclear matter in the whole of *The Zohar* without interpreting it, but the clarifications are based on a straightforward analysis, which any intermediate student can understand. (Baal HaSulam, "A Speech for the Completion of The Zohar")

ACKNOWLEDGEMENT OF SPIRITUAL LEADERS OF THE WRITINGS OF BAAL HASULAM

Baal HaSulam made it so that if an ordinary person were to walk in his path, he would be able to discover the Creator.

Rav Baruch Ashlag, "The Works of the Greatest in the Nation"

When Baal HaSulam began to publish his writings, he was greeted with enthusiasm by the spiritual leaders of his time:

> A Godly sage of great understanding has come, a sacred treasure ... and the spirit of the Lord was upon him to compose the sacred book ... to the truth of the Torah and in true foundations ... happy is the woman who bore him.

The Rav Kook

> The great priest of the study of Kabbalah, whose name is renowned.

Rav Yosef Chaim Zonenfeld

> How glorified is the day when the bright light has appeared before us, the Sulam commentary on the Holy Zohar ... and with the hand of the Lord upon him, the great Kabbalist ... the minister of the house of Zohar.

Rav Yaakov Moshe HARLAP

> He illuminated the eyes of sages with the words of the Holy Zohar ... which is a ladder placed on the earth, and its top reaches the heaven.

Rav Ben-Zion Meir Hai Uziel

It was possible to obtain *The Book of Zohar* even before Baal HaSulam wrote the *Sulam* commentary, but people did not understand what it said. The role of *The Book of Zohar* as a means to reveal the Creator is the thing that was hidden, and that is now revealed. The *Sulam* commentary opens before us the ability to correct ourselves and to discover the Creator. This is why Baal HaSulam disclosed *The Zohar*. And because he concluded thousands of years of concealment of *The Book of Zohar*, these and other acknowledgements[35] soon appeared.

The following words, which were found among his writings, give us a clue into the spiritual level of Baal HaSulam:

> And God said unto me: "Get thee out of thy country,* to the pleasant land, the land of the Holy Fathers, where I will make you a great sage and all the sages of the land shall be blessed in you, for I have chosen you for a righteous sage in all this generation, to heal the human suffering with lasting salvation."
>
> Baal HaSulam, "The Prophecy of Baal HaSulam"

> And by a Higher Will, I have been awarded the impregnation of the soul of the Ari ... and I cannot elaborate on this matter, as it is not my way to speak of the incomprehensible.
>
> Baal HaSulam, Letter no. 39

ZOHAR FOR ALL

The wisdom of truth, ...like secular teachings, must be passed on from generation to generation. Each generation adds a link to its former, and thus the wisdom evolves. Moreover, it becomes more suitable for expansion in the public.

Baal HaSulam, "The Teaching of the Kabbalah and Its Essence"

Bnei Baruch—Kabbalah Education and Research Institute is an organization with vast experience in studying and teaching

---

* At the time, Baal HaSulam was still in Poland, prior to his immigration to Israel in 1921.

The Book of Zohar. The experience accumulated through teaching different people in different countries, and through different mediums, has brought us to a decision that was not easy to take—to slightly change the typesetting of the text for the contemporary reader. We learned that in its original setting, *The Zohar* was approachable only to very few, due to an archaic structure and the unfamiliar use of bold letters or different fonts. As a result, *The Zohar* remained inaccessible to most people.

The difficulties in reading made many readers leave the book and thus deny themselves the correction of their souls. After much hesitation, we have come to the decision that because of the necessity to bring *The Zohar* closer to all, we must rearrange the original text of Baal HaSulam.

We did this with the greatest care, without removing anything substantial, changing only the *appearance* of the text, not its content.

At times, Baal HaSulam wrote his commentaries in between the words of *The Zohar*, and at times he added broader explanations after the words of *The Zohar*. Our experience has shown that while reading in *The Zohar*, it is best to include the text of *The Zohar*, the *Sulam* commentary that is in *The Zohar* itself, as well as the *Sulam* commentary after the words of *The Zohar*. Hence, to make it easier on the reader to read the text smoothly, we unified the texts.

To illustrate what we did, below is an example of text from *The Zohar* (in Hebrew) from the portion, *Aharei Mot* [After the Death]. First comes the original text of *The Zohar*, which is almost entirely in Aramaic [and hence will be left without translation], followed by *The Zohar* with the *Sulam* commentary, and finally, *Zohar for All*, which is what we did to make the source—the light that reforms—closer to you.

The Original Zohar:

צד) פתח רבי חייא ואמר, ט) מה שהיה כבר הוא ואשר להיות וגו'. מה
שהיה כבר, היינו דתנינן, עד לא ברא קודשא בריך הוא האי עלמא, הוה בארי
עלמין וחריב לון, עד *) דקב"ה סליק ברעותיה, למברי האי עלמא, ואמליך
באורייתא. כדין אתתקן הוא בתקונוי, י ואתעטר בעטרוי, וברא האי עלמא.
וכל מאי דאשתכח בהאי עלמא, הא הוה קמיה, כ ואתתקן קמיה.

צה) ותאנא, כל אינון ל דברי עלמא, דאשתכחו בכל דרא ודרא, עד לא
ייתון לעלמא, הא הוו קיימי קמיה בדיוקניהון. ם אפילו כל אינון נשמתין דבני
נשא, עד לא יחתון לעלמא, כלהו גליפין קמיה ברקיעא, בההוא דיוקנא ממש,
דאינון בהאי עלמא. וכל מה דאולפין בהאי עלמא, כלא ידעו עד לא ייתון
לעלמא.

The Book of Zohar with the Sulam commentary:

94) Rabbi Hiya started, etc.: Rabbi Hiya started and said, "That
which is has been already, and that which will be..." "That which
is has been already," meaning before the Creator created this
world, He created worlds and destroyed them, which is the
breaking of the vessels, until the Creator desired to create this
world, and He consulted with the Torah, which is the middle
line. Then He was corrected in His corrections, decorated in His
decorations, and created this world. And then, everything that
exists in this world was before Him, at the time of creation, and
was established before Him.

95) *VeTaana Kol Inun* [Aramaic], etc.: We learned that all the
leaders of the world in every generation stand before the Creator
in their forms, before they come into the world. Even all the
souls of people, before they come to the world, are engraved
before Him in the heaven, in the very same form they have in
this world. And all that they learn in this world, they know
before they come into the world...

Commentary. Upon the creation of the souls, while they are
still above, before they come down to this world under time, they
are in the eternity, above time, where past, present, and future
exist as one, as is the nature of eternity. It follows that all the

deeds that the souls do one at a time, when they come into this world, they will be there at the same time. This is the meaning of what is written (Item 95), *Kol inun nishmatin*, etc., *behahu dyokna mamash de inun behai alma*, that is, according to their actions in this world.

Zohar for All:

94) "That which is has been already, and that which will be..." "That which is has been already..." Before the Creator created this world, He created worlds and destroyed them. This is the breaking of the vessels. Finally, the Creator desired to create this world, and consulted with the Torah, the middle line. Then He was corrected in His corrections, decorated in His decorations, and created this world. And then, everything that exists in this world was before Him at the time of creation, and was established before Him.

95) All the leaders of the world in every generation stand before the Creator in their forms, before they come into the world. Even all the souls of people, before they come to the world, are engraved before Him in the heavens, in the very same form they have in this world. And all that they learn in this world, they know before they come into the world...

Upon the creation of the souls, while they are still above, before they come down to this world under time, they are in eternity, above time, where past, present, and future exist as one, as is the nature of eternity. It follows that all the deeds that the souls do one at a time, when they come into this world, will be there at the same time. This is the meaning of the words, "All the souls of people, before they come to the world, are engraved before Him in the heaven, in the very same form they have in this world," that is, according to their actions in this world.

As you can see, we tried to break down as many of the barriers that separate *The Zohar* from the people and offer a slightly briefer and easier version to read. If you can be assisted by *Zohar for All* to grow accustomed to *The Book of Zohar*, and then move to the *Sulam* commentary itself, our work will have been like a ladder to the Ladder commentary.

The great spiritual questions, which used to be solved only by the great and the excellent, must now be solved on different degrees for the entire nation, to lower exalted and sublime matters from the height of their tower to the depth of the common and ordinary. This requires tremendous and great richness of spirit along with constant, regular engagement, for only then the mind will expand and the language will be made clearer, to the point of expressing the deeper matters in a light and popular style to revive thirsty souls.

Rav Raiah Kook, *Ikvei Ha'Tzon*, [*By the Footsteps of the Flock*], 54

THE NECESSITY TO ENGAGE IN THE ZOHAR

Below is a quote from the Ari's *The Tree of Life*, written in the 16th century. These are the words of Rav Chaim Vital in his introduction to the book, *Gate of Introductions*.

I am sitting here, bewildered, with my thoughts confused, for no cure has been found to the ruin of our Temple, which has been in ruin for 1,504 years now. We have come to the end of our rope, yet the Messiah has not come. It is known that in each generation when the Temple is not built, it is as though it was ruined in that generation.

I have looked into the reason for the length of our exile, and I have found an answer in *The Book of Zohar* (in the corrections, "Correction no. 30"): "Those who do not wish to exert in the wisdom of Kabbalah, who make the Torah dry, woe unto them, for thus they inflict poverty, ruin, looting, killing, and destruction in the world. And the spirit of the Messiah departs, the holy spirit, the spirit of wisdom and understanding, the spirit of counsel and might, the spirit of knowledge and the fear of the Lord.

"Any grace that they do, they do for themselves. They engage in Torah to receive many rewards, as well as to be heads of seminaries. In their actions, they are similar to the people of the generation of Babel who built a tower whose top was in heaven, as it is written, 'And let us make us a name.' The Zohar calls them 'Mixed multitude'" (Ex, 12:38).

THE WISDOM OF KABBALAH—THE TRUE, INNER MEANING OF THE TORAH

Each day, a voice comes out of Mount Horev and calls out, "Woe unto the people from the affront of Torah," for when they engage only in its literal part and its stories, it robes in its widow garments and all the nations shall say unto Israel, "How is your law better than our law? After all, your law, too, is but stories of worldly vanities." Indeed, there is no greater affront to the Torah than that. Thus, woe unto them from the affront of Torah. They do not engage in the wisdom of Kabbalah, which gives glory to the Torah, and they extend the exile and all the evils that are about to come upon the world.

In *The Book of Zohar*, Rabbi Shimon says about it, "Woe unto one who says that the Torah comes to tell literal tales. This tale in the Torah is the clothing of the Torah, and one who thinks that that garment is the actual Torah, and there is nothing else within it, his spirit will be cursed and he will have no part in the next world."

This is so because in the literal Torah, when its tales and judgments are treated literally, there is no recognition or information in them to know their Maker. Moreover, there are commandments and laws within them that reason cannot tolerate.

REDEMPTION DEPENDS ON THE STUDY OF KABBALAH

Had we engaged in the wisdom of Kabbalah, redemption would have drawn closer, for everything depends on the study of this wisdom, and avoiding to engage in it delays and hinders the building of our Temple. ...It explicitly explains that one does not do one's share by merely reading in the Bible, the Mishnah, the legends, and the Talmud. Rather, one must engage as much as one can in the secrets of Torah and the wisdom of Kabbalah, for there is no pleasure to the Creator in all that He has created, except when His children engage in the secrets of Torah, to know His greatness, beauty, and virtue.

DISCLOSING THE WISDOM TO ALL

The Book of Zohar, VaYera [The Lord Appeared]: "When it is near the days of the Messiah, even infants in the world will find the secrets of the wisdom." It is explained that thus far the words of the wisdom of *The Zohar* have been concealed. But in the last generation, this wisdom will be revealed and become known, and they will understand and perceive the secrets of Torah that our predecessors did not attain.

II

The World
Was Created
for Me

5

THE ACTUAL REALITY

We were as those who dream

Psalms, 126:1

The most complicated, yet fascinating topic connected to
The Book of Zohar, and indeed to life, is "the perception
of reality."

It is known that around us are numerous waves that we do
not perceive. However, there is also a field of higher information
called "the upper nature" or "the Creator." We can come in
contact with that field and receive everything from it—emotions,
understanding, information, love, sensation of eternal life, and
the sensation of wholeness that exists in that field, which fills
everything around us.

The very purpose of the wisdom of Kabbalah is to teach us
how to develop our own tools so we can perceive that field of
higher information. This can be done only if we change within;

hence, when we change, we ourselves become like that field, and thus like the Creator.

There is nothing simpler than that. The field is here, around us, yet we are blocked; we are not receiving it.

> *There is nothing more natural than coming into contact with one's Maker... In fact, every creature has contact with his Maker, as it is written, "The whole earth is full of His glory," except that one does not know and does not feel it. Actually, one who attains contact with Him attains only the awareness. It is as though one has a treasure in his pocket, and he does not know it. Along comes another who tells him what is in his pocket, and now he really has become rich.*
>
> Baal HaSulam, "Writings of the Last Generation," Part 2

We are unaware of the Creator, of the actual reality, just as a person is dreaming, experiencing all sorts of events, believing oneself to be awake. This is how we are in this world.

In his "Introduction to The Book of Zohar," Baal HaSulam compares this situation to a worm that hatched into a radish, believing that the entire world was the radish it was born in. This is how we are, living in our world, oblivious to the fact that there is a vast world around us, enlightened, expansive, and beautiful. This is where Kabbalists—those who have already awakened from the dream to reality—are found. According to them, what we now sense is called "an imaginary world," and only when we rise above it will we be able to truly understand that previously, "We were as those who dream."

Experience over time and the advancement of science has greatly distilled the human spirit.

The Raiah Kook, *Lights of Faith*, p 67

The Book of Zohar is being revealed to explain to us how to perceive reality correctly, and it is not at all a coincidence that science is also signaling that reality is far broader and richer than we can currently perceive. Scientists are saying that there is a kind of "dark energy," that there are all kinds of white or black spots in the universe, that there are other dimensions that we cannot perceive in our senses or develop tools to perceive.

Also, when we examine other animals, we see that their perception of reality is different from ours. Bees, flies, bears, frogs, snakes, and even cats and dogs, which live near us, perceive reality differently. A dog, for instance, perceives the world primarily as patches of scent. The world image of the bee is the sum of visions received by each of the numerous units that compose its eyes

Different creatures perceive reality differently, but in the end, they are all perceiving the same reality. What reality? This is a good question. And here is another good question: If a person were to miss one of the senses, would that person perceive less of reality? And what if that person did not miss any senses, but instead had another, additional sense? Would he or she see a broader reality? Perhaps the only question is, "Which sense is that?"

With the world we perceive now, we can say that we need glasses or a hearing aid because we know what it means to see well or to hear well. However, if we did not know which additional sense we lacked, how could we acquire it? Just as we do not feel that we need a sixth finger, we cannot feel that we need a sixth sense. As a result, we are living in our world without a need to sense true reality.

Let us examine ourselves from the side for a moment. We exist in the world for several decades, yet we have no idea what happened before us or what will happen after we are gone. In truth, we have no idea what is happening *during* our lives. For example, do we know where our desires come from? Where our thoughts come from? It could be said that we are living in the dark, except that while we are in it, we have a false sensation that we understand and control our lives.

In previous generations, people's lives were simple. They were concerned with food, tried to lead their lives as comfortably as they could, had children, and left for them the rewards of their work. Their children continued on the same route, generation after generation. When we lived in this way, there really was no need to know what was happening around us.

But today we are beginning to ask questions about life. These questions move us from within until we cannot be calm and continue with the flow of life as before. We are beginning to feel that without knowing what we are living for, life simply makes no sense. This is what requires us to discover the actual reality.

To move a step forward in a scientific manner here, all we need is the wisdom of Kabbalah, for all the teachings in the world are included in the wisdom of Kabbalah.

Baal HaSulam, "The Freedom"

To better understand the news that Kabbalah introduces in regard to the perception of reality, let us briefly review how science has approached this topic over the years.

The classical approach, represented by Newton, said that the world exists independently, regardless of man, and that the shape of the world is fixed. Then came Einstein, who discovered that our perception is relative and depends on our senses. In consequence, we cannot say precisely what comprises the world outside of us, as it all depends on the observer's perception of reality.

The contemporary approach to our perception of reality is based on quantum physics, and holds that the observer affects the world, and thus affects the picture one perceives. The picture of reality is a kind of "average" between the qualities of the observer and the qualities of the object or phenomenon being observed.

To better understand the matter, let us look at a familiar example. A speaker stands in a spacious hall and lectures to an audience. They listen to his words through waves that come from the speakers into their ears, and through them to the eardrum. Then the waves traverse an electrochemical mechanism, followed by the brain's examination to see if there is something similar in the memory, and accordingly, it decodes this electrochemical phenomenon.

Thus, according to the contemporary scientific approach, the picture of reality is depicted within us. We cannot say anything about what exists outside of us, since we never perceive what is outside of us. The wisdom of Kabbalah takes us one step forward. Thousands of years ago, Kabbalists discovered that the world actually *has no picture* whatsoever!

In his "Preface to The Book of Zohar," Baal HaSulam writes, "Take our sense of sight, for example: we see a wide world before us, wondrously filled. But in fact, we see all that only in our own interior. In other words, there is a sort of a photographic machine in our hindbrain, which portrays everything that appears to us and nothing outside of us." Baal HaSulam explains that in our brain, there is "a kind of polished mirror that inverts everything seen there, so we will see it outside our brain, in front of our face."[24]

To illustrate the issue, think of a human being as a closed box with five inlets: eyes, ears, nose, mouth, and hands. These organs represent the five senses—sight, hearing, smell, taste, and touch, through which we perceive that there is seemingly something outside of us.

All kinds of stimuli come in through those five inlets in the box, which are all processed in relation to the existing information in that person's memory, and in relation to one's will. The result is some picture of reality, which is then projected onto "a screen" in the back of the brain.

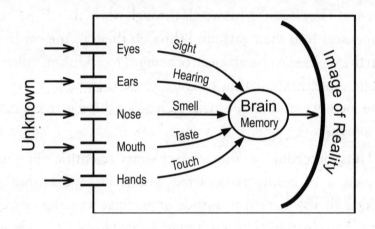

Drawing no. 4

We were deliberately made in a way that our senses create for us an illusory image of a world that *seems* to exist outside of us. This allows us to gradually study what is the real picture on the outside.

I was looking at that eternal world, and the world stood only on those righteous that reign their hearts' desire.

Zohar for All, VaYera [The Lord Appeared], Item 239

If we wish to advance from our present state, to expand our reality, and to know where we truly are and what for, we need only to tend to what is within us—our will. Deep inside there is the will, and it is what operates all our tools of perception, as well as our minds and our thoughts.

Sometimes, we seemingly don't see the world. We shut ourselves within and do not pay attention to what is happening around us. But what actually happens is that our desire becomes detached, as though unconscious. Sometimes, our desire is so intense that it causes us to "devour" the whole world. And sometimes, it just quenches like a candle.

Why do people grow old? It is because they no longer want to perceive the world. It is hard for them, and as a result, their bodies stop functioning. In truth, we begin to decline, to gradually die in the *middle* of our lives. And yet, it is not the body, but our will that dies, losing its motivation to move onward. People who begin to evolve spiritually receive energy and the desire to advance. They are like children, always full of wishes, waking up each day with renewed vigor.

The desire is what evokes needs in us, and what determines what we see or don't see around us. For example, a person who becomes a parent begins to notice the presence of stores for baby products around each corner. The stores were there before, but because he or she had no need for them, their existence went unnoticed.

Our will is self-centered and hence directs us to perceive only what is good for us or what is bad for us, so we can stay away from it. The more the ego develops, and with it the mind, the more we understand, perceive, and control. Accordingly, our perception of reality expands.

Yet, however expansive, in the end our perception is very limited because it depends on the five senses that give us the sensation of physical life. Our body is no different than that of any other animal; hence, this kind of perception is defined as "perception of reality on the animate level." Perceiving the broader reality, the one that is not limited by our egos, is precisely the subject matter of *The Book of Zohar*–the perception of reality on the human level.

What we perceive through our will, our memory, and our five senses is called "this world." Because our will and our memory are only our own, we are as limited as individual cells. To feel the entire reality, the higher realm of information, we must connect to the desires of others–those who are seemingly outside of us but who are actually parts of us. In other words, to perceive the true reality we must replace our will and shift from the inner, egoistic will, to the outer one.

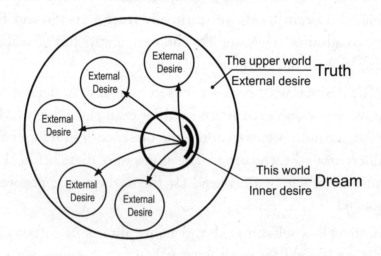

Drawing no. 5

The rule, "Love thy friend as thyself" is not a moral law that aims to force us to love other people. It is rather a means by which we connect the whole of reality to ourselves.

Usually, we love some people, are indifferent to others, and dislike others. This type of approach stems from the sensation that others are outside of us. However, when we can join those parts to us, we become whole and feel the actual reality.

Why were we created this way, detached from the true reality? It is so that we ourselves would gradually connect all these parts of ourselves. In this process, we study laws and phenomena that exist within the actual reality, and thus become equal to the Creator.

Baal HaSulam describes this in the following way:

> All you need is to collect all of those limp organs that have fallen out of your soul, and join them into a single body. In that complete body, the Creator will instill His Divinity permanently, incessantly, and the fountain of great understanding and high streams of light shall be as a never ending spring. Then, each place upon which you cast your eyes shall be blessed.
>
> Baal HaSulam, Letter no. 4

The correct perception of reality is of paramount importance to us. It is not merely another theoretical topic for sophisticated discussions. What we see is only a projection of our inner qualities. The Baal Shem Tov spoke a lot about the world being a mirror of the person:

> One who sees any fault in one's friend, it is as though one is looking in the mirror. If one's face is dirty, this is what one sees in the mirror. If one's face is clean, one sees no faults in the mirror. As one is, so one sees. This is "Love thy friend as thyself."[25]

It is an unbending rule for all Kabbalists that, "Anything we do not attain, we do not define by a name and a word."

Baal HaSulam, "The Essence of the Wisdom of Kabbalah"

The perception of reality is a topic that clearly distinguishes the wisdom of Kabbalah from philosophy, religion, and science. Kabbalah is a practical study method that leads a person stage by stage through one's personal development. Like any other scientific method, Kabbalah instructs the researcher what to do, identifies which results can be expected, and explains the reasons for them. It does not offer descriptions of theoretical states whatsoever—states that one cannot perform *de facto* and in complete awareness.

The "Preface to The Book of Zohar"[26] divides the recognition of reality into four levels: matter, form in matter, abstract form, and essence. Also, it defines the boundaries within which correct perception of reality is possible: in matter and in form in matter.

Abstract form and essence cannot be perceived clearly or in a way that can be monitored, hence *The Zohar* does not deal with them at all. Conversely, philosophy does discuss abstract form, and religion deals with the essence. Thus, the wisdom of Kabbalah completely differs from philosophy and religion in that it deals only with what can be realistically, scientifically perceived.*

And what about the wisdom of Kabbalah compared to science? There are similarities and there are differences. The similarity is that a person does not imagine what comes into

---

* One of the Kabbalists who stressed the differences between the wisdom of Kabbalah and religion was Ramchal [Rav Mohse Chaim Luzzato]: "There is a great need for the wisdom of truth. First, I shall tell you that we must know it because so we are commanded, as it is written, "And know today and reply to your heart that the Lord He is the God." Thus, we must know it by knowing, not merely by believing, but by things that the heart agrees with, as it is written explicitly, "And reply to your heart." ...Thus, there are two things we must know: that the only Master is the one who watches over and leads everything, whether above or below, and two—that there is none other, meaning to know the truth of His uniqueness. Those two things that we must know, you tell me, whence shall we know them? Which wisdom shall teach them to us?

We cannot understand it from the literal Torah, for what does the literal Torah revolve around? Only the commandments, how they should be done, and all their ordinances, or the narration of tales that took place, which are mentioned in it... and if you do not draw this knowledge from all those, you must still keep this commandment, and you must find a way to keep it. Thus, it is only found in this wisdom of truth" (Ramchal, Rules of the Book Moses' Wars, "First Rule").

the desire, but studies it. The difference is the *type* of desire. Worldly science, the science of the corporeal world, studies what comes into the internal, egoistic desire. The wisdom of Kabbalah studies what comes into the outer desire.

In Kabbalah, research begins only after a person has bonded with the other desires. The wisdom of Kabbalah is called "the wisdom of truth" because it studies the true reality, not the imaginary one, which depends upon and is limited by our will.

In corporeal science, a person might be a cruel and mean individual, yet a great scientist. In Kabbalah, the research depends on the extent to which we change. The more we can depart from self-love toward love of others, the more we will succeed in studying what is found outside of us.

Our personal correction and the attainment of wisdom are inseparable. Only if one corrects oneself does one perceive the whole of reality. The 125 degrees of spiritual attainment are actually 125 degrees of correcting the connection between the attaining individual and all the others.

Whether one is a person who cannot read or write, or a brilliant scientist, a complete fool or a great scholar, is completely irrelevant. Only when one corrects oneself in relation to others does one actually become wise. This does not mean that Kabbalah does not require intellect. However, it is a different kind of intellect, one that comes as a result of correcting the desire.

To perceive the actual reality, the world of truth, we must come out of ourselves and begin to know what really exists. Then we will discover that life does not depend on one's body, one's senses, one's inner, egoistic will, or one's memory. Rather, life depends only on the extent to which one is connected to all that exists outside—to others' desires.

Using *The Book of Zohar*, which provides us with the powers
to realize the law of Nature called "love thy friend as thyself,"
we transcend this fictitious reality and move towards perception
of the real world. Although our corporeal body may die, it will
not interrupt our ability to live in the real world. Our spiritual
life continues because we will already be living in a great will, a
higher one, and there is where our true self is found.

Through the secrets of Torah, the value of the power of man's will is
yet to be revealed in the world, and how crucial is its level in reality.
This revelation will be the crown of the whole of science.

The Rav Raiah Kook, *Sacred Lights*, 3, p 80

6

Outer Is Inner

All who fault, fault in their own defect

Babylonian Talmud, *Kidushin* 70b

It is no coincidence that we were made to perceive reality as divided into two parts—me and what is outside of me. If our perception were only internal we would never be able to rise above our egos toward the quality of love and giving. We would be wedged in one place, "chasing our own tails."

Here is an example to clarify what this means. Each of us has a certain amount of self-centered tendencies such as desires for domination or pride. When we examine ourselves, we don't really notice them. But when we see others acting out of a craving to dominate or to boast, for the most part it annoys us.

We have been preordained with hatred and repulsion of others to allow us not to be biased and to define our attitude toward these tendencies in a wise and critical manner. Like a strict and perceptive judge, our ego helps us examine the evil that appears before us in others, to judge it meticulously, profoundly, and in great detail.

Our initial external perception opens our eyes and allows us to detect bad things outside of us. Afterwards, we realize that in truth, it is all within us. It is said that "All who fault, fault in their own defect." However, we are destined to discover that it's not that "he is overbearing" and "she is a snob," but that it is we who are seeing them this way because of our own spoiled desires.

The Creator's desired goal for the creation He had created is to bestow upon His creatures so they will know His truthfulness and greatness, and receive all the delight and pleasure He had prepared for them.

Baal HaSulam, "Introduction to The Book of Zohar," Item 39

As stated above, it is desire that shapes our perception of reality. Now we will try to understand what parts make up the desire, why we were created specifically as we are, and how we can change our reality for the better.

Along the way, we will discover why such emotions as hatred and love toward others appear in us, what causes us to be glad when someone else is suffering, and why we are envious when the neighbor buys a new car.

Question: if the purpose of Creation is to be delighted, why does it seem that matters are constantly getting worse? *The Book of Zohar* explains that in truth, we exist in a perfect system that was created by the Creator. The whole of the substance of Creation is the will to receive, and the perfect system is actually the comprehensive will that was created. This will is also called "the general soul" or "the soul of Adam HaRishon." However, the Creator broke the general soul into many pieces, and in each of us there is only a tiny fraction of the general soul.

Prior to the breaking, we all felt like organs of a single body in this system. Everything was perfect and unbounded; hence, at that time, the system was called "the world of *Ein Sof* [infinity]." In the world of *Ein Sof*, all parts of the system are connected with love and are filled with light. However, the Creator placed 125 "filters" on this system, which conceal the worlds so now we cannot sense that there is any light there.

It is like a beautiful picture covered with a stained nylon sheet, on top of which there is another stained sheet, and another one, so the original picture becomes increasingly hidden.

We are on the outermost layer and have no sense whatsoever of the previous layers, hence the connection between us is completely distorted. Instead of feeling the love that connects us in the world of *Ein Sof*, there is hatred and repulsion among us. We do not feel the comprehensive connection between us; instead, we are separated and detached.

The Creator wanted us to return to the good and enlightened state by ourselves, to the world of *Ein Sof*. This is the program of the evolution of Creation, which divides into three stages:

- Stage One: the initial state (the world of *Ein Sof*);
- Stage Two: the broken state (this world);
- And Stage Three: the perfect state, which we must create by ourselves (returning to the world of *Ein Sof*).

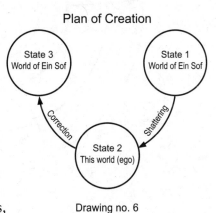

Plan of Creation

State 3
World of Ein Sof

State 1
World of Ein Sof

Correction

Shattering

State 2
This world (ego)

Drawing no. 6

It is quite similar to the way we behave with children. We take a picture, cut it into pieces, then let them put the pieces back together. The reassembly process develops the child.

As a result of the shattering, the will (known as *Kli* [vessel]) of every person was divided into two main parts: internal *Kelim* [vessels], known as "root," "soul," and "body," and external *Kelim*, known as "clothing" and "palace." I perceive my inner *Kelim* as "me," therefore I care for them, and I perceive the external *Kelim* as alien, not my own. The inner *Kelim* and the outer *Kelim* contradict each other, so the more I love my inner *Kelim*, the more I hate my outer *Kelim*.

There is a boundary between those two types of *Kelim*—the border of the shattering. It is a kind of partition that causes me to look outward only in a mindset of "What can I receive from there to improve my situation? What does that give me?" It compels me to always relate to others egoistically, desiring to exploit them.

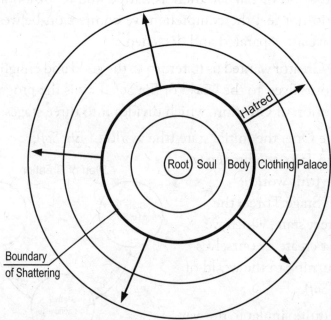

Drawing no. 7

I always evaluate my situation by the difference between myself and the rest of the world. Hence, as surprising and as odd as it may sound, the worse it is for the world, the better it is for me—provided it does not put my personal safety in any danger.

I cannot tolerate fulfillment in the external *Kelim*. I cannot remain indifferent toward another or behave as though I do not care about him or her. When another person succeeds, it is very painful to me, it really destroys me. I constantly compare.

If, for instance, I earn $100,000 a year, and the people around me earn $50,000, I feel great satisfaction. But if someone earns $200,000 a year, I feel great disappointment. I cannot rid myself of this thought and settle for what I have because it is so important to me that others have less than me.

We cannot simply ignore those external *Kelim* because we feel them as belonging to us. If there were no connection between us, it would be another story. However, the shattering created a negative connection between us so that even if we did nothing bad to one another, the force of the shattering makes us *de facto* enemies.

But the equal side in all the people of the world is that each of us stands ready to abuse and exploit all the people for his own private benefit with every means possible, without taking into any consideration that he is going to build himself on the ruin of his friend.

Baal HaSulam, "Peace in the World"

Understanding how these matters work is extremely important because it serves as a means for change, a lever for development. Let us examine another example that, precisely because it is extreme, helps us understand the issue more precisely.

All of humanity's villains acted on the same inner drive to expand the gap between their own internal *Kelim* and their external *Kelim*. Nazi Germany, for instance, could not settle for realizing the great human potential of the German people to create a thriving country. Instead, a drive appeared in it to be superior to others, to govern them, to destroy them. Only then would it feel that it was truly great.

Human egoism feels that killing other people, exploiting them, and dominating them is pleasurable for it. This is the result of the shattering—man is hurting himself, his own external *Kelim*, but he doesn't know it. When we find out that all the evil we have been trying to inflict on others was really inflicted on ourselves, will experience immense disillusionment and pain. Yet, it is precisely this pain and disillusionment that will help us carry out the actual correction.

We are unaccustomed to discussing these matters and we tend to hide them, but where it is distinctly visible is in politics. We even found a respectable name to this world of lies— "diplomacy." Each side strives to dominate the other, but for lack of other choices, signs an alliance with the other side.

In human society, we have built many systems to allow us to live with minimal friction between the inner *Kelim* and outer *Kelim* of each. We understand that otherwise we will all be harmed. We have established Social Security, welfare systems, and charities because we are all terrified that tomorrow we, too, will be in that state of need. Hence, we prepare the cure ahead of the blow.

Hatred between inner and outer *Kelim* is a human phenomenon that doesn't exist in the animal kingdom. When a lion eats a zebra, it doesn't hate it, and the zebra doesn't hate the lion. The lion regards the zebra as food and the zebra tries not to be eaten. But there is no hatred between them. Nature governs both of them perfectly.

If there were no connections between us, we would not be able to discover the reason for what is bad in our lives. However, because we are discovering that the connections between us are bad, we can then turn them into good.

Let us examine the current state of humanity. In the past, ties among countries barely existed. Each country was connected only to a few other countries. When we were far from each other, there was not much contact, hence the evil was not so evident. But as the world became more globalized, everyone became connected, affecting everyone else. Suddenly, there was nowhere to run. We do not have another earth, hence the hatred between us is surfacing. Yet, it is precisely this hatred that will compel us to correct our relationships.

Even though we see everything as actually being in front of us, every reasonable person knows for certain that all that we see is only within our own brains.

Baal HaSulam, "Preface to The Book of Zohar"

Now that the picture of our relations with others has been made a little clearer, we can move on. As we said above, the force that divides our picture of reality into two parts—internal and external—is the force of the shattering. After the shattering, part of our desires (our outer *Kelim*, "clothing" and "palace") were no longer sensed as our own. It is like a person who received an anesthetic to the leg, and while his leg was being amputated, he laughed and talked, behaving as though nothing was happening to him because he felt nothing.

In these parts of the will, "clothing" and "hall," we actually feel all that is not us, meaning the outside world. Around us are people, processes unfolding, and the entire world when in fact, they are all parts of our own desire.

We are living in a long feature film in which our desires our projected before our eyes, and what determines the image we see each moment in the film is the *Reshimot* [recollections]. As mentioned in Chapter 2, *Reshimot* are information bits that define our personal plan of development.

Let us review what we have said before to restore some order. Reality consists of three elements: the light, the power of love and giving (the Creator), the will to receive (the creature), and the *Reshimot* (the creature's plan of development). First, the Creator created the creature, meaning a desire to receive pleasure. Then the Creator broke the desire into an inner part (root, soul, body) and an outer part (clothing, palace), and created in it an egoistic sensation of "me vs. the world."

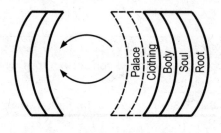

Drawing no. 8

Within the desire is its development plan, which consists of *Reshimot*. Each such *Reshimo* [singular of *Reshimot*] constitutes a certain state that the creature must experience until it corrects the shattering—equalizes with the qualities of the Creator and realizes the purpose of Creation.

If we return to the film, what I see now is a realization of the *Reshimo* that I feel in the five parts of my desire, and there is nothing else but that.

Each moment, new *Reshimot* awaken in my desire and evoke new impressions in me, which immediately makes me see a different world. My whole life, the whole of reality are *Reshimot* that pass through me and become realized. The light affects me, my desire, through which the *Reshimot* begin to traverse in a chain as though in frames on celluloid film.

I feel that it is my life that I am living, but is it really me living it? If look back a few years, will I believe that it was really me? It seems as though some motion picture ran through me. <u>Many people feel that way—that life passes through them as though in a dream, that it was not them</u> doing and experiencing, but some projection, a film that was projected and they were playing their roles in it.

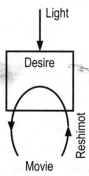

Drawing no. 9

The Zohar explains that there is nothing but *Reshimot*, light, and desire. Each *Reshimo* that passes divides the desire into two—internal and external. We experience ourselves and something other, which seems to be outside of us—trees, sun, moon, people. We have children, we are at work, there is always us and something other. Why?

The sensation of reality as though it were divided into two allows us to recognize that besides us there is another force—the light, the Creator—which compels us to search for it.

All the worlds, Upper and lower, are included in man.

Baal HaSulam, "Introduction to the Preface to the Wisdom of Kabbalah," Item 1

The Book of Zohar is hidden in the sense that people don't know how to read and understand what is written in it because the key to reading it is in the perception of reality. <u>*The Zohar* demands that we understand that the reality we perceive is happening within, not without.</u>

Even the upper world, to which *The Zohar* is leading us, will be experienced within us. It is pointless to search for the outlet to the upper world beyond the horizon. Rather, it is only a change in our inner qualities.

The Zohar speaks of a reality that exists "above" what we feel at the moment, "above" time, space, and motion. This external reality that it describes and which appears to be outside of us is nowhere to be found. It is all within our will. All phenomena, sensations of the past, present, and future are depicted within it. History is merely a process that we picture as something that occurred sometime in the past, when in truth, there is no time at all, no motion, and all places are imaginary. There is only one place where everything occurs—the desire.

The natural course of things, the different parts of our desire (internal and external, me and others) collide with one another. *The Book of Zohar* assists us in correcting the connection between them, in joining them until they become one and we feel no difference between them. This is the longed-for change in our perception of reality.

This is how we discover the upper world, also known as "the next world." It is not that we prepare ourselves here and subsequently reach some other place. Rather, the more we show love toward others instead of hatred, the more we begin to feel what is called "the upper world" or "the next world." All the worlds are here in the connection between us and what currently seems to be outside of us, remote.

Desires that seem to us as others are divided into several circles with respect to our ego. In the closest circle are family, relatives and friends. In the next circle are people who help us and who benefit us by their existence, such as doctors. Then there are the people that we only want to use, to harm, but to keep them alive. And the farthest are the people that we truly hate and may even be prepared to kill.

Yet, they are all our own desires. When we reconnect them to ourselves, we will become the general soul that the Creator created and will return to the world of *Ein Sof*.

It is important to stress that the process of correcting the perception of reality is not meant to be carried out artificially. If my neighbor were to yell at me tomorrow, I would not reply with something like, "Relax, my friend. After all, we are all one will." It is also not a simplistic shift of "inward instead of outward."

Rather, it is a profound transformation, and to execute it we need *The Book of Zohar* to help us build that new perception within us, as well as the company of people who will support us in the correction process.

The most hidden is given to the wise at heart.

Zohar for All, Lech Lecha [Go Forth], Item 96

7

As One Man in One Heart

The Creator created one Kli [vessel] called Adam HaRishon, and shattered it into numerous tiny fragments, so that they would learn together what it means to love, and together reach all the way to Him.

From the book, *The Wise Heart*

One of the necessary means for spiritual development is the group.

To be prepared for spiritual development, the Creator evokes two sensations within us. The first is one of emptiness with regard to this world, and the second is a longing to attain the source of life. This is the awakening of the "point in the heart."

The point in the heart connects us to the place where we can feed and nourish it—the group. Indeed, you can see that those whose point in the heart has awakened are naturally drawn toward one another. This always happens in human society: birds of a feather flock together.

The group allows for true bonding to others according to the new principles of love and giving, as opposed to hatred and separation. Hence, group work is a necessary means for achieving the revelation of the Creator. It allows one to measure one's true relationship with others, and prevents one from falsely believing that one has already obtained personal contact with the Creator because after all, the Creator is the quality of love and giving that exists within the corrected connection between us.

Such groups have always existed throughout history. By changing relationships among group members into one of bonding and mutual love, they created the necessary conditions for us to sense the actual reality. From the vast experience they have acquired, they wrote about the world that opened before them. The books they left behind them allow us to reach this new life in the shortest and most efficient way.

A group of this kind is called a "group of Kabbalists," and its only purpose is to unite them, as it is written, "As one man in one heart," "That which you hate, do not do to your friend," and "Love thy friend as thyself."

The atmosphere created in a group of Kabbalists is very special. To somewhat sense it, let us examine a few examples of bonds among the members of known groups from the past:

> We have all taken it upon ourselves to behave with love and brotherhood, and to spare one's friend's honor as one's own.

The group of the sages of Egypt, among which was the Ari, 1558[27]

> Tie a strong and unfailing tie of love, brotherhood, and peace among us ... as though we were a single body, as though we were brothers to the same father and mother from conception and from birth, all the days of our lives.

The group of the sages of Egypt, 1564[28]

Let each think of one's friend as though he is truly a part of him with all his might and soul.

Let us unite as one man, friends in every which way, to help and to assist, to strengthen and to support one another.

The Rashash group, Kabbalists of Beit El, Jerusalem, 1757[29]

They have taken it upon themselves to love one another ... and to all try to come to the study of The Zohar each day.

The Ramchal group, Padua, Italy, 1731[30]

Correcting the relations in the group from self-love to love of others can only be done by that same higher force that created our egoism. It is the only thing that can transform the evil inclination into a good inclination. The Creator says, "I have created the evil inclination, I have created for it the Torah as a spice, for the light in it reforms it,"[31] changing it to bonding and love.*

Even now, we are within the corrected reality—tightly connected among us as parts of a single organism, but we haven't awakened to the recognition of that state. This awakening, that reviving power, the light that reforms, can be obtained when we come together.

In the group, we read together in *The Book of Zohar*. The *Zohar* speaks of our connected state; hence, reading together with the aim of achieving unity and love evokes the light that reforms.** Gradually, we begin to rise above our natural self-centered feelings and feel the connection of love that is among us. And within that, we feel the Creator. This is the way to realize the essence of the wisdom of Kabbalah, the revelation of the Creator to the creature.

---

* One can never have the strength to go against nature alone, since regarding the mind and heart, in which one must be complemented, one must be assisted in that, and the assistance is through the Torah, as our sages said, "I have created the evil inclination, I have created the spice of Torah." By engaging in it, the light in it reforms them. (Rav Baruch Shalom HaLevi Ashlag, the Rabash, The Writings of Rabash, essay, 'What Are Torah and Work in the Way of the Lord")

** When engaging in this composition ... Divinity shines and illuminates from that Light as when it was first created. And all who engage in it reawaken that same benefit and that first Light, which Rashbi and his friends had revealed while composing. (Ramak, *Ohr Yakar* [*Precious Light*], Gate 1, Item 5)

THEY HELPED
EVERY MAN HIS FRIEND

Each of them had a spark of love of others, but the spark could not ignite the light of love to shine in each, so they agreed that by uniting, the sparks would become a big flame.

Rav Baruch Shalom Ashlag, *Rabash—the Social Writings*[32]

In our generation, the whole of humanity must become a single, large group, and correct itself. For this reason, Rav Baruch Shalom HaLevi Ashlag (the Rabash), the firstborn son and successor of Baal HaSulam, wrote dozens of articles on the work in the group. He bequeathed to the world a detailed method for bonding, with instructions related to each of the states that arise in the relationship within the group. By his writings, we study and evolve in the spiritual.

> *Since man is created with a Kli [vessel] called "self-love" ... and without annulling self-love, it is impossible to achieve ... equivalence of form. And since it is against our nature, we need a society that will form a great force so we can work together on annulling the will to receive.*

Rabash, *Rabash—the Social Writings*, "Purpose of Society (2)"

It is impossible to advance in spirituality without a group. Today's advanced technology allows us to convey the correction method through the Internet to any place in the world. Lessons in the wisdom of Kabbalah about *The Book of Zohar* and essays of Rabash are broadcast daily at www.kabbalah.info, and through them, thousands of people join the study group. Some of them gather in local groups around the world, and some connect online from their homes.

Today's ability to connect to the group from anywhere in the world opens the possibility for spiritual development to any person who is interested. Even the physical distance between people is no longer an obstacle. Since we are dealing with internal bonding with people, we can connect through the media, since it is not the bodies that need to bond, but the hearts. Within this global group, people may be very different in appearance, yet are very similar inside.

When humankind achieves its goal ... bringing them to the degree of complete love of others, all the bodies in the world will unite into a single body and a single heart. Only then will all the happiness intended for humanity become revealed in all its glory.

Baal HaSulam, "The Freedom"

A PRAYER OF MANY

A prayer of many rises before the Creator and the Creator crowns Himself with that prayer, since it rises in several ways. This is because one asks for *Hassadim*, the other for *Gevurot*, and a third for *Rachamim*. And it consists of several sides: the right side, the left, and the middle. This is so because *Hassadim* extend from the right side, *Gevurot* from the left side, and *Rachamim* from the middle side. And because it consists of several ways and sides, it becomes a crown over the head of the Righteous One That Lives Forever, *Yesod*, which imparts all the salvations to the *Nukva*, and from her to the whole public.

But a prayer of one does not comprise all the sides; it is only on one way. Either one asks for *Hassadim* or *Gevurot* or *Rachamim*. Hence, a prayer of one is not erected to be received like the prayer of many, as it does not include all three lines like the prayer of many.

Zohar for All, VaYishlach [Jacob Sent], Item 45

A prayer of many does not depend on the number of people, but on the content of the prayer. Billions of people may cry out but if the cry is an egoistic one, the prayer is not answered.

A prayer of many is a request to reconnect the numerous pieces of the broken soul. This is the only prayer that the Creator answers.

III

Unlocking
The Zohar

8

BEING LIKE THE CREATOR

When we equalize in every conduct with our root,
we sense delight.

Baal HaSulam, "The Giving of the Torah"

We are standing at a crucial point in history. Tens of thousands of years of human development, and billions of years of evolution have all occurred only to bring us to these moments of transformation, to the birth of the new humanity.

If we examine Nature, we will see that it is constantly evolving. First, the inanimate evolved, then the vegetative, and finally the animate. Each such evolution is based on the evolution of the desire in the creature.

The desire that wishes only to sustain itself without change takes the form of inanimate. When the desire wishes to evolve, to move toward what is good for it and away from what harms it, the vegetative form appears. An even greater desire, which

97

approaches the benefiting and turns away from the harmful by its own movement, takes on the animate form. All the forms we see before us in reality are only external envelopes that express the evolution of the only force that was created, "the will to receive delight and pleasure" or in short, "the will to receive."

The most developed creature in the animate degree is the human species. However, as we said earlier, a little over 5,770 years ago a new evolution began in Nature: One of the creatures evolved into the speaking degree, to the degree of Adam, who is *Domeh* [similar] to the Creator. Within the desire of that person appeared a craving that was not of this world—the point in the heart, a spark that pushed him to discover the Creator.

> We find that the only need in man's wishes, which does not exist in the whole of the animate species, is the awakening towards Godly Dvekut (adhesion). Only the human species is ready for it, and none other.
>
> Baal HaSulam, "This Is for Judah"

Unlike lower degrees, evolution to the speaking degree does not happen by itself. It occurs only when we have a desire, a craving to rise to it. That craving is called "intention." To develop within us an intention to be similar to the Creator, we need a means to help us. This is why *The Book of Zohar* was written.

The Zohar is a very special book. Throughout history, Kabbalists have used it to attain the recognition of the highest level of the overall Nature. This is why it is considered such an important book. In fact, when Kabbalists refer to a book without mentioning its name, they are always referring to *The Book of Zohar*.

In a generation that would be the start of a 2,000 year exile, ten Kabbalists gathered to compose *The Book of Zohar*. They were special souls who represented the ten *Sefirot* [from the word "sapphires"], the ten foundations in the general system of Creation, and they were able to express the entire structure of reality. Rabbi Shimon Bar Yochai was their leader, and he was considered the *Sefira* [singular of *Sefirot*] *Keter* [crown]. The others corresponded to the rest of the *Sefirot—Hochma, Bina, Hesed, Gevura, Tifferet, Netzah, Hod, Yesod,* and *Malchut.*

To describe the shape of the system, the authors of *The Zohar* used signs that we call "letters." When we read the letters and the words, if we desire to be connected to this system, it begins to affect us.

Studying *The Zohar* makes us grow and evolve in the spiritual sense. It gradually provides us with the right intention and the special power of development called "the light that reforms." To be reformed means to achieve the degree of the Benevolent One—the Creator.

THE MIDDLE LINE

One should believe that one has a point in the heart, which is a shining spark. Sometimes, it is only a black point and does not shine. That spark must always be awakened ... for it can light up one's deeds so they will shine.

Rabash, *The Writings of Rabash*, "What Is 'The Herdsmen of Abram's Cattle and the Herdsmen of Lot's Cattle' in the Work"

Let us now approach an excerpt from *The Book of Zohar*. The excerpt is taken from the portion *Lech Lecha* [Go Forth], and talks about the middle line, the MAN of the righteous. MAN is one's intention to develop into being similar to the Creator, and righteous are those who wish to be right. They wish to say that the Creator was right to create them, to justify Him, and justification is possible only by truly seeing and sensing what is happening in reality, out of the highest degree to which a person rises. This is what we wish to achieve through *The Zohar*.

He even plays with the souls in this world, since at midnight, all those true righteous awaken to read in the Torah and to sound the praises of the Torah. And the Creator and all those righteous in the Garden of Eden listen to their voices. And a thread of grace stretches over them during the day, meaning that by the MAN that they raise through the Torah and the praises, the middle line—the light of Hassadim [mercy]—extends to the Nukva [Aramaic: female]. And since they caused that light, they are rewarded with the same amount they have induced in the Nukva. This is the meaning of, "By day the Lord will command His mercy, and in the night His song shall be with me," for because of the singing at night, one is rewarded with His mercy during the day.

Zohar for All, Lech Lecha [Go Forth], Item 132

Within the overall system, some souls are already corrected. If we wish to discover the Creator but feel that He is hidden from us, then we are in spiritual darkness, a state called "night." In that state, we should make efforts and evoke our pleas, and then those high souls will affect us as we read in *The Book of Zohar*.

The Book of Zohar was written specifically to connect us with those souls. When reading *The Zohar*, we create that connection and they send us the light that reforms.

That light still does not permeate and fill our souls, since the equivalence of form between our souls and the light is still absent. But it does affect us as though we were in a womb, surrounding us, caressing us, embracing us.

Thus, the light gradually corrects us until we begin to feel it, meaning those corrected souls to which we have connected, and the Creator, Who is in the system of the souls.

That light surrounding us is called "surrounding light." To the extent that we become corrected, it permeates us and fills us, and becomes the "inner light" of the soul, our spiritual life.

Within the womb, which is the light that surrounds us, grows the middle line. The middle line is my own precise calculation, which best combines Nature's two forces—the power of the will and the power of the light—so that the light will correct the will.

The part of the desire that has been corrected in this process and has become Creator-like is the middle line. In other words, the extent to which I have become similar to the Creator is called "my middle line." It is the image of the Creator that I have built within me, in a process that began with a request that I made during the state of "night."

FROM DARKNESS TO LIGHT

In our world, day and night interchange by themselves as a result of the turning of the earth. In spirituality, it works differently: I myself turn the night into day because by reading in *The Zohar* and the work in the group, I invert the direction of the operation of my will to receive from inward to outward. That is, darkness and light depend on the way in which the desire operates.

Let us explain the above statement: The will to receive may operate in one of two ways—in order to receive or in order to give (also known as "in order to bestow"). When the desire operates in order to receive, it cannot contain anything. The pleasure cannot permeate the desire; it only touches the desire and we feel as though we are enjoying it, but it only seems so. In truth, the sense of pleasure disappears promptly after we receive it. This is so because the will to receive and the pleasure are opposites—the desire is like minus and the pleasure is like plus—neutralizing each other.

We can never keep pleasure within. If, for example, we buy something that we've been craving for a long time, something really special, a week later the sense of satisfaction disappears.

There are pleasures, like the pleasure of sex, which disappear immediately, at the very moment we obtain them because of the oppositeness between the nature of the desire and the nature of the pleasure. This is how Baal HaSulam summarizes this futile pursuit:

> This world is created with a want and emptiness of all the good abundance, and to acquire possessions we need movement. ...Hence, we choose the torment of movement in order to acquire the fulfillment of possessions. However, because all their possessions are for themselves alone, and "One who has a hundred wants two hundred," one finally dies with less than "half one's desire in one's hand." In the end, they suffer from both sides: from the pain of increased motion, and from the pain of deficiency of possessions, half of which they lack.

Baal HaSulam, *Talmud Eser Sefirot* [*The Study of the Ten Sefirot*],
Part 1, "Inner Reflection," Chapter 4

This darkness, which is felt in the will to receive, can be turned to light only if we change the *modus operandi* of the will to receive into "in order to bestow." In other words, if we use the will to receive in order to give to others, and enjoy the giving, we will become unbounded in our actions because one can give indefinitely.

If we enjoy loving and giving to others as much as the Creator enjoys it, we will become similar to Him and we will feel life as eternal and whole. What do we need in order to realize it? We need to acquire love of others and find abundance that we can give to others.

Love of others can be obtained from the Creator through the light that reforms. Once love for others is created within us and we have become similar to the Creator, the abundance of the Creator appears in us. When we act out of love for others, we realize the thought of Creation and become the Creator's "partners" with respect to the creatures. This is the correction process of how the will to receive operates.

A corrected act of the will follows the formula: "Israel, the Creator, and the Torah are one." Israel means the desire in me to reach straight to the Creator, *Yashar El* [Straight to God], meaning to become similar to the Creator. The Creator is the Creator, the goal to which I aspire, and the Torah is the entire corrected mechanism, the ties of love that connect the souls together.

To illustrate the above, think of the human body. In the body, different parts work in unison and with mutual guarantee. Each part helps the others and there is bonding and unity among them. Our souls must function similarly—unite in a bond of loving and giving. This is the Torah. The Torah contains 613 correct connections between each soul and all the other souls.

If the connection between the souls is one of hatred and not one of love, there is no Torah and it is hidden. The souls that do not feel the ties of love among them are in exile from the Torah and from the Creator, meaning detached from the right connection (Torah) and from the light that fills the right connection (the Creator). We can compare it to the difference between a healthy body and a body whose systems are dysfunctional.

The corrections we perform on our desire—to shift from the corrupted form to the corrected one—are called *Mitzvot* [commandments].* This is why it is said that "Love thy friend as thyself" is the great rule of the Torah, for it contains the entire system of correct relations among the souls.**

---

*   "When one can aim in order to bestow, this act is called a *Mitzva* [commandment]" (Rabash, *The Writings of Rabash*, "Regarding the Received Reward").
**   For more on the topic, see Letter no. 17 and "Introduction to the Book, From the Mouth of a Sage" by Baal HaSulam.

TEARS

If my people heeded me ... they would delve all their lives in the study of The Book of Zohar ... and would extend abundance and Light.

Rav Yitzhak Yehuda Yehiel of Komarno[33]

In reading *The Zohar*, we must intend for the upper force to affect us. *The Zohar* is built in such a way that it oozes into us bit by bit. Time and time again, with the same intention to grow, we should let *The Zohar* affect us. Then we will feel how it leads us from darkness to light.

The following excerpt from *The Zohar* discusses tears:

> When this prayer in tears rises through those gates, that angel comes ... whose name is Yerachmiel. He takes a prayer in tears, the prayer enters and becomes connected above, and the tears remain here, inscribed in the door that the Creator opens. The prayer in tears raises MAN for the correction of the Miftacha [Aramaic: key], to raise the Malchut to Bina, and therefore the prayer is answered and the tears remain inscribed on the door, causing there the mitigation of Malchut in Bina. Tearing comes from the word "mixing" because he drips and mingles the Malchut in Bina.
>
> *Zohar for All*, *Pekudei* [Accounts], Item 490

What Are Tears?

In this world, a person cries because he is sad, in pain, has no control over a situation, or feels small and weak. We cry when we are in a situation that we don't know how to cope with—fate, chance, force majeure.

In the spiritual world, however, the state of "tears" is the most active of states. Throughout that state, we activate the entire mechanism of our correction and ascension.

"The prayer in tears raises MAN for the correction of the *Miftacha* [Aramaic: key], to raise the *Malchut* to *Bina*," says *The Zohar* in the above excerpt. *Miftacha*, in Aramaic, means "key." The tears open the gate to the spiritual world, through which we enter in order to correct our will, *Malchut*, to become a giver like the Creator, *Bina*. Although our desire is a desire to receive, and hence opposite from the Creator, we mitigate it with the intention to bestow, making it similar to the Creator.

The above excerpt also writes, "Therefore the prayer is answered and the tears remain inscribed on the door." A prayer is a request to become similar to the Creator, and the tears are what keeps the door open. It follows that tears are an act that enables us to be similar to the Creator.

Being allowed to study the sublime matters, called "the wisdom of Kabbalah," is only as a remedy, for they can bring one to desire and crave adhesion with the Creator ... When one studies the sublime matters so they will bring one closer to sanctity, it causes the nearing of the lights. This means that this study causes one that through it, one will come to aim all one's actions to be in order to bestow.

Rabash, *The Writings of Rabash*, "Three Lines"

When we engage in *The Zohar*, all the lights and power hidden within it traverse us. Even if we still cannot detect or sense those things, they do travel through us, affect us, and change us. There is no other way to grow. It is like a baby who still does not understand how it grows and develops, but has an inner drive to run around from corner to corner to search, examine, and know everything.

It makes no difference what emotions our reading in *The Zohar* may evoke in us. At times it will be pleasant and at other times less so; at times we will laugh, and at times we will cry; at times we will be excited, and at times indifferent. Yet, in the end, only perseverance will yield results. We must let the power of *The Zohar* affect us so we may grow and thrive in spirituality.

ETERNAL PLEASURE

Even if one lived a thousand years, on the day he departs from the world, it will seem to him as though he lived only one day.

Zohar for All, *VaYechi* [Jacob Lived], Item 293

After the demise of the body, if we did not rise from the animate level to the human level during our lives, if we did not achieve equivalence of form—acquired the quality of love and giving and became similar to the Creator, and thus revealed the Creator—nothing remains of us. The spiritual point that was in us, and which we did not develop, reincarnates into our world, acquires a new clothing (additional egoistic desire), and a new cycle of life begins. Only by studying the wisdom of Kabbalah can we rise to the degree of man.

> *It is known from books and from authors that the study of the wisdom of Kabbalah is an absolute must for any person from Israel. And if one studies the whole Torah and knows the Mishnah and the Gemarah by heart, and if one is also filled with virtues and good deeds more than all his contemporaries, but has not learned the wisdom of Kabbalah, he must reincarnate into this world to study the secrets of Torah and wisdom of truth. This is brought in several places in the writing of our sages.*
>
> Baal HaSulam, "Introduction to The Mouth of a Sage"

In the spiritual sense, only our efforts to evolve beyond the animate degree are written for all eternity. When our animate degree ceases to exist, meaning when our bodies die, we remain only with what we have acquired from the degree above it. Thus, it is clear that engagement in *The Zohar* is the greatest thing we can do in our lives, far above and beyond anything that can be attained in this world.

And considering profits, it is important to understand that the source of all pleasures is in the world of *Ein Sof*. The pleasures come as upper light and travel through a system of five worlds in which the light diminishes from 100 to zero percent. Then, through the boundary that separates the spiritual world from ours, a tiny spark breaks in.

Incidentally, science has also discovered that our universe began with a spark of special energy. That spark, explains *The Zohar*, is all the pleasure that exists in our world, and there is nothing else.

In our world, the pleasure that exists in that spark divides into two primary kinds: physical pleasures—food, sex, family, and so on, and human pleasures—wealth, respect, domination, and knowledge.

What is the difference between those pleasures and the pleasures in the spiritual world? First, all the pleasures in our world, of all the people and at all times, add up to a tiny spark of light. The gap between that spark and the pleasure that is sensed in the spiritual world is unfathomable. *The Zohar* compares that gap to the gap between a tiny candle and a huge light, or between a tiny grain of sand and the entire world.

Second, in our world, pleasures come and pleasures go. They are inconstant, as eventually we disappear, we die. But in the spiritual world, pleasure is eternal; we experience our existence above time, motion, and place.

To summarize, we are standing at the threshold of a wondrous development to the highest level of reality. *The Book of Zohar* has been revealed today to bring us the light that will help us get there.

A wisdom that one must know: to know and to observe the meaning of his Master, to know himself, know who he is, how he was created, where he comes from, and where he is going ... and one should see all that from the secrets of the Torah.

New Zohar, Song of Songs, Items 482-483

9

The "Rabbi Shimon" System

This book shall be called The Zohar ["The Radiance"]
because of the impact of that light
from the upper radiance.

The Ramak, *Know the God of Your Father*

*T*he Zohar is a gift that humanity has received from the Creator through the great Kabbalist, Rabbi Shimon Bar Yochai. Rabbi Shimon was a special soul. He combined within him all the souls that preceded him. This is why he succeeded in leading the group that authored *The Zohar* to such unprecedented and never-repeated attainment—the end of correction.

The authors of *The Zohar* lived at a special time, which incorporated two completely opposite points: the end of their correction, on the one hand, and the spiritual ruin of the entire people, on the other hand. This is the reason why they succeeded in connecting the great light, called "upper radiance," with our world. We can learn about their greatness from the following words:

> *Happy are you in this world and in the next world. You are all holy; you are all sons of the Holy God. It is written about you, "One shall say, 'I am the Lord's'; and another shall call himself by the name of Jacob." Each of you is tied and connected to the High and Holy King, and you are appointed ministers with a shield from that land, called "the land of the living," the Nukva [female] that clothes upper Ima [mother], whose ministers eat from the MAN of the Holy dew.*
>
> Zohar for All, Lech Lecha [Go Forth], Item 445

The Book of Zohar, which they granted us, is the primary source that we have for the correction of the soul. Among all the holy scriptures ever written, beginning with the book, *Angel Raziel*, through the Bible and to the present day, there has not been a single book that compares to *The Zohar* in its spiritual power. All the Kabbalists wrote that there is a very powerful light in this book, a special "powerhouse," and when they say that the Kabbalah is "the interior of the Torah" or "the true Torah," they are referring first and foremost to *The Book of Zohar*.

One who reads in it, even without understanding a word of it but by simply wishing to know what the book says, will arouse an immense force that initiates internal changes within him. This is the reason why people who join *Zohar* lessons often feel that there is something very powerful about these lessons. They cannot always tell what it is, but something happens to them from within.

The authors of *The Zohar* have prepared for us a system of development. In our world, we see it as a book. But in truth, it is a complete system that they have prepared for us.

It is like a newborn baby. It doesn't know that everything has already been prepared for it—diapers, a cradle, special food, and toys for each stage in its development. The world has worked and is working for it all the time. Every generation, we prepare more things for newborns; it is a compulsion of our love for them.

The work that the authors of *The Zohar* did was enormous. They did not compose a technical science book, but transferred all the upper light through each of them, as though through a special mechanism, and prepared it to be received within our souls.

If you look at *The Book of Zohar*, you will see only paper and letters. But our desire to grow unconsciously activates the spiritual mechanism they prepared for us, and the light reaches us through it. This is why we are so influenced by these writings.

Why did the Kabbalists obligate each person to study the wisdom of Kabbalah? Indeed, there is a great thing within it, worthy of being publicized: There is a wonderful, invaluable remedy for those who engage in the wisdom of Kabbalah. Although they do not understand what they are learning, through the yearning and the great desire to understand what they are learning, they awaken upon themselves the Lights that surround their souls ... which bring one much closer to achieving perfection.

Baal HaSulam, "Introduction to The Study of the Ten Sefirot," Item 155

A SPIRITUAL SUPPORT SYSTEM

While reading in *The Zohar*, we should want to connect to all the people in the world whose point in the heart has awakened, and who wish to receive from *The Zohar* the strength to develop, too. Thus, even if we are just beginners, we receive in return for our desire an enormous power that will push us forward.

This is a huge force that can invoke a significant change in the world. All we need is to approach *The Zohar* with a desire to bond with everyone.

> There is none to begin and say songs, and there is none to complete his singing. That is, those who stand in the middle of the singing do not complete their song because they all become attentive to the voice of Rabbi Shimon until an utterance of a mouth is heard through all the firmaments above and below.
>
> When Rabbi Shimon concludes engaging in the Torah, who saw songs? Who saw the joy of those who praise their Master? Who saw the voices that walk in all the firmaments? It is for Rabbi Shimon that all the souls and angels come and kneel and bow before their Master, and raise the fragrances of the perfumes in Eden—illumination of Hochma—all the way to Atik Yomin. All this is for Rabbi Shimon.
>
> *Zohar for All, Shemot* [Exodus], Item 242

Rabbi Shimon is not a flesh and blood person being praised here, but a spiritual system called "Rabbi Shimon." What does that mean? The general soul consists of many parts with many different functions, like organs in a human body such as a brain, a heart, kidneys, and so forth. The soul of Rabbi Shimon, discussed in this chapter, is a very important part of the general soul because it leads the correction of the rest of the souls.

The great souls that preceded him led the correction in regard to Israel. But the soul of Rabbi Shimon is a system that passes the correction onto the entire world. Unlike Moses' Torah, whose purpose was only to correct the people of Israel, *The Zohar* is intended to correct the whole of humanity. The degree that continues the soul of Rabbi Shimon is the soul of Rabbi Elazar, his son, and it already aims at the end of the general correction.[34] This is the structure of the system of the souls through which the light that corrects our souls comes down and fills them.

The fathers came–Moses, Aaron, David, and Solomon–and blessed Rabbi Shimon. They said, "You are a holy light, and your friends, ...which shine from you. And in each of it, it is said, 'The candle of the Lord is man's soul.' Moses shines in you and you in your friends, and you are all one, without any separation. And from there onward all these illuminations spread to all who attain the wisdom."

Zohar for All, Pinhas, Item 824

In the current state of the world, it is vital that we cling to the system of Rabbi Shimon because it leads us toward the corrections. This is also the reason why *The Book of Zohar* is now becoming so well known throughout the world.

Until recently, while everyone knew that there was something special about *The Zohar*, very few actually felt a need to open it. Today, when the world is in a global crisis, *The Zohar* must be revealed. It is the only means for the correction of the world. Through it, we can and should obtain the power to reach the highest level of Nature, the upper world.

Happy are those who sit before Rabbi Shimon and are rewarded with hearing the secrets of the Torah from his mouth. ...Rabbi Shimon said, "Happy are you, friends, for no secret is hidden from you."

Zohar for All, Yitro [Jethro], Item 170

Anyone who wishes to receive strength from this system is regarded as "sitting before Rabbi Shimon." Even a person who slightly touches the system of Rabbi Shimon is already under its influence.

If you were not Rabbi Shimon, it would not be conveyed to be revealed. The Zivug [coupling] in that world bears fruit more than a Zivug that is done in this world. With their Zivug, the Zivug of that world, with their desire as one, when the souls cling to one another, they bear fruit and lights come out of them and become candles. ...All those souls that are born out of these Zivugim [couplings] enter the same hall.

Zohar for All, Shlach Lecha [Send Out], Item 202

When speaking of Rabbi Shimon as a system, it may be a bit confusing. Therefore, let's put some order into our words. Some 1,800 years ago, there indeed lived a man whose name was Shimon, and he did write the book known as *The Book of Zohar* along with friends-students. However, besides living in our world and writing the book physically, their souls actually experienced all the impressions that they described in the book.

If the authors of *The Zohar* had not lived in our world, they would not have been able to write the book. But if they had not lived in the upper world, they would not have been able to correct anything and the book would give us no spiritual value. In other words, along with the writing, they performed internal corrections at the level of the souls in the upper world. Writing is just a superficial expression of a corrected connection of love and bonding among souls, which allows the light to come down from the world of *Ein Sof* through their system, almost all the way to us.

Why almost? Because the light is standing right above us, and what is required of us is only for us to want to receive it.

One who parts from Rabbi Shimon,
it is as though he parted from everything.

Zohar for All, Yitro [Jethro], Item 411

10

THE UPPER WORLDS

> Behold that before the emanations were emanated and
> the creatures were created, the upper simple light had
> filled the whole existence. And there was no vacancy,
> such as an empty air, a hollow, but all was filled with
> that simple, boundless light.
>
> ...And when upon His simple will, came the will to cre-
> ate the worlds and emanate the emanations, to bring
> to light the perfection of His deeds, His names, His
> appellations, which was the cause of the creation of
> the worlds, then the Ein Sof restricted Himself, in His
> middle point, precisely at the center, and ... a place was
> formed, where the Emanations, Creations, Formations,
> and Actions might reside.
>
> The Ari, *The Tree of Life*[35]

In this chapter, we will deal with the structure of reality and the upper worlds. This information will allow us to better understand life and help us see what hides behind the words in *The Book of Zohar*. We exist in a reality that includes the Creator, the creatures, and the system through which the Creator connects to the creatures. Through that system, the Creator leads us toward the purpose of Creation—to do good to us, meaning to allow us to be like Him.

Like a loving father, the Creator wishes to share with us all that He has. But the Creator must make us evolve to become independent; hence, He must activate His influence on us from both sides, with mercy and with judgment. Although both stem from Him, they appear to us as contradictory forces and are perceived by us as effects of good or bad, mercy or judgment, light or darkness.

When we experience life's events we must keep in mind that even in what appears to be the most detrimental situation, He wishes only to do good to us.

If we remember to connect everything to Him, and remember that He is benevolent, then we reconnect those two lines—mercy and judgment—to the same source. And since we are the ones who connect them in our hearts and minds, we are the ones who achieve *Dvekut* [adhesion] with the Creator, meaning to become like the Creator.

However, when we try to do it, we discover that it is very difficult to connect all the bad and good things to the Creator, to understand that everything comes from Him only for a good purpose. We find ourselves asking Him for the strength to be able to unite everything to Him.

Studying the wisdom of Kabbalah in a group is the means that promotes us and directs us in this process. During the study and the work in the group, our egos grow and seem more intense, meaner, and crueler with each stage. Our egos try to mislead us into thinking that there is someone other than Him, and that He is not only benevolent. As a result, we are compelled to turn more and more to the Creator to receive more strength from Him to overcome the ego.

We overcome, and the ego intensifies. We overcome again, and it intensifies again. Stage by stage we rise until we succeed in exposing and correcting all the ego that was hidden in us to begin with. At that point, we achieve complete bonding with the Creator, *Dvekut*. We become like Him. This makes us infinite as well, allowing us to see the whole of reality without any boundaries between life and death, to understand and to feel everything, to be filled with light.

To allow us to perform the entire process, the Creator created a communication system between Him and us. Through it He leads us from above, and through it we can ask from below and receive His assistance.

This system is divided into several parts:

1. Its top is the world of *Ein Sof* [Infinity], where the Creator's power is out in the open.

2. Below it is the world of *Adam Kadmon* [Primordial Man], where the Creator divides His bestowal into five types, according the level of our egos.

3. Below *Adam Kadmon* is the world of *Atzilut* [Emanation], which is a system of guidance and governance that divides into five parts: *Keter* [Crown], *Hochma* [Wisdom], *Bina* [Understanding], *Zeir Anpin* [Small Face], and *Malchut* [Kingship]. They are also called *Atik* [Ancient], *Arich Anpin* [Long Face], *Aba* and *Ima* [Father and Mother], *Dechar* [male] and *Nukva* [female].

- *The Zohar* refers to *Atik* and *Arich Anpin* as the "hidden head" or *Atzilut*.
- *Aba* and *Ima* are those from whom all the lights come to us.
- These lights traverse *Zeir Anpin* and reach the *Nukva*, *Malchut* of *Atzilut*, who is called "Divinity," since all the light that is intended for the souls comes from her, from Divinity. *Malchut* is also called "the Assembly of Israel" because she assembles within her all the souls that wish to reach *Yashar El* [straight to God], meaning rise to the world of *Ein Sof*.

4. Below the world of *Atzilut* are the worlds *Beria, Yetzira*, and *Assiya (BYA)*, where our souls exist.

5. Finally, there is this world.

In the language of *The Zohar*, *Malchut* is also called "land," and *Bina (Ima)* is also called "heaven." *Zeir Anpin* and *Malchut* have different names in *The Zohar*: *Shochen* [Dweller, in masculine form] and *Shechina* [Divinity, in feminine form], the Creator and the Assembly of Israel, groom and bride, male and female.

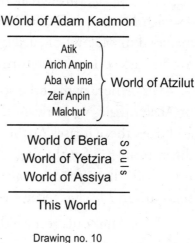

World of Ein Sof

World of Adam Kadmon

Atik
Arich Anpin
Aba ve Ima   } World of Atzilut
Zeir Anpin
Malchut

World of Beria
World of Yetzira
World of Assiya

This World

Drawing no. 10

These are only a few examples because each of these elements of reality has many names in *The Zohar*, taken from the language of interpretations [Midrash]. To help us connect to the heart of the matter, Baal HaSulam consistently attached Kabbalistic terms to the different names.

All the worlds, Upper and lower and everything within them,
was created only for man.

Baal HaSulam, "Introduction to the Preface to the Wisdom of Kabbalah"

These worlds do not exist in any physical place. Rather, they are as qualities that have no place, volume, or weight.

A person who still resides in the inborn egoistic desires is regarded as being in this world, in terms of one's qualities. If the point in the heart awakens and one begins to wish to grow in spirituality, if one aspires for a higher dimension, it is considered being in the worlds *BYA*, in one's qualities.

Working on oneself in a group that studies the wisdom of Kabbalah, one begins to evoke the light that reforms from the degree of *Ein Sof*, through all the worlds. That light creates a desire to reach *Malchut* of *Atzilut* along with one's group. When one is included in *Malchut* of *Atzilut*, one evokes the desire to feel Him, to give back to Him, in return for the Creator's giving.

This general will of the souls rises from *Malchut* to *Zeir Anpin* of *Atzilut*. *Zeir Anpin* raises that will to *Aba* and *Ima* of *Atzilut*, and from there it rises further through *Ein Sof*. Then, light pours down from *Ein Sof* through the entire system down to *Aba* and *Ima*, from them to *Zeir Anpin*, and from there to *Malchut*, and the souls in *Malchut* receive the filling.

When the souls receive the filling, they grow and unite with *Zeir Anpin*. This is called "the unification of Divinity with the Creator," or "the unification of the souls with the Creator."

It requires many such operations before all the desires in the souls realize themselves. When all the desires are corrected and aim to give to the Creator as the Creator gives to them, the end of correction will arrive.

What causes this process? The Creator has an inherent desire to give. Hence, there is no need to ask Him to give abundance and pleasure, as we normally do. The Creator has what to give, as well as an infinite desire to give it, but He wants us to not merely be receivers, inferior to Him, but for us to be like Him—great, independent, giving—similar in qualities to the Creator.

We are accustomed to asking for fulfillment. Instead, we should be asking for *correction*. When we acquire the correction, meaning become givers ourselves, we will immediately begin to feel all the abundance of the Creator and be filled with it. In other words, our problem is that we don't understand *what* to ask of the Creator. We are in an ocean of bounty, goodness, and delight, but we lack the proper receptacle in which to sense it. That *Kli* [vessel] is the quality of love and giving, and this is what we should ask of the Creator to give us. The more we have of this quality, the more we will feel the abundance that fills us.

On the Creator's part there is only one limitation on our reception of abundance—we should be like Him. He wishes for us to enjoy as much as He enjoys.

What does that mean? Let us assume that I come to visit a respectable personality. The host serves me all kinds of delicacies, invites me to play golf with him, listen to classical music ... but alas, I am an uncultured person. I have no interest in any of these offerings. I never experienced these sophisticated delights and I have no desire for them. I look at the host, bewildered, and say, "What do you want from me? I didn't come to you to enjoy what you like. I came to enjoy what *I* like!"

And the host replies, "My friend, I wish to give you pleasures beyond your imagination. Make a little effort, get used to them and believe me, you will see the beauty in them. You will feel that they are giving you much greater pleasure than you are feeling now."

What should I do? I can go along with the host and try to learn those new pleasures, although I have no desire for them, and then I will indeed gradually begin to experience a very special pleasure in them, a real taste of heaven. I can also tell the host, "You know what? It's too hard for me to get used to these new things. I can't, so let's drop it. I'm going back to my simple life."

"Fine, go back," he'll reply.

But when I return to my old life, I now feel that it's not such a bargain after all. And then I remember those words of the host about those other pleasures, the superior ones, and I return to him after all.

And perhaps I will go back to my old life once more, and then again to him several times. But in the end, I will understand that I have no choice but to return to the host to change my taste into his, because I already know that in them I will feel the taste of life.

Indeed, if we set our hearts to answer but one very famous question, I am certain that all these questions and doubts would vanish from the horizon, and you will look unto their place to find them gone. This indignant question is a question that the whole world asks, namely, "What is the meaning of my life?"

In other words, these numbered years of our life that cost us so heavily, and the numerous pains and torments that we suffer for them, to complete them to the fullest, who is it who enjoys them? Or even more precisely, whom do I delight?

It is indeed true that historians have grown weary contemplating it, and particularly in our generation. No one even wishes to consider it.

Yet the question stands as bitterly and as vehemently as ever. Sometimes it meets us uninvited, pecks at our minds and humiliates us to the ground before we find the famous ploy of flowing mindlessly in the currents of life as always.

Indeed, it is to resolve this great riddle that the verse writes, "Taste and see that the Lord is good."

Baal HaSulam, "Introduction to The Study of the Ten Sefirot," Items 2-3

ALL ARE HIS WORDS

If you only listen,
If you only open your heart,
You will begin to see
That He wishes to speak with you,
That He is speaking to you.

Everything that passes
Through your mind and heart
Within you and around you,
Is all His words.

All that you hear,
All that you see,
Are only
Him.

There is nothing,
No people,
No one else.
You are speaking only with Him,
And it is His language.

The world's appearance,
The sensation of reality,
The sensation of the self,
Are all the Creator
Speaking with you.

The Understanding Heart

11

THE EXPERIENCE OF READING
IN THE ZOHAR

*The language of The Zohar remedies the soul, even
when one does not understand what it says at all. It is
similar to one who enters a perfumery; even when he
does not take a thing, he still absorbs the fragrance.*

Rabbi Moshe Chaim Ephraim of Sudilkov,

Degel Machaneh Ephraim [The Banner of the Camp of Ephraim], Excerpts

The Book of *Zohar* is a wonderful tool. It can open an entire world of wonderful and surprising revelations before us. *The Zohar* is like a gate to the actual reality, currently hidden from our senses. However, to use the power within it effectively, we must learn how to read in *The Zohar* properly. The five rules below will summarize the entire contents of the book and will help you prepare for the great journey in the paths of *The Zohar*.

FIRST RULE—THE HEART UNDERSTANDS.
Do Not Seek Intellectual Understanding

The Book of Zohar is studied with the heart, meaning through will and emotion. What does that mean? Unlike ordinary forms of study, which are based on intellectual processing of facts and data, here we must adopt a completely different approach. Studying *The Zohar* aims to evoke an internal change in us, and prepare us to receive the hidden reality.

The measure of our success depends only on the measure of our longing to discover and to feel that reality. Hence, there is no need for prior knowledge, skill, or any special intelligence. All that is required is to have a genuine desire to open one's eyes wide, to open the heart, and to "devour" everything.

SECOND RULE—MAN IS A SMALL WORLD
Interpret the Words Correctly

The Book of Zohar contains many descriptions and concepts that we are familiar with from our world, such as "sea," "mountains," "trees," "flowers," "animals," "people," and "journeys." It is important to understand that all those details, images, and events mentioned in the book do not speak of the outside world around us, but only about what occurs within us.

Hence, while reading *The Zohar* we should try to interpret the words within it as expressions of those internal actions that take place in the soul, to see the text as a bridge to our deepest desires and qualities.

THIRD RULE—THE LIGHT IN IT REFORMS
Seek the Light

We often hear that there is a special quality to *The Zohar*. This quality is a natural law of development that acts in all of life's processes, and not some mystical, imaginary power.

Kabbalists explain that the corporeal world is entirely governed by the egoistic desire to exploit others, while in the spiritual world, only the intention to love and to give operates. Hence, we were given a special means whose function is to connect between the opposite worlds, or in other words, to direct our qualities according to the quality of loving and giving of the spiritual world—"the light that reforms."

The way the light affects us is currently hidden from our understanding. This is why we refer to it as a *Segula* [power, remedy, virtue] or as a miracle. However, to Kabbalists, who know the spiritual world, there are no miracles here at all, only a perfectly natural process.

They explain that all we need is to read *The Book of Zohar* and wish for the power within it to affect us during the study. Gradually, we will begin to feel the inner change taking place in us thanks to that light. The spiritual world will be opened, and what first seemed to us a miracle will become a clear and straightforward rule.

FOURTH RULE—NOTHING DEFEATS THE WILL

We all know what efforts are required of babies to take their first steps in the world, and with what inspiring persistence they do it. They never give up, repeatedly trying until they succeed. Likewise, we should continue studying *The Zohar* with patience and persistence until we begin to "walk" by ourselves and discover the spiritual world. The system required for advancement has already been prepared for us in advance, and the only thing we must bring in is our great desire.

FIFTH RULE—AS ONE MAN IN ONE HEART
Bonding Is Key

The Book of Zohar was written by a group of ten Kabbalists who built a perfect *Kli* among them, a united will to discover the highest force in reality—the Creator. Only the internal connection between them, the love and the bonding, enabled them to breach the boundaries of the corporeal world and rise to the level of eternal existence that *The Zohar* speaks of. If we wish to follow them, we must try to build a similar bond among us, to search for the power of connection that existed among the students of Rabbi Shimon Bar Yochai. *The Zohar* was born out of love, hence its renewed disclosure today will be made possible only out of love.

* * *

For this chapter, which summarizes the book, we have selected special excerpts from *The Zohar*. In between the excerpts we added explanations, guidance as to the right intention during the reading, and more to help you connect to the light imbued in *The Zohar*.

It is recommended that you read this section slowly. *The Book of Zohar*, our guide to spiritual development, was not meant for superficial reading, but for relaxed reading joined with deep inner search.

"We create nothing new.
Our work is only to illuminate
what is hidden within."

Menachem Mendel of Kotzk

WHY MAKES SALT SO IMPORTANT?

"Neither shall you lack the salt of the covenant of your God from your offering." Why is salt so important? It is because it cleanses and perfumes the bitter, and makes it tasty. Salt is *Dinim* [judgments] in the *Masach* [screen] of *Hirik*, on which the middle line emerges, which unites the right with the left. It cleanses, perfumes, and sweetens the *Dinim* of the left, which are bitter, with the *Hassadim* [mercies] on the right line. Had there not been salt, the middle line would not have been extended and the world would not have been able to tolerate the bitterness.

Zohar or All, VaYechi [Jacob Lived], Item 666

Salt is the basis of all the spices, adding flavor to the food. In spirituality, when we begin to receive the upper light into the soul, it is regarded as flavors spreading within us.

Our evil inclination, the egoistic material of which we are made, is like a stew without spices. We derive no pleasure from it. This is why it was said (Babylonian Talmud, *Kidushin*, 30b), "I have created the evil inclination; I have created for it the Torah as a spice." With the additional spice that the upper light brings—using the right intention—that same substance acquires wondrous flavors. Then, we have an evil inclination, and next to it, *The Zohar* as a spice. The combination between them yields the middle line.

If there weren't salt, the middle line would not have been drawn and the world would not be able to tolerate the bitterness, says *The Zohar*. In other words, if we could not mitigate the ego, we would not be able to tolerate it.

O FAIREST
AMONG WOMEN

The soul says to the Creator, "Tell me the secrets of the sublime wisdom, how You lead and govern the Upper World; teach me the secrets of the wisdom that I have not known and have not learned thus far, so I will not be shamed among those high degrees, among which I come."

The Creator replies to the soul, "'If you know not, O fairest among women,' if you have come and did not gaze in the wisdom before you came here, and you do not know the secrets of the upper world, 'go thy way,' for you are not worthy of entering here without knowledge. 'Go thy way by the footsteps of the flock,' reincarnate in the world and become knowing by these 'footsteps of the flock,' who are human beings that people trample with their heels, for they consider them lowly. However, they are the ones who know their Master's sublime secrets. From them will you know how to observe and to know, and from them will you learn."

New Zohar, Song of Songs, Item 485-486

When beginning to study *The Book of Zohar*, it compels us to "rearrange" our minds, to perceive reality differently. *The Zohar* "sculpts" us from within, according to that inner world that we should enter, like a key that must match its lock.

Even now the spiritual world is in us, except we simply don't feel it. We must build within us a different nature, new tools of perception, and new senses so we may feel it.

JACOB, ESAU, LABAN, AND BALAAM

We study ourselves and wish to find within us all the distinctions *The Book of Zohar* describes.

"Thus shall ye say unto my lord Esau: 'Thus says thy servant Jacob: 'I have lived with Laban.'''" Jacob immediately opened, to turn into a slave before him so Esau would not look upon the blessings that his father had blessed him, because Jacob left them for the end of days.

What did Jacob see that he sent for Esau and said, "I have lived with Laban"? Did he do it on a mission from Esau? Rather, Laban the Aramean, a voice walked in the world, as no man has ever been saved from him, because he was the soothsayer of soothsayers and the greatest charmer, and the father of Be'or, and Be'or was the father of Balaam, as it is written, "Balaam... son of Be'or, the soothsayer." And Laban was more versed in soothsaying and wizardry than them, but he still could not prevail over Jacob. And he wanted to destroy Jacob in several ways, as it is written, "A wandering Aramean was my father." For this reason, he sent for him and said, "I have lived with Laban," to let him know of his strength.

The whole world knew that Laban was the greatest of all sages and soothsayers and charmers. And one who Laban wished to destroy could not be saved from him. And all that Balaam knew came from Laban. It is written about Balaam, "for I know that he whom thou blesses is blessed." It is all the more so with Laban. And the whole world feared Laban and his magic. Hence, the first word that Jacob sent to Esau was, "I have lived with Laban." And not for a short time, but for twenty years was I belated with him.

Zohar for All, VaYishlach [Jacob Sent], Items 21-23

If we picture before us all those forms and explanations that we heard in school and in life in general about the stories of the Bible—about Jacob, Esau, and all the other familiar names—and approach the study of *The Zohar* with them, we fall into a great confusion and cannot focus on what *The Zohar* really says.[*]

While reading, we should seemingly go out to space, as if planet earth does not exist, as if we are only imagining that anything ever took place on it. After all, time, motion, and space are illusions that exist only in our current perception.

The fact that we imagine that someone was here thousands of years ago, and proceed to dig and find archeological findings, is just in our minds. Yet we call it "reality." Now we want to change that perception. We want to see this world as existing only in our will, which is where it truly is.

Since we were born, we have been accustomed to seeing the film of life in this way—that there is seemingly something outside of us. However, the whole of this film is happening only in our will. We must fight against our habit and convince ourselves time and time again that in fact, it is all happening within the desire.

This approach does not deny reality because the desire *is* reality. Even now, when we run into something, we are actually running into a desire. Even the sensation that there are things happening around us is a manifestation of desires, forces that appear this way before us.

The more we try to live this inner picture through *The Zohar* and refrain from sinking into historic images of familiar Bible stories, the more *The Zohar* will promote us to the interior of the Torah, to the true Torah—the real perception of reality.

---

[*] Yet, there is a strict condition during the engagement in this wisdom—to not materialize the matters with imaginary and corporeal issues, for thus they breach, "Thou shall not make unto thee a graven image, nor any manner of likeness" (Baal HaSulam, "Introduction to The Study of the Ten Sefirot," item 156).

We will gradually begin to see everything as forces and qualities, and the overall force that operates them—the Creator. This is the revelation to which we aspire. It happens within our will to the extent that we equalize with the Creator. This is the revelation toward which *The Zohar* is directing us.

FEAR NOT,
YOU WORM OF JACOB

The Creator placed all the idol worshipping nations in the world under appointed ministers, and they all follow their gods. All shed blood and make war, steal, commit adultery, mingle among all who act to harm, and always increase their strength to harm.

Israel do not have the strength and might to defeat them, except with their mouths, with prayer, like a worm, whose only strength and might is in its mouth. But with the mouth, it breaks everything, and this is why Israel are called "a worm."

"Fear not, you worm of Jacob." No other creature in the world is like that silk-weaving worm, from which all the garments of honor come, the attire of kings. And after weaving, she seeds and dies. Afterwards, from that very seed, she is revived as before and lives again. Such are Israel. Like that worm, even when they die, they come back and live in the world as before.

It is also said, "as clay in the hands of the potter, so you, the house of Israel, are in My hands." The material is that glass; even though it breaks, it is corrected and can be corrected as before. Such are Israel: even though they die, they relive.

Israel is the tree of life, ZA. And because the children of Israel clung to the tree of life, they will have life, and they will rise from the dust and exist in the world.

Zohar for All, *VaYishlach* [Jacob Sent], Items 250-254[36]

The point in the heart, the inner predilection that can awaken within each person, wherever he is, to reach directly to the quality of love and giving of the Creator, this is called Israel, *Yashar* [straight] *El* [God]. The rest of our self-centered inclinations are called "the nations of the world."

On the way to the Creator, the point in the heart traverses many different states until it is finally rewarded with clinging to the "tree of life."

THE SEA MONSTERS

"Come unto Pharaoh." It should have said, "Go unto Pharaoh." But He allowed Moses into rooms within rooms, to one high sea monster, from which several degrees descend.

And Moses feared and did not approach, except to those Niles that are his degrees. But he feared the monster itself and did not come near because he saw it rooted in the upper roots.

Since the Creator saw that Moses was afraid and no other appointed emissaries above could approach it, the Creator said, "Behold, I am against you, Pharaoh king of Egypt, the great monster that lies in the midst of his rivers." The Creator needed to wage war against him, and no other, as it is written, "I, and no emissary." And they explained the wisdom of the monster that lies in the midst of his Niles to those "who travel on the road," who know the secret of their Master.

Zohar for All, *Bo* [Come], Items 36-38

The Book of Zohar speaks about us. It tells us about what happens within us and only within us—albeit in a very peculiar way that often seems like a fairytale story or a history book. We have lungs, kidneys, spleen, and other organs. But in addition, in our feelings, there are many desires, qualities, thoughts, and drives. In other words, besides the physical body, there also exists the human in us.

Who is the human in us? If we open our souls up and examine them, we will find what the authors of *The Zohar* write about. In the human in us there are qualities known as "Moses," "Pharaoh," "monsters," "Niles," etc.. We must try to find them within.

What does searching for them within give us? In truth, it gives us nothing. However, by trying to find these qualities within we draw upon ourselves "the light that reforms," and this is what we are meant to want. There is no danger of misunderstanding. Even if we understand everything backwards, it will make no difference. What counts is the *effort*.

Let us assume that a person walks out at the end of a *Zohar* lesson and thinks, "I did well today! I felt that I really understood what Moses and what Pharaoh mean within me." Yet, this is completely meaningless. It may well be that next time, that same person will feel, "I didn't get any of it today; it's all dry. Except for a minute or two, I couldn't even concentrate." However, those few minutes are exactly what that person gained.

It is with good reason that Baal HaSulam wrote in the "Introduction to The Study of the Ten Sefirot" that the states of concealment are the states in which one can toil. One who strains during the darkness and feels that it is pointless should understand that states in which one is made to labor without receiving something to refresh the ego, pride, understanding, the mind, and the feeling are very good for one's spiritual progress.

We must welcome states that feel bland, since it is through them that we grow.

"And God created the great sea-monsters," which is the whale and its female partner. The word "monster" [in Hebrew] is written without a *Yod*, since he killed the female, and the Creator elevated her to the righteous. Hence, only one great monster remained. Also, know that a whale is a pure fish.

The whale and his female partner are of a very high root. This is because the sea is *Malchut* from the discernment of *Hochma*, and the most important of all sea creatures is the whale. Thus, he is the whole of the *Hochma* in the sea, although he does not extend from *Hochma* herself, but from *Bina* that returned to *Hochma*, the left line in her, called, "the point of *Shuruk*." This is why it is written about them, "And God created the great sea-monsters," since *Bina* is called *Beria*.

And yet, his place was not determined as the sea itself, which is *Malchut de* [of] *Atzilut*. Rather, a place was prepared in the world of *Beria*, outside of *Atzilut*, below *Malchut de Atzilut*, which are the ten Niles.

Zohar for All, *Bo* [Come], Item 39

What does that depiction give us if we do not understand it and do not know how to connect it to us? Baal HaSulam could have explained the words of *The Zohar* in a little more emotional style, a little closer to us, in addition to the explanation of the language of Kabbalah. Yet, he leaves us room for effort, for searching for its meaning, what it is for, and where it is happening within us.

We are in *Ein Sof*, and there are 125 concealments from our current sensation to *Ein Sof*. We must try to feel our real state more and more vividly to "regain consciousness." We are given this story specifically so we will begin to search. The search will yield within us new qualities and discernments with which we will begin to feel what we currently can't. Otherwise, the ability to sense spirituality will not develop in us.

There must be an effort on our part here, as it is written, "The reward is according to the effort." There is nothing else but effort here, which is why it was said, "You labored and found, believe." When will finding come? When the upper light affects us sufficiently and the spiritual sense is complemented within us at its first degree.

Knowing has no significance here, only wanting. We must *want* to feel what is really happening here, and not the words. "Spiritual attainment," as the Hazon Ish[36] said, "Is a subtle leaning of the fineness of the soul." It is impossible to acquire it with the intellect, but only with the will of the heart.

It is with good reason that *The Book of Zohar* is abstruse. When we open that closed gate, we enter spirituality. Time and time again, day after day, without understanding what is happening, we will advance toward a state where all of a sudden, we will begin to feel something. At that point, internal responses to the words will awaken in us. And thus, we will naturally feel how a reality is formed within us and how a new world is being structured within.

WHAT IS HELL?

"Better is he that is ignoble and has a servant, than he that plays the man of rank and lacks bread." This verse the evil inclination because it always complains against people. And the evil inclination raises man's heart and desire with pride, and man follows it, curling his hair and his head, until the evil inclination takes pride over him and pulls him to Hell.

Zohar for All, VaYishlach [Jacob Sent], Item 16

Should we also feel that state of Hell? And how do Kabbalists know about it? They experienced it themselves. After all, it is impossible for one to discover anything if not through experience. So do we all have to be in Hell? Apparently, we do.

We always sink into the evil inclination first, and only then discover what it truly is. At first, we do not see that it is evil. If we did, we would not get into it. At first, it is appealing, shining, glittering, and wonderful. Thus, our egoism deceives us.

Here *The Zohar* speaks of a person who scrutinizes the various parts in one's soul. He must be entangled, and out of that entanglement he must come down to a state of Hell. That state exists in every degree, and it is said about it, "There is not a righteous man on earth who does good and does not sin" (Ecclesiastes, 7:20). Only when one is in that state can one scrutinize the evil that lies within, and discover how much one is losing because of one's evil, how impotent one is, when it comes to doing something with oneself without the help of the Creator.

We should remember that each word that was written by Kabbalists is based on their own personal attainment, for "What we do not know, we do not define by a name or a word."[37] The authors of *The Zohar* experienced all those states in themselves. Let us hope that we, too, will obtain these states. After all, they are part of the road to discovering the truth.

THE GATE OVER THE DEEP

These three sons of Noah are the persistence of the entire world ... and from these the whole earth dispersed, for all the souls of people come from them because they are the meaning of the three upper colors in *Bina*, the three lines...

When the river that stretches out of Eden, *Zeir Anpin*, watered the garden, the *Nukva* [female], it watered her by the power of these three upper lines from the upper *Bina*, and from there the colors spread—white, red, and black...

And when you look in the degrees, you will find how the colors spread to all those sides, right, left, and middle, until they enter below, in *Malchut*, as twenty-seven channels of doors that cover the deep.

Zohar for All, Noah, Items 302-303

The more we can resemble the light, meaning its quality of giving and love, the more we will connect to it and discover its channels of bounty. In fact, even now we are in the world of *Ein Sof*, but it is hidden from us by all the worlds—*Haalamot* [concealments]—that exist within us, in our desire, because it is in contrast to the quality of the world of *Ein Sof*.

> The twenty-seven letters, with the five final letters of Malchut, are twenty-seven channels that bring the abundance to it. They have been made into doors to cover the Dinim in Malchut, which are called "deeps."

Zohar for All, Noah, Item 303

We ourselves are the ones who are building these channels and the doors above them. Once, these doors open a way for the light, and once they close it, like valves that open and close to the extent of our similarity with the light. Our efforts should be aimed at only one purpose—to make all our qualities resemble the spiritual qualities and receive light in them.

To the extent that we make the egoism in us similar to the light, we will discover within us the qualities of the Creator and the thought of Creation. There is a special part in *The Book of Zohar*, called *Safra de Tzniuta* [*Book of Humbleness*], which talks about it. This is also why it was said, "Wisdom is with the humble" (Proverbs, 11:2).

ON MY BED AT NIGHT

"On my bed night after night I sought him whom my soul loves." The assembly of Israel spoke before the Creator and asked Him about the exile, since she is seated among the rest of the nations with her children and lies in the dust. And because she is lying in another land, an impure one, she said, "I ask on my bed, for I am lying in exile," and exile is called "nights." Hence, "I sought him whom my soul loves," to deliver me from it.

"I sought him but did not find him," since it is not His way to mate in me, but only in His palace, and not in exile. "I called him but he did not answer me," for I was dwelling among other nations, who do not hear his voice except for His sons. "Did ever a people hear the voice of God?"

"On my bed night after night," said the assembly of Israel, Divinity. "On my bed I was angered before Him, asking Him to mate with me to delight me—from the left line—and to bless me—from the right line—with complete joy—from the middle line." When the king, ZA, mates with the assembly of Israel, several righteous inherit inheritance of a holy legacy, upper *Mochin*, and several blessings are found in the world.

Zohar for All, *Ki Tazria* [When a Woman Inseminates], Items 1-3

We should try to translate each word in *The Zohar* into its spiritual, internal meaning, and not perceive it in its familiar, corporeal sense. If we remain with the corporeal meaning, we degrade the Torah from the upper world to this world, and this is not why it was written. We must aspire to rise through it from this world to the upper world.

If we wish to reach *Zeir Anpin*, the Creator, to be in contact with Him, we must go through the mechanism called *Malchut* of *Atzilut* or "the Assembly of Israel," through the collection of souls that are united directly to the Creator, meaning with love and giving. There is no other way.

If I do not see myself connecting all the broken souls within me and bringing them all to the Creator, to contact and to *Zivug* [coupling] with Him, then there is no "me." This is a necessary picture that must always be kept in front of me. Otherwise, I am not going in the right direction.

Also, "me" means that I have taken myself through that mechanism of bonding among all the souls. This is the only way I can open up to *The Book of Zohar*. Why? Because the power of *The Zohar* was intended to keep the bonding among all those parts of me, which currently appear as not mine.

THE FRIENDS

All those friends who do not love each other depart the world before their time. All the friends in Rashbi's time had love of soul and love of spirit among them. This is why in his generation, the secrets of Torah were revealed. Rabbi Shimon would say, "All the friends who do not love each other cause themselves to stray from the right path." Moreover, they put a blemish in the Torah, since there is love, brotherhood, and truth in the Torah.

Abraham loved Isaac; Isaac loved Abraham; and they were embraced. And they were both gripped Jacob with love and brotherhood and were giving their spirits in one another. The friends should be like them and not blemish them, for if love is lacking in them they will blemish their value above, that is, Abraham, Isaac, and Jacob, which are *Hesed, Gevura, Tifferet*.

Zohar for All, *Ki Tissa* [When You Take], Item 54

The Zohar was written by a group of Kabbalists; hence, it can only be understood within the framework of a group. To connect to what is hidden in it, we must bond with all the other people who are craving it. Together, we form a group.

Only the connection between us will allow us to open the book because all that the book talks about is found among the souls. If we wish to bond, our desires will be called "souls," and in the connection between them, we will discover the Creator, the light that ties us all together.

"How good and how pleasant it is for brothers to dwell together in unity, as well." These are the friends, as they sit together inseparably. At first, they seem like people at war, wishing to kill each other. Then they return to a state of brotherly love.

The Creator, what does He say about them? "How good and how pleasant it is for brothers to dwell together in unity, as well." The words, "as well" indicate the presence of Divinity with them. Moreover, the Creator listens to their words and He is pleased and content with them.

And you, the friends who are here, as you were in fondness and love before, you will not part henceforth, until the Creator rejoices with you and summons peace upon you. And by your merit there will be peace in the world. This is the meaning of the words, "For the sake of my brothers and my friends let me say, 'Let peace be in you.'"

Zohar for All, *Aharei Mot* [After the Death], Items 65-66

If we do not consider the unity between us while reading in *The Zohar*, we will be missing out on the main point.

But wait! Until now, we said that we must feel these things within us, to look for the details mentioned in *The Zohar* within us, and now we are talking about bonding with other friends, bonding with a group outside of us. Isn't there a contradiction here?

The thing is that even the group is not really outside. We must remind ourselves every moment that all that we feel as external to us is really within us.

We must tie the concept of "self" within us with the concept of "other" within us. We do not feel "others" who are outside of our bodies. Rather, they, too, are inside of us, within our desires. This is how our desires are divided. There are internal *Kelim* [vessels] and there are external *Kelim*, and we need only mend the connection between them. And the other people in the group are the first people that we will connect to ourselves.

SELECTED QUESTIONS ABOUT THE STUDY OF THE ZOHAR

The *Segula* [Power] in *The Book of Zohar*

There is another magnificent power in it: All who engage in it, although they still do not understand what is written in it, are purified by it, and the Upper Lights draw closer to them.

Baal HaSulam, "The Teaching of the Kabbalah and Its Essence"

Question: I am not really sure how the *Segula* in *The Book of Zohar* works.

Answer: In our current situation, it's hard to understand it. This is why it is called *Segula.*

Let us say that I am told that if I jump on one spot ten times, the lamp on the ceiling will switch on. I don't know what the connection is between them. Perhaps a switch was placed under the floor, and there is a counter that counts to ten and switches it on after ten counts, but I don't know that. There must be a connection, but it's hidden from me. In Kabbalah, such a hidden connection is called *Segula*.

In other words, *Segula* is a law that exists in Nature, but one that I still don't know. Those who have already studied themselves and it are telling me, "If you use it in such and such a way, you will activate it. You do not see it, but this is how you activate it."

If an alien were to come to our world from another planet, he would look at a human baby and at a newborn calf and say that the calf will grow up to become a prominent figure, and the baby will grow up to small and helpless. However, we know that if you give both of them what they need, one will grow up to be a cow or an ox, and the other to be a human. This is a miracle, a *Segula*. We have grown accustomed to it happening, but it really is a miracle.

The little baby suddenly begins to understand, to react, to perform all kinds of actions. Each day, new abilities appear. How does it happen? After all, we didn't do anything to make it happen. We have become used to the existence of a process of development, but in fact, it is a manifestation of the force of life, a spiritual force that acts in the creature and appears in such a way.

The same thing happens with our spiritual development. After all, the laws of spiritual development are no different, only this development is still hidden from us; we are not accustomed to it. But the day when people use these laws just as they do all other laws of Nature is not far.

Kabbalists are telling us that there is a force in Nature whose impact we can draw by studying *The Book of Zohar*. The more you study it, the stronger, wiser, more sensitive, and more understanding you will become. By that process, spirituality will appear to you because this book has the ability to change you.

But aren't there other books that change me? There are, indeed. There are other books that change our perception of reality and help us discover the hidden realms. But *The Book of Zohar* affects the change more potently, yet more smoothly than any other book.

The World of Desires

A person who is in the dark and has always been in the dark. When you want to give him light, you first need to light a small light, like the eye of a needle, and then a little bigger. Thus, every time some more until all the light properly shines for him.

Zohar for All, VaYishlach [Jacob Sent], Item 91

Question: If I hear that everything is inside of me, how should I relate to those around me? How should I see the world? How should I consider those who love me, those who hate me, and generally relate to what happens around me?

Answer: We need to understand that there is the ideal, and there is reality. The ideal is what we will discover in the future, in our corrected states. For now, we are only learning that another reality exists in which everything is happening within us. For now, none of it is real for us, and perhaps everything that we imagine as a future picture is nothing like we see it.

We have no idea how our lives will change once we discover this picture. It is not that our world will change to some extent, but that a new world will appear before us. Hence, when we read in *The Book of Zohar* we must detach ourselves from everything we know and simply try to "dive" into it. At the moment, we cannot be in two worlds simultaneously. For now, we can only be in one world.

Therefore, we detach ourselves from the material reality and try to build a different picture, much like a child who wants to grow. Children want to be grownups in every way—in how they dress, how they behave, and in the eyes of others. They want everyone to treat them as adults.

We, too, should imagine in every way we can that *The Book of Zohar* speaks about our own new world, and that we are in it. In other words, this book discusses our internal qualities within which we exist, and within which we see a new reality. This game yields the impact of the light of correction upon us, and this new world appears.

So when the new world appears, does the old world disappear and we fly into heaven? Not quite. We discover a new life in our desires. Two desires—our own and that of the Creator—appear in us one opposite the other. We feel them, and we are in between them like a middle line, as our "selves," and there is nothing else but that. Between the two forces there is me.

The Difference Between the Torah and *The Zohar*

"Open my eyes, that I may see wonders from Your law." How foolish are people, for they do not know and do not consider engaging in the Torah. But the Torah is the whole of life, and every freedom and every goodness.

Zohar for All, Hayei Sarah [The Life of Sarah], Item 219

Question: Why do we need *The Zohar* if we already have the Torah?

Answer: The Zohar is a Kabbalistic interpretation of the Torah. Moses laid down the foundation, but the Torah is a coded book. There is a single code in it, but it is very deep. The Torah is written in "the language of the branches."* The wisdom of

---

* Kabbalists study the upper world, which is beyond the range of perception of an egoistic individual. According to them, from every object in the spiritual world, which is called "a root," a force cascades into our world and produces an object here, which is called "a branch." In his essay, "The Essence of the Wisdom of Kabbalah," Baal HaSulam explains it in the following way: "There is not an element of reality, or an occurrence of reality in a lower world, that you will not find its likeness in the world above it, as identical as two drops in a pond. And they are called 'Root and Branch.' That means that the item in the lower world is deemed a branch of its pattern, found in the higher world, which is the root of the lower element, as this is where that item in the lower world was imprinted and made to be."

Kabbalah explains the language of the branches and helps us read the Torah and understand what Moses really meant.

We are accustomed to relating to the Torah as a historic narrative about the feats of an ancient tribe. But Kabbalah allows us to see the upper roots through all that, the forces that evoke such actions in our world. Through Kabbalah, we can rise to the level of the system of forces that governs our world, and from there, we can correct and manage reality.

The Torah served as a correction method for those who lived since Moses' time until the ruin of the Temple, which symbolized humankind's detachment from the spiritual world. At that time, it became evident that Moses' Torah was so remote from us that we could not correct ourselves directly through it.*

The Torah is simply too encrypted to be a guide for the souls that have fallen into corporeality. That fall created a need for another source of guidance. This is the time when *The Book of Zohar* was written. However, *The Zohar* was not written for the people who lived in those days—the beginning of the exile—but for our days—the end of the exile.

"Woe unto one who says that the Torah comes to tell literal tales and the uneducated words of such as Esau and Laban. If this is so, even today we can turn the words of an uneducated person into a law, and even nicer than theirs. And if the Torah indicates to mundane matters, even the rulers of the world have among them better things, so let us follow them and turn them into a law in the same way. However, all the words of the Torah have the uppermost meaning.

"The upper world and the lower world are judged the same. Israel below correspond to the high angels above. It is written of the high angels, "Who makes winds His

---

* For more on this topic, see Baal HaSulam's "Introduction to The Study of the Ten Sefirot"

messengers," and when they come down, they clothe in dresses of this world. Had they not clothed in dresses such as in this world, they would not be able to stand in this world and the world would not tolerate them.

"And if this is so with angels, it is all the more so with the law that created the angels and all the worlds, and they exist for it. Moreover, when it came down to this world, the world could not tolerate it if it had not clothed in these mundane clothes, which are the tales and words of the uneducated.

"Hence, this story in the Torah is a clothing of the Torah. And one who considers this clothing as the actual Torah and nothing else, cursed will be his spirit and he will have no share in the next world."

Zohar for All, BeHaalotcha [When You Raise], Items 58-60

* * *

This chapter is only a taste of *The Zohar*. We tried to walk you through reading excerpts from *The Zohar* to make it easier for you to join the study. In the appendices you will find selected excerpts from *The Zohar*, as well as quotes from the greatest Kabbalists about the importance of the study of *The Zohar*. If you wish to delve deeper into the words of Baal HaSulam about the approach to studying *The Zohar*, you can do that in the appendix, "Introductions of Baal HaSulam to The Book of Zohar."

Even if we first feel that we are not feeling anything while reading *The Zohar*, after only ten lessons over the Internet you will be able to feel very distinctly how *The Zohar* affects you.

The impact of the study of *The Zohar* is very powerful indeed, and as we said above, it does not depend on the level of our understanding, but rather on our efforts to perceive what *The*

Zohar speaks of. We only need to listen, to *want* to feel. This is the only way to know the world—our world, as well as the spiritual world.

The Book of Zohar is a lifeline that has been thrown to us by the Creator. If we grab the end of that line, we will be able to climb all the way to *Ein Sof*.

"How great is Your goodness, which You have stored up for those who fear You."

"How great is Your goodness," meaning how sublime and precious is the Upper Light called, "good."

This is the hidden light, with which the Creator does good in the world. He does not deny it every day, in it is the world sustained, and upon it does it stand.

Zohar for All, *Emor* [Say], Item 3

ENDNOTES

1 Rabbi Tzvi Hirsh Eichenstein of Ziditshov, *Ateret Tzvi*, *Behaalotcha* [When You Raise]

2 Abraham Ben Mordechai Azulai, Introduction to the book, *Ohr HaChama* (*Light of the Sun*), p 81

3 The Rav Raiah Kook, *Orot* [*Lights*], 57

4 Rav Yitzhak Yehuda Yehiel Safrin of Komarno, *Notzer Hesed* [*Keeping Mercy*], Chapter 4, Teaching 20

5 Rav Yitzhak Yehuda Yehiel Safrin of Komarno, *Notzer Hesed* [*Keeping Mercy*], Chapter 4, Teaching 20

6 Rabbi Moseh Bar Elijahu, *Gate of Connection*, Gate 1, Preaching 5, Article no. 2

7 Rabbi Shalom Ben Moshe Buzzaglo, *The King's Throne*, *Tikkun* [Correction] 43, Item 60

8 *Zohar for All*, *VaYikra* [The Lord Called], Item 1

9 Isaiah, 14:14

10 "The world exists for six thousand years." Babylonian Talmud, Sanhedrin 97a

11 Genesis, 11:1

12 Genesis, 25:6

13 Based on Midrash Rabah, Eicha Rabah, Introduction, Paragraph 2

14 Johannes Reuchlin, *De Arte Cabbalistica*

15 *The Book of Zohar*, *VaYera* [The Lord Appeared], Item 460

16   The Gaon, Rabbi Eliyahu of Vilna (GRA), *Even Shlemah* [*A Perfect and Just Weight*], Part 11, 3

17   Rav Moshe Chaim Luzzato (Ramchal), *Shaarey Ramchal* [*Gates of the Ramchal*], "The Debate," p 97

18   Rabbi Shalom Sharabi, (The Rashash), *Light of the Rashash*, p 159

19   Baal HaSulam, "The Teaching of the Kabbalah and Its Essence"

20   Baal HaSulam, "The Teaching of the Kabbalah and Its Essence"

21   "I am the Lord, I have called You in righteousness, and I will hold You by the hand and watch over You, and I will appoint You as a covenant to the people, as a light to the nations" (Isaiah, 42:6).

22   Baal HaSulam, *Shamati* [*I Heard*], Article No. 89, "To Understand the Words of the Holy Zohar."

23   Baal HaSulam, "Messiah's *Shofar*"

24   Baal HaSulam, "Preface to The Book of Zohar," Item 34

25   Presented in the name of the Baal Shem Tov in the book *Light of the Eyes*, beginning of the portion Hukot [ordinances]

26   For more on this topic, see Baal HaSulam's "Preface to The Book of Zohar"

27   From the magazine, *Collections*, a yearbook for Jewish studies, ninth book, Jerusalem, 1995, Editor: Meir Benayahu, pp 152-154

28   From the magazine, *Collections*, a yearbook for Jewish studies, ninth book, Jerusalem, 1995, Editor: Meir Benayahu, pp 152-154

29   From the magazine, *Collections*, a yearbook for Jewish studies, ninth book, Jerusalem, 1995, Editor: Meir Benayahu, pp 152-154

30   From the book, *Let Moses Raise*, pp 11-15

31   Babylonian Talmud, *Kidushin*, 30b

32   *Rabash—the Social Writings*, "One Should Always Sell the Beams of His House"

33   Rav Yitzhak Yehuda Yehiel Safrin of Komarno, *Notzer Hesed* [*Keeping Mercy*], Chapter 4, Teaching 20

34   For more on this see "The Giving of the Torah" and "The Arvut [Mutual Guarantee]" by Baal HaSulam

35   The Ari, *The Tree of Life*, Gate 1, Branch 2

36   Rabbi Abraham Isaiah Karlitz (1878-1953), *Faith and Confidence*

37   Baal HaSulam, "The Essence of the Wisdom of Kabbalah"

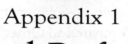

Appendix 1
Selected References
in Praise of
The Zohar

CONTENTS

ZOHAR FOR ALL

The prohibition from Above to refrain from open study of the wisdom of truth was for a limited period, until the end of 1490. Thereafter is considered the last generation, in which the prohibition was lifted and permission has been granted to engage in The Book of Zohar. And since the year 1540, it has been a great Mitzva (precept) for the masses to study, old and young.

Abraham Ben Mordechai Azulai,
Introduction to the book, Ohr HaChama (Light of the Sun) 81

The words of the Holy *Zohar* have power for the soul, and are approachable for every soul of Israel, small or great, each according to one's understanding and the root of one's soul.

Rabbi Tzvi Hirsh Horovitz of Backshwitz,
Hanhagot Yesharot (Upright Guidance), Item 5

The livelihood of the person of Israel depends on *The Book of Zohar*, studying with joy and pleasantness, and with fear and love, each one according to his attainment and sanctity, and all of Israel are holy.

Rav Yitzhak Yehuda Yehiel Safrin of Komarno,
Notzer Hesed [Keeping Mercy], Chapter 4, Teaching 20

The Ari said that at that time the hidden will become revealed, and learning the secrets of the Torah and revealing the secrets to everyone from Israel gives joy to the Creator.

Rav Yitzhak Yehuda Yehiel Safrin of Komarno,
Heichal HaBrahch (The Hall of Blessing), Devarim (Deuteronomy) 208

This composition, titled, *The Book of Zohar*, is like Noah's ark, in which there were many species, and those species survived only by entering the ark. Just so ... the righteous will permeate the meaning of the light of this composition to survive. And so, the power of the composition is that one who willingly engages, the love of the Creator will suck him in like the suction of the magnet that pulls the iron. And he will come inside it to save his mind and soul and spirit, and his correction. And even if he is wicked, there is no fear should he come inside.

Rav Moshe Kordovero (the Ramak),
Ohr Yakar [*Precious Light*], Gate 1, Item 5

Let us hope that all our brothers in the house of Israel will study of *The Book of Zohar* together, rich and poor, young and old. And how good and how pleasant if they try to establish friendships for the study of *The Zohar*. Particularly now, when the sparks of redemption have begun to blossom, we should exert in this sacred study.

Introduction of the Rabbis to *The Zohar*, Jerba Printing

When the days of the Messiah draw near, even infants in the world will find the secrets of the wisdom, knowing in them the end and the calculations of redemption. At the same time, it will be revealed to all.

This is the meaning of what is written, "For then I will turn to the peoples." What is "Then"? It is the time when the Assembly of Israel rises from the dust and the Creator raises her, then "I will turn to the peoples a clear language, that they may all call upon the name of the Lord, to serve Him shoulder to shoulder."

The Book of Zohar with the *Sulam* [Ladder] Commentary, *VaYera*, Item 460

THE NECESSITY OF STUDYING THE ZOHAR IN OUR DAYS

This point in time requires accelerated acquisition of the inner Torah. *The Book of Zohar* breaks new paths, makes a highway in the desert, the *Zohar* and all it harvests are ready to open the doors of redemption.

The Rav Raiah Kook,
Orot [Lights], 57

My aim in all my notebooks and in all that I write is only to evoke the hearts of disciples of the wise, old and young, to engage in the study of the internality of the Torah.

The Rav Raiah Kook,
Igrot (Letters), Vol. 1, pp 41-42

Hence, it is said in *The Zohar* that *The Book of Zohar* will be revealed only at the End of Days, the days of the Messiah... And since The Zohar appeared in our generation, it is a clear proof that we are already in the days of the Messiah, at the outset of that generation upon which it was said, "for the earth shall be full of the knowledge of the Lord."

Baal HaSulam,
"A Speech for the Completion of The Zohar"

And the books of Kabbalah and *The Zohar* are filled with corporeal parables. Therefore, people are afraid lest they will lose more than they will gain... And this is what prompted me to compose a sufficient interpretation to the writings of the Ari, and now to the Holy *Zohar*. And I have completely removed that concern, for I have evidently explained and proven the spiritual meaning of everything, that it is abstract and devoid of any corporeal image, above space and above time, as the readers will see, to allow the whole of Israel to study *The Zohar* and be warmed by its sacred Light.

Baal HaSulam,
"Introduction to the book of Zohar" item 58

THE APPEARANCE OF
THE ZOHAR

The Zohar was destined to be concealed ... until the arrival of the last generation at the end of times, at which time it was to appear.

Rav Isaiah Horowitz (the Holy Shlah),

In Ten Utterances, "First Article," p 17

Studying *The Zohar* at this time is much needed to save and to protect us from all evil, since the disclosure of this wisdom now, in flawed generations.

The Sage Yaakov Tzemach
in his introduction to *The Tree of Life*

At the time of the Messiah, evil, impudence, and vice will increase, led by the heads of the mixed multitude. Then the Hidden Light will appear out of Heaven—*The Book of Zohar* and the *Tikkunim* [Corrections], followed by the writings of our teacher, the Ari. And that study will root out the evil in his soul, he will be rewarded with adhering to the Upper Light, and will be rewarded with all the virtues in the world.

Rav Yitzhak Yehuda Yehiel Safrin of Komarno,
Heichal HaBerachah [*The Hall of Blessing*], *Devarim* (Deuteronomy), 208

This study has been revealed so brightly and expansively at this time primarily because the evil is greatly increasing and the assembly of Israel is falling. Through this study, the soul is purified. Indeed, while studying the secrets, and particularly *The Book of Zohar* and the *Tikkunim* [corrections], the soul illuminates.

Rabbi Yitzchak Isaac Yehuda Yechiel Safrin of Komarno,
The Path of your Commandments, Introduction, "The Path of Unification," 1, Item 4

Rabbi Shimon Bar Yochai testified in the corrections that the book itself will be hidden until the last generation, the generation of the Messiah, for engagement in this wisdom to unite the Creator with His Divinity and to attach it to the exile is a great need. Hence, *The Book of Zohar* appeared in this last generation, to see if it shall be delved in truthfully, to give Divinity assistance and support.

Abraham Ben Mordechai Azulai,
Ohr HaChama (*Light of the Sun*) p 105, in the name of Ramak

FROM EXILE
TO REDEMPTION

Because Israel is destined to taste from the Tree of Life, which is the holy *Book of Zohar*, through it, they will be redeemed from exile.

Rabbi Shimon Bar-Yochai,
The Book of Zohar, Portion *Naso*, Item 90

Redemption will come through the study of the holy *Zohar*.

Rabbi Eliahu Ben Sulimani,
Elijah's Throne, gate 4

Studying the corrections of the Holy *Zohar* purifies the body and the soul and is capable of bringing redemption soon in our days.

Rabbi Efraim Ben Avraham Ardot,
Mateh Efraim (*Efraim's Wand*), *The Tip of the Mateh* (wand), Item 23

The redemption of Israel and the rise of Israel depend on the study of The Zohar and the internality of the Torah.

Baal HaSulam,
"Introduction to the book of Zohar" item 69

Anyone who engages in this book brings redemption closer and brings great contentment to one's Maker ... for so the Creator has sentenced—that it will not be revealed and will remain concealed until the end of days, and that by its merit, freedom will come, for it has this power and none other.

Rabbi Shalom Ben Moshe Buzaglo,
The King's Temple, on the corrections of *The Zohar*

THE ZOHAR BRINGS ABUNDANCE

The words and the speaking of the holy *Zohar* themselves tie a person to the infinite.

Rabbi Moshe Israel Bar Eliahu,
The Remnants of Israel, Gate of Connection, "Gate One," Midrash 5, Essay 2

Many fools escape from studying the secrets of the Ari and *The Book of Zohar*, which are our lives. If my people heeded me in the time of the Messiah, when evil and heresy increase, they would delve in the study of *The Book of Zohar* and the *Tikkunim* and the writings of the Ari all their days. They would revoke all the harsh sentences and would extend abundance and Light.

Rav Yitzhak Yehudah Yehiel of Komarno,
Notzer Hesed (Keeping Mercy), Chapter 4, Teaching 20

The study of *The Zohar* cancels all sorts of tragedies.

The Rabbis of Jerusalem, 1921

One who says *The Zohar* each and every day will have provision.

Rav Pinhas Shapira of Kuritz, *Midrash Pinhas*

THE LIGHT OF
THE ZOHAR

"And the wise shall shine as the brightness of the firmament" are the authors of the Kabbalah. They are the ones who exert in this brightness, called *The Book of Zohar*, which is like Noah's ark, gathering two from a town, and seven kingdoms, and sometimes one from a town and two from a family, in whom the words, "Every son that is born you shall cast into the river" come true... This is the light of this *Book of Zohar*.

The Book of Zohar with the *Sulam* [Ladder] Commentary, *BeHaalotcha*, Item 88

Happy and so blessed are we for having been rewarded with going by its light and contemplating the pleasant words from the upper brightness, the holy light. It is sweet to the palate and it is all delights, endless, infinite water, to understand and to be educated with the act of creation and the work of the *Merkava* [structure/assembly], and how to become a *Merkava* for uniting and returning the soul to its origin and root. This has been resolved and engraved in my soul: One who has not seen the Light of *The Book of Zohar*, has never seen Light.

The Rav Tzvi Hirsh of Ziditshov,
Ateret Tzvi [A Crown of Glory] Parashat BeHaalotcha

A new Light is renewed every moment, until it actually becomes a new creation, through *The Zohar* and our teacher the Ari.

Heichal HaBracha (Hall of Blessing), *Devarim* (Deuteronomy), p 11

And this book shall be called *The Book of Zohar* due to the influence of that Light from the Upper Radiance [*Zohar*]. Through its Light, all who engage in it impart by Divine Providence, for the Upper Light and abundance above the reason would was imparted in the secrets of the Torah. Since it flowed from there, this composition was called *The Book of Zohar*, meaning that it extended from that *Zohar* [Radiance].

Ramak,
Know the God of Thy Father, 2

To excite the hearts of Israel to Torah and to work in the wisdom of internality, which is sweeter than honey and nectar, opens the eyes, and revives the soul, hidden delight, sweet as the light to the eyes, and good for the soul, refining and illuminating it with good and upright qualities, tasting the flavor of the hidden Light of the next world in this world through the wisdom of *The Zohar*.

Rav Yitzhak Yehuda Yehiel Safrin of Komarno,
Netiv Mitzvotecha [The Path of Your Commandments], Introduction

One who studies *The Zohar*, his face radiates. This is why it is called *The Book of Zohar* [Book of Radiance]. ...It is an intimation of sublime affairs, for the word *Zohar* in *Gematria* is the *Ein Sof* [infinite].

Zohar, Livorno, publisher's introduction

When engaging in this composition, one evokes the power of the souls with the power of Moses. This is so because while engaging in it, they renew the generated Light, which was created during its composition. And Divinity shines and illuminates from that Light as when it was first created. And all who engage in it reawaken that same benefit and that first Light, which Rashbi and his friends had revealed while composing.

Ramak,
Ohr Yakar [Precious Light], Gate 1, Item 5

THE ZOHAR AFFECTS EVEN WHEN NOT UNDERSTANDING

The language of *The Zohar* remedies the soul, even when one does not understand what it says at all. It is similar to one who enters a perfumery; even when he does not take a thing, he still absorbs the fragrance.

Rabbi Moshe Chaim Ephraim of Sudilkov,
Degel Machaneh Ephraim [*The Banner of the Camp of Ephraim*], Excerpts

One who was not rewarded with understanding *The Zohar* should read nonetheless, for the words can purify the soul and illuminate it with wondrous brightness.

The prayer book of Rabbi Shabtai Rashkovar, "Order of the Study," p 17

The study of *The Zohar* is great completeness for the soul. And even when one does not understand, the words of *The Zohar* alone are very able.

Rabbi Hanoch Hanich of Alsek,
The Order of the Study, Item 2

One who engages extensively should dedicate the majority of his studies in *The Zohar* even though he does not understand, for why should he care if he does not understand if it is *Segula* [special cure] in any case?

Rabbi Schneier Zalman of Laddi,
Short Essays of the Old ADMOR, p 571

It is true that we accept that even for one who knows nothing, the words of *The Zohar* can still cleanse the soul.

Rav Tzvi Elimelech Shapira (MAHARTZA),
The MAHARTZA Additions, Item 9

Since the time the precious light of the two great lights, *The Book of Corrections* and *The Book of Zohar* has shone, the Jews, the congregation of Israel, have taken it upon themselves to maintain the sacred study of the corrections and *The Zohar*, alone and with others, young and old. And although they are unable to attain and to understand the meaning of the pure sayings in these holy books, nevertheless, they drink their words with thirst and read with great enthusiasm.

Rabbi Yosef Chaim of Bagdad,
The Son of the Living Man, Benaiahu, introduction

The study of *The Book of Zohar* is very sublime to purify and sanctify the soul. Even if one does not know what he is saying and errs in it many times, it counts before the Creator, as it is written, "And his banner over me is love." Our sages interpreted, "And his skip over me is love."

What is this like? It is like a little baby who knows nothing and speaks half words with a stammering language, and his father and mother laugh with him and rejoice at his voice. So is the One who dwells above: He laughs and rejoices when the Israeli man is fond of the Torah and wishes to study, yet his mind does not attain or he has none to teach him, and he learns when he knows. He certainly brings contentment to his Maker and receives his reward. Thus, there is no room for excuses for one who does not know how to study; this argument does not exempt him on judgment day, for he could learn as he knew.

Rabbi Eliezer Bar Yitzhak Pappo,
Wonderful Counselor, entry: *Zohar*

Who can say the great sanctity of *The Book of Zohar* and its benefit, whose words are hidden and concealed as burning torches, illuminating and shining. Opener of eyes, the origin of life, the life of the souls, its contents is unbroken love, its words excite the hearts to love and to fear the honorable and terrible Lord.

And even one who does not understand the internal content of its words, any palate that tastes and learns its language, its words are able for the soul: to illuminate it and to purify it.

Introduction of the Amsterdam Courthouse publication of *The Book of Zohar*, 1804

We heard explicitly from the Old Admor in Liazni that there is dumbness of the mind, etc., and that reading of *The Book of Zohar* is good for that, even when he does not know what it is saying.

Rav Yitzhak, Isaac HaLevi Epstein of Hamil,
Ariel Has Camped, Exodus, p 64

CORRECTION OF THE SOUL

The Baal Shem Tov says ... Saying *The Zohar* is good for the soul.

The Path of RASHI, in the name of Rabbi Hillel of Paritch

Each and every letter in *The Book of Zohar* and the writings of our great teacher, the Rav Chaim Vital ... are great corrections for the soul, to correct all the incarnations.

Rav Yitzhak Yehuda Yehiel Safrin of Komarno,
Notzer Hesed [*Keeping Mercy*], Chapter 4, Teaching 20

My sons and my brothers, accustom yourselves to delve into the study of the words of *The Zohar* and the corrections. One who has never seen the Light of *The Zohar*, sweeter than honey, has never seen Lights in his life, and has never tasted the flavor of the Torah. Moreover, it purifies the soul and cleanses it. Even a mere utterance through the lips is a great remedy and correction for the soul. In particular, the book of corrections, which are the actual corrections of the soul from any flaw, blemish, and disease.

Rav Yitzhak Yehuda Yehiel Safrin of Komarno,
"Introduction to Atzei Eden [Trees of Eden]"

He should grow accustomed to studying in the Kabbalah, for reading the Kabbalah is a correction for this iniquity. This is why the Kabbalists were called "harvesters of the field," for they cut off all the *Klipot* [shells]. And the study of *The Book of Zohar* is part of that correction.

Horns of the Righteous, Item 53

Five pages from the holy *Zohar* each day is a great benefit and a great correction for the soul, to illuminate, purify, and correct it. It heals and corrects the sins and transgressions of the soul.

The Staff of Ephraim, Item 516, Sub item 7

The interpreters wrote as follows: One who studies in the holy *Zohar* corrects the upper worlds, and one who studies in the corrections chases away the *Klipot* [shells] and corrects the world of *Assiya*. This is the reason why Rabbi Shimon Bar Yochai established the holy book of *Zohar* in a great number and the book of corrections in a small number. This is the meaning of the words "And God created the two great lights," implying to the holy book of *Zohar* and the book of corrections ... Thus, studying in them is a great thing for correcting worlds in heaven and in the earth.

Rav Chaim Huri,
Mercy and Truth

PURIFYING THE HEART

Saying *The Zohar* can purify the heart.

Light of the Upright, "Pure Myrrh"

Always cleave your soul to *The Book of Zohar* and the writings of our teacher, the Ari. And cleave your soul with fear, love, and humility, lest your aim will be to become a rabbi and a leader, for this is truly idol-worship. Hence, my brothers, my sons, dear souls, sublime and elevated, cleave your souls to *The Book of Zohar*.

Rav Yitzhak Yehuda Yehiel Safrin of Komarno,
Notzer Hesed [Keeping Mercy], Chapter 4, Teaching 1

He also said that he asked his rav to be saved from pride and constantly pleaded to him about that. He told him "Study *The Zohar*," and he replied, "I am studying *The Zohar*." And his rav replied, "Study *The Zohar* a great deal."

Rav Pinhas Shapira of Kuritz,
Midrash Pinhas, 36, Item 73

STUDYING THE ZOHAR COMPARED TO OTHER STUDIES

Reading the words of *The Zohar* is more beneficial for Divinity and for the soul than the whole engagement in the Torah.

Correction of the night of Hoshaana Rabah [Great Supplication]

Who is greater to us than this holy book, *The Book of Zohar*, interpreting the ways, removing the stones from the trail, admitting love and fear in one's heart, teaching, guiding in the circles of justice, and leading us to the rest and inheritance.

The Zohar, Mentoba printing, The Publisher's Introduction

[A person] Will not achieve life but only through the study of *The Zohar*... And in this generation it is impossible to draw the Higher *Shechina* (Divinity) but through *The Zohar* and the writings of the Ari and Rav Chaim Vital, which were said in the spirit of holiness. And in this generation, "Who is the man who desires life and loves days" without wasting a day without holiness? To see the good of the next world in this world, let him cleave his soul only to *The Book of Zohar* and the writings of the Ari and Rav Chaim Vital.

Heichal HaBracha (Hall of Blessing), Devarim (Deuteronomy), 58

The virtue of the study of *The Book of Zohar* is already known, as the Ari said, "A single day of studying *The Book of Zohar* and the secrets of Torah equals an entire year of studying the literal. By this merit, the Creator will prolong their days in goodness and their years in pleasantness, wealth, and honor. They will be whole with sons and sons of sons, and houses filled abundantly, filled with the blessing of the Lord and the blessing of Elijah."

The Zohar, Livorno Press, Intro

Studying *The Zohar* ... builds worlds. It is all the more so if one is rewarded with studying and understanding the meaning of an article. It will correct him in an hour more than the study of the literal will do in a year.

Rabbi Shalom Ben Moshe Buzzaglo,
The King's Throne, Tikkun [Correction] 43, Item 60

The reason why our sages wrote that the study of *The Zohar* is awe-inspiring and exalted ... in all the Torah there is *PARDESS* and in all the studies, the concealed is not apparent whatsoever. On the contrary, a reader who repeats only the literal does not understand that there is a secret to the Torah at all. This is not so in *The Book of Zohar*, in which the secrets are open and the disciple knows that it speaks of the wonders and secrets of the Torah, which he does not know, and this is very instrumental for the correction of the soul.

Rabbi Chaim of Voluzhin,
Nefesh HaChaim [The Soul of Life], Set no. 7

There is no doubt that any study in the holy Torah is sublime and elevated and uplifting, especially if it is truly *Lishma* [for Her name]. It builds one's ascents in heaven and corrects the worlds, and unites the lovers.

However, the study of *The Zohar* is great. That is, the Bible and the Mishnah and the Talmud are very clothed and the meaning is unapparent in them at all. This is not so with *The Zohar*, which speaks the secrets of the Torah explicitly, and there is not a fool who will read and not understand its words in the depth of the secrets of the Torah. Hence, since the secrets of Torah are revealed without clothing, they brighten and illuminate the soul.

Rabbi Chaim Yosef David Azulai (The CHIDA),
The Great Ones for the CHIDA, "A System of Books," Item 2

The study of *The Book of Zohar* elevates more than any other study, even when one does not know what it says, and even if one errs in one's reading. It is a great correction for the soul because although the whole Torah is the names of the Creator, it is clothed in several stories, and one who reads and understands the stories considers the simple literal meaning, but *The Book of Zohar* is the revealed secrets themselves, and the reader knows that they are the secrets and the meaning of the Torah, but it is not perceived for the lack of the attaining and the depth of the attained.

Rabbi Chaim Yosef David Azulai (The CHIDA),
Pointing with the Finger, Item 44

What we see—that there are people whose mind is not drawn to holy and very terrible books such as *The Book of Zohar* and the books of the Ari, although there are terrible, terrible innovations in them, which illuminate the eye and are sweeter than honey, yet they are drawn after other matters, such as scrutiny—know that it is due to their temper that they cannot tolerate the truly holy matter. Indeed, one does have choice and has the power to break one's bad temper, but since he has already been born with such a bad temper, he must suffer great bitterness to break his bad temper and nature.

Rabbi Nachman of Breslev,
Talks of Rabbi Nachman, 40

One who studies *The Zohar* brings redemption closer. This is what the Rav Truth unto Jacob wrote in the introduction to his book in the name of *The Zohar* and the corrections. The rav warned extensively that one who studied the written and oral Torah would be severely punished he if did not study in *The Book of Zohar* and the wisdom of Kabbalah.

The Zohar, Livorno Press, Publisher's Introduction

There is no comparison between the livelihood and delight in the study of the revealed and the study of *The Zohar* and the corrections.

Rav Pinhas Shapira of Koritz,
Midrash Pinhas, 72, Item 3

The most important is *The Zohar* and the corrections.

Integrity, Words of Truth, Item 39

THE ZOHAR AS A MEANS TO DISCOVER THE CREATOR

Know that the entire Book of *Zohar* and the obligation to study it etc., is all a positive *Mitzva* [commandment to do a certain action], to cleave to it and to know that God is found, in sacred knowledge in the particular and in the unifications, and with love, fear, and unity.

Rav Yitzhak Yehuda Yehiel Safrin of Komarno,
Netiv Mitzvotecha [*The Path of Your Commandments*], Path 2, Item 3

Hear me my brothers and companions, the friends, who are craving and seeking the truth, the truth of the work of the heart—to behold the pleasantness of the Creator and to visit His Hall: My soul shall bend and cling unto *The Book of Zohar*, as the power of engaging in the holy book is known from our ancient sages.

Rabbi Tzvi Hirsh Eichenstein of Ziditshov,
Sur MeRa [*Depart from Evil*], p 4

It is known that the study of *The Zohar* is capable indeed. Know that the study of *The Zohar* creates desire, and the holy words of *The Zohar* strongly evoke to the work of God.

Rabbi Nachman of Breslev,
Talks of Rabbi Nachman, 108

The merit of one who contemplates the words of the living God, *The Book of Zohar* and all that accompany it, the words of the sages of truth, and the writings of the Ari is immeasurable. Through the constant engagement, they will discover the gates of light and the doors of wisdom for all who sincerely follow the path of God, whose soul desires to approach the palace of the King of Honor who lives forever, blessed be He. Hence, all who volunteer to engage in the wisdom for even an hour or two a day, each day ... and the Creator adds a good thought to an action. It will be considered as though he stands all day always in the courts of the Lord, and his dwellings are in the secrets of the Torah.

The Rav Raiah Kook,
Letters of the Raiah, Part One, p 85

One who studies *The Zohar*, which is the wisdom of Kabbalah, becomes a son to the Creator.

Zohar, Livorno, publisher's introduction

Let every son of Israel grow strong in the holy *Zohar*, even if he shall undergo several attempts to separate him from studying the holy *Zohar*. Also, if he has been through several attempts by people who are materialized in their substance, who are the harlequins of the generation, and he sits among them as a lily among the thorns...

Let one who has a soul of Israel, who wishes to cleave adherently to the Creator ... although at times it seems to him that he is as a lily among thorns, let him pay no heed to that. Let us be strong and grow stronger in the power of the *Ein Sof* blessed be He and blessed be His name.

Rabbi Eliezer Bar Yitzhak Pappo, (Eliezer of Damascus),
Introduction, *Path of Holiness, Item 12*

STUDY HOURS
PRESCRIBED BY SAGES

The Baal Shem Tov ordered his people to study the words of *The Zohar* prior to praying.

Rav Yitzhak Bar Yishaiah Atia,
Doresh Tov (Seeking Good), "Concerning *The Zohar*"

Prior to prayer, speak as little as possible and study an item in the holy *Zohar* or the corrections, or the new *Zohar*.

"Order of the Day and Cautions of Holiness" in the House of Aaron prayer book

One should not pray before he studies in the holy *Zohar*, whether much or little.

The Pure Table, Paragraph 93, Item 2

Be sure to study the holy *Zohar* or the legends each night before going to sleep.

Rabbi Yehiel Michal of Zlotchov,
Conducts of Rabbi Michal of Zlotchov, item 21

Our teacher, the Baal Shem Tov wrote an advice to the rav Rabbi David of Michaelikov, how not to have nightmares: study one of the corrections of *The Zohar* before going to sleep.

The Crown of Shem Tov, in the name of Rabbi Israel Baal Shem Tov, the BAASHT

If one is rewarded with studying the holy *Zohar* in watches, thanks to him Israel will be redeemed from exile, which is like a night.

Prayer book, *Gate of Heaven*, in the order of the study that the ancient ones wrote

My soul so clings to *The Book of Zohar* that when I lay and when I rise I am attached to it. My heart is neither restful nor at ease for indeed, the power of engagement in it is known and famous; it is the source of all the books of the fearful.

From a letter of the author of *Ateret Tzvi* to his rav, The Raiah of Afta

Some study the holy *Zohar* all year long, dividing the pages over the days of the entire year. Happy are they and happy is their lot.

Rabbi Eliahu Ben Sulimani,
Elijah's Throne, gate 4

The righteous Gaon, Rabbi Shlomo Bloch, said in the name of his rav, The Hafetz Chaim, "There are no limitations on studying *The Zohar* because it is mostly *Midrash* (commentaries). The *Hafetz Chaim* used to evoke everyone to study *The Zohar* of that *Parasha* (weekly portion of the Torah) every Shabbat, even unmarried men."

Rabbi Yosef Ben Shlomo of Pojin,
Hosafot Binian Yosef (*Yosef's Building Supplements*)

The first rule is to establish constant study, so this sacred study in the holy book of *Zohar* and the corrections will not stop, each of them learning his part one by one.

When Moses Raised, wondrous issues from
Rav Moshe Chaim Lozzato, the Ramchal

In his seminary, he established constant study of *The Zohar*, the corrections, and the *New Zohar* from dawn to dusk.

When Moses Raised, wondrous issues from
Rav Moshe Chaim Lozzato, the Ramchal

Also, be sure, my sons, to study or at least say each day in the early morning on an empty heart, a lesson in the holy *Zohar*. This is very good for the purification of the soul.

A Father's Mercy, Paragraph 3

One should determine to study five pages of *The Zohar* each day. This is very beneficial and a great correction for the soul, to illuminate it, to cleanse it, to correct it, and to wipe out the thorns, bad qualities and ill wills, and to be rewarded with the pleasantness of the Creator.

Rabbi Yitzchak Isaac Yehuda Yechiel Safrin of Komarno,
The Path of your Commandments, Introduction, "The Path of Torah," 1, Item 31

My teacher (the Ari), gave Rabbi Abraham HaLevi good advice pertaining to attainment—to study *The Zohar* only for knowledge, without deep study, forty or fifty pages each day, and to read *The Book of Zohar* many times.

Rav Chaim Vital,
The Writings of the Ari, "The Gate of the Holy Spirit"

One should see that he completes the old *Zohar* and the *New Zohar* and the corrections each year. However, should he study the order of the portions of the holy *Zohar* by the order of weeks, sometimes he will need more than two or three weeks for one portion, that is, with longer portions.

Hence, one should establish the amount of study from the holy *Zohar* and the corrections as three pages each day, so he can complete the whole of the old *Zohar* the *New Zohar* and the corrections each year. And after studying three pages, he will establish his studies in the rest of the books of the Kabbalists and will study the books of Kabbalists in an order that he can, until he completes all the available books of Kabbalists. However, one should be sure to complete the holy *Zohar* and the corrections each year, and to do so for the rest of his life.

Rabbi Alexander Ziskind of Hrodna,
The Basis and the Root of the Work, "Sixth Gate, the Gate of the Sparkle"

EXERTION IN STUDYING THE ZOHAR

The Book of Zohar has a different meaning every day.

Rabbi Moshe Chaim Ephraim of Sudilkov,
Degel Machaneh Ephraim [*The Banner of the Camp of Ephraim*],
Portion: *Bo* [Come], p 84

While studying *The Zohar*, one should deem each and every word as wisdom of truth.

The prayer book of Rabbi Shabtai Rashkovar, "Order of the Study," p 17

When studying *The Zohar*, one should contemplate each and every word, for each letter is an innovation in and of itself, and things that seem literal are actually a secret, for *The Zohar* is all light.

Rav Chaim HaCohen, *Good Conducts*, Item 46

While studying *The Zohar*, one should cry a lot until he is granted understanding.

About Rabbi Nachman of Breslev, *Talks of Rabbi Nachman*, 8

THE WISDOM OF THE ZOHAR
AND WORLDLY WISDOMS

Anyone who tastes from *The Book of Zohar* will taste for himself
that there is such wisdom in the world as the wisdom of the
depth of the secrets of the flavors of Torah, and all the wisdoms
besides it are regarded as naught and formless.

The Rav Tzvi Hirsh of Ziditshov,
Depart from Evil and Do Good

He would elaborate extensively with praise of the greatness of the
sanctity of the *Tikkuney Zohar* [corrections of *The Zohar*]. He was
accustomed to engage in it extensively ... and he said that all the
wisdoms in the world are included in the book of corrections.

About Rabbi Nachman of Breslev,
Talks of Rabbi Nachman, 128

RASHBI AND THE GROUP THAT
AUTHORED THE ZOHAR

We would never have the power to strip the Torah of its clothing,
were it not for Rashbi and his friends.

Ramak, *Know the God of Thy Father*, 16

And Rabbi Shimon Bar-Yochai would reveal the secrets of the
Torah, and his friends listened to his voice, joining him in this
composition, each answering his part... And here, Rabbi Shimon
Bar-Yochai instructed Rabbi Abba to be the writer and organizer
of all the words that the sages, students of the seminary would say.

The Ramchal,
Adir BaMarom [*The Mighty One on High*], 24

The Rashbi composed *The Book of Zohar* according to the illumination that came to him while he was corrected in the cave ... It is a great and terrible composition, which reveals the depth of the secrets of the Torah itself with great clarity, and this is called "The revelation of the internality of the Torah."

The Ramchal,
Adir BaMarom [*The Mighty One on High*], 24

Only during the days of Rashbi, after 13 years of being in the cave, the gates of wisdom opened upon him, to shine for all of Israel through the end of days.

The Ramchal, *Adir BaMarom* [*The Mighty One on High*], 13 duction, 1892

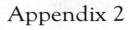

Appendix 2

Introductions
of Baal HaSulam
to The Book of Zohar

Selected Excerpts

CONTENTS

INTRODUCTION
TO THE BOOK OF ZOHAR

1) In this introduction, I would like to clarify matters that are seemingly simple. Matters that everyone fumbles with, and for which much ink has been spilled, attempting to clarify. Yet we have not reached a concrete and sufficient knowledge of them. And here are the questions:

1. What is our essence?
2. What is our role in the long chain of reality, of which we are but small links?
3. When we examine ourselves, we find that we are as corrupted and as low as can be. And when we examine the operator who has made us, we are compelled to be at the highest degree, for there is none so praiseworthy as Him. For it is necessary that only perfect operations will stem from a perfect operator.
4. Our mind necessitates that He is utterly benevolent, beyond compare. How, then, did He create so many creatures that suffer and agonize all through their lives? Is it not the way of the good to do good, or at least not to harm so?
5. How is it possible that the infinite, that has neither beginning nor end, will produce finite, mortal, and flawed creatures?

3) Our sages said, that man is the center of reality, that the Upper Worlds and this corporeal world and everything in them were created only for him (*The Zohar, Tazria*, 40), and obliged man to believe that the world had been created for him (*Sanhedrin* 37). It is seemingly hard to grasp that for this trifling human, whose value is no more than a wisp, with respect to the reality

of this world, much less with respect to all the Upper Worlds, whose Height and Sublimity is immeasurable, that the Creator had troubled Himself to create all these for him. And also, why would man need all that?

4) To understand these questions and inquiries, the only tactic is to examine the end of the act, that is, the purpose of Creation. For nothing can be understood in the middle of the process, but only at its end. And it is clear that there is no act without a purpose, for only the insane can act purposelessly.

6) Our sages have already said that the Creator created the world for no other reason but to delight His creatures. And here is where we must place our minds and all our thoughts, for it is the ultimate aim of the act of the creation of the world. And we must bear in mind that since the Thought of Creation was to bestow upon His creatures, He had to create in the souls a great measure of desire to receive that which He had thought to give them. For the measure of each pleasure and delight depends on the measure of the will to receive it. The greater the will to receive, the greater the pleasure, and the lesser the will, the lesser the pleasure from reception.

Thus, the Thought of Creation itself necessarily dictates the creation of an excessive will to receive in the souls, to fit the immense pleasure that His Almightiness thought to bestow upon the souls. For the great delight and the great desire to receive go hand in hand.

9) And you find that in spirituality the disparity of form acts like the ax that separates in the corporeal world, and the distance between them is proportional to the oppositeness of form. From this we learn that since the will to receive His delight has been imprinted in the souls, and we have shown that this form is absent in the Creator, because from whom would He receive, that disparity of form that the souls acquired separates

them from His essence, as the ax that carves a stone from the mountain. And because of that disparity of form the souls were separated from the Creator and became creatures. [...]

10) [...] To mend that separation, which lays on the *Kli* of the souls, He created all the worlds and separated them into two systems, as in the verse: "God has made them one against the other," which are the four pure worlds ABYA, and opposite them the four impure worlds ABYA. And He imprinted the desire to bestow in the system of the pure ABYA, removed the will to receive for themselves from them, and placed it in the system of the impure worlds ABYA. Because of that, they have become separated from the Creator and from all the worlds of holiness.

For that reason the *Klipot* are called "dead," as in the verse: "sacrifices of the dead" (Psalms 106, 28). And the wicked that follow them, as our sages said, "The wicked, in their lives, are called 'dead,'" since the will to receive imprinted in them in oppositeness of form to His Holiness separates them from the Life of Lives, and they are remote from Him from one end to the other. [...]

11) And the worlds cascaded onto the reality of this corporeal world, to a place where there is a body and a soul and a time of corruption and a time of correction. [...]

14) Thus you necessarily find that on the whole, there are three states to the soul:

The First State is their presence in *Ein Sof*, in the Thought of Creation, where they already have the future form of the End of Correction.

The Second State is their presence in the six thousand years, which were divided by the above two systems into a body and a soul. They were given the work in Torah and *Mitzvot*, in order to invert their will to receive and turn it into a will to bestow contentment upon their Maker, and not at all to themselves.

During the time of that state, no correction will come to the bodies, only to the souls. This means that they must eliminate any form of self-reception, which is considered the body, and remain with but a desire to bestow, which is the form of desire in the souls. [...]

The Third State is the end of correction of the souls, after the revival of the dead. At that time the complete correction will come to the bodies, too, for then they will turn reception for themselves, which is the form of the body, to take on the form of pure bestowal. And they will become worthy of receiving for themselves all the delight and pleasure and pleasantness in the Thought of Creation.

And with all that, they will attain strong adhesion by the force of their equivalence of form with their Maker, since they will not receive all that because of their desire to receive, but because of their desire to bestow contentment upon their Maker, since He derives pleasure when they receive from Him. [...]

16) Therefore, one must not wonder at how it was that the choice had been taken from us, since we must be completed and come to the third state, since it is already present in the first. The thing is that there are two ways the Creator has set for us in the second state to bring us to the third state:

1. The Path of Keeping Torah and *Mitzvot*.
2. The Path of Suffering, since the pain itself purifies the body and will eventually compel us to invert our will to receive into the form of a will to bestow, and cleave to Him. It is as our sages said (*Sanhedrin*, 97b), "If you repent, good; and if not, I will place over you a king such as Haman, and he will force you to repent." Our sages said about the verse, "will hasten

it in its time": "If they are rewarded, I will hasten it;
and if not, in its time."

This means that if we are granted through the first path, by
keeping Torah and *Mitzvot*, we thus hasten our correction, and
we do not need the harsh agony and the long time needed to
experience them, so they will compel us to reform. And if not,
"in its time," meaning only when the suffering will complete our
correction and the time of correction will be forced upon us [...]

18) And we must not ponder the state of other beings in the
world but man, since man is the center of Creation, as will be
written below (item 39). And all other creatures do not have any
value of their own but to the extent that they help man achieve
his perfection. Hence, they rise and fall with him without any
consideration of themselves.

19) Indeed, when all human beings agree to abolish and eradicate
their will to receive for themselves, and have no other desire but
to bestow upon their friends, all worries and jeopardy in the
world would cease to exist. And we would all be assured of a
whole and wholesome life, since each of us would have a whole
world caring for us, ready to fulfill our needs.

Yet, while each of us has only a desire to receive for ourselves,
it is the source of all the worries, suffering, wars, and slaughter
we cannot escape. They weaken our bodies with all sorts of sores
and maladies, and you find that all the agonies in our world are
but manifestations offered to our eyes, to prompt us to revoke
the evil *Klipa* of the body and assume the complete form of the
will to bestow. And it is as we have said, that the path of suffering
in itself can bring us to the desired form. Bear in mind that the
Mitzvot between man and man come before the *Mitzvot* between
man and God, because the bestowal upon one's friend brings
one to bestow upon his Maker.

33) Now remains the clarification of the sixth inquiry, which is the words of our sages who said that all the worlds, Upper and lower, were created only for man. It seems very peculiar that for man, whose worth is but a wisp compared to the reality before us in this world, much less compared to the Upper, Spiritual Worlds, the Creator would go to all the trouble of creating all that for him. And even more peculiar is what would man need all these vast Spiritual Worlds for?

And you must know that any contentment of our Maker from bestowing upon His creatures depends on the extent that the creatures feel Him—that He is the giver, and that He is the one who delights them. For then He takes great pleasure in them, as a father playing with his beloved son, to the degree that the son feels and recognizes the greatness and exaltedness of his father, and his father shows him all the treasures he had prepared for him, as it is written (Jeremiah 31): "Ephraim, my darling son, is he joy of his parents? For whenever I speak of him, I earnestly remember him still. Hence, My heart yearns for him, I will surely have compassion upon him, says the Lord" (Jeremiah 31, 19).

Observe these words carefully and you can come to know the great delights of the Lord with those whole ones that have been granted feeling Him and recognizing His greatness in all those manners He has prepared for them, until they are like a father with his darling son, the joy of his parents. And we need not continue on that, for it is enough for us to know that for this contentment and delight with those whole ones, it was worth His while to create all the worlds, Higher and lower alike.

39) Now we have shown that the Creator's desired goal for the Creation He had created is to bestow upon His creatures, so they would know His truthfulness and greatness, and receive all the delight and pleasure He had prepared for them, in the

measure described in the verse: "Ephraim my darling son, is he joy of his parents?" (Jeremiah 31, 19). Thus, you clearly find that this purpose does not apply to the still and the great spheres, such as the earth, the moon, or the sun, however luminous they may be, and not to the vegetative or the animate, for they lack the sensation of others, even from among their own species. Therefore, how can the sensation of the Godly and His bestowal apply to them?

Humankind alone, having been prepared with the sensation of others of the same species, who are similar to them, after delving in Torah and *Mitzvot*, when they invert their will to receive to a will to bestow, and come to equivalence of form with his Maker, they receive all the degrees that have been prepared for them in the Upper Worlds, called *NRNHY*. By that they become qualified to receive the purpose of the Thought of Creation. After all, the purpose of the creation of all the worlds was for man alone.

40) And I know that it is completely unaccepted in the eyes of some philosophers. They cannot agree that man, which they think of as low and worthless, is the center of the magnificent Creation. But they are like a worm that is born inside a radish. It lives there and thinks that the world of the Creator is as bitter, as dark, and small as the radish it was born in. But as soon as it breaks the shell of the radish and peeps out, it claims in bewilderment: "I thought the whole world was the size of the radish I was born in, and now I see a grand, beautiful, and wondrous world before me!"

So, too, are those who are immersed in the *Klipa* (singular for *Klipot*) of the will to receive they were born with, and did not try to take the unique spice, which are the practical Torah and *Mitzvot*, which can break this hard *Klipa* and turn it into a desire to bestow contentment upon the Maker. It is certain that they must determine their worthlessness and emptiness, as they truly are, and cannot comprehend that this magnificent reality had been created only for them.

Indeed, had they delved in Torah and *Mitzvot* to bestow contentment upon their Maker, with all the required purity, and would try to break the *Klipa* of the will to receive they were born in and assume the desire to bestow, their eyes would immediately open to see and attain for themselves all the degrees of wisdom, intelligence and clear mind, that have been prepared for them in the Spiritual Worlds. Then they would themselves say what our sages said, "What does a good guest say? 'Everything the host has done, he has done for me alone.'"

41) But there still remains to clarify why would man need all the Upper Worlds the Creator had created for him? What use has he of them? Bear in mind that the reality of all the worlds is generally divided into five worlds, called a) *Adam Kadmon*, b) *Atzilut*, c) *Beria*, d) *Yetzira*, and e) *Assiya*. In each of them are innumerable details, which are the five *Sefirot KHBTM* (*Keter*, *Hochma*, *Bina*, *Tifferet*, and *Malchut*). The world of AK (*Adam Kadmon*) is *Keter*; the world of *Atzilut* is *Hochma*; the world of *Beria* is *Bina*; the world of *Yetzira* is *Tifferet*; and the world *Assiya* is *Malchut*.

And the Lights clothed in those five worlds are called YHNRN. The Light of *Yechida* shines in the world of *Adam Kadmon*; the Light of *Haya* in the world of *Atzilut*; the Light of *Neshama* in the world of *Beria*; the Light of *Ruach* in the world of *Yetzira*; and the Light of *Nefesh* in the world of *Assiya*.

All these worlds and everything in them are included in the Holy Name, *Yod-Hey-Vav-Hey*, and the tip of the *Yod*. We have no perception in the first world, AK. Hence, it is only implied in the tip of the *Yod* of the Name. This is why we do not speak of it and always mention only the four worlds ABYA. *Yod* is the world of *Atzilut*, *Hey*—the world of *Beria*, *Vav*—the world of *Yetzira*, and the bottom *Hey* is the world of *Assiya*.

42) We have now explained the five worlds that include the entire spiritual reality that extends from *Ein Sof* to this world. However, they are included in one the other, and in each of the worlds there are the five worlds, the five *Sefirot KHBTM*, in which the five Lights *NRNHY* are dressed, corresponding to the five worlds.

And besides the five *Sefirot KHBTM* in each world, there are the four spiritual categories—Still, Vegetative, Animate, and Speaking. In it, man's soul is regarded as the speaking, the animate is regarded as the angels in that world, the vegetative category is called "dresses" and the still category is called "halls." And they all robe one another: the speaking category, which is the souls of people, clothes the five *Sefirot*, *KHBTM*, which is the Godliness in that world. The animate category, which are the angels clothes over the souls; the vegetative, which are the dresses, clothe the angels; and the still, which are halls, revolve around them all.

The dressing means that they serve one another and evolve from one another, as we have clarified with the corporeal still, vegetative, animate and speaking in this world (Items 35-38): the three categories—still, vegetative, and animate—did not extend for themselves, but only so the fourth category, which is man, might develop and rise by them. Therefore, their role is only to serve man and be useful to him.

So it is in all the spiritual worlds. The three categories—still, vegetative, and animate—appeared there only to serve and be useful to the speaking category there, which is man's soul. Therefore, it is considered that they all clothe over man's soul, meaning to serve him.

43) When man is born, he immediately has a *Nefesh* of *Kedusha* (Holiness). But not an actual *Nefesh*, but the posterior of it, its last discernment, which, due to its smallness, is called a "point." It dresses in man's heart, in one's will to receive, which is found primarily in one's heart. [...]

55) Thus, we have clarified what we asked, "Why does man need all the Upper Worlds, which the Creator had created for him? What need has man of them?" Now you will see that one cannot bring contentment to one's Maker, if not with the help of all these worlds. This is because he attains the Lights and degrees of his soul, called *NRNHY*, according to the measure of the purity of his will to receive. And with each degree he attains, the Lights of that degree assist him in his purification.

Thus, he rises in degrees until he achieves the amusements of the final aim in the Thought of Creation (Item 33). It is written in *The Zohar* (*Noah*, Item 63), about the verse, "He who comes to be purified is aided." It asks, "Aided with what?" And it replies that he is aided with a holy soul. For it is impossible to achieve the desired purification for the Thought of Creation, except through the assistance of all the *NRNHY* degrees of the soul.

57) Now you can understand the aridity and the darkness that have befallen us in this generation, such as we have never seen before. It is because even the worshipers of the Creator have abandoned the engagement in the secrets of the Torah.

Maimonides has already given a true allegory about that: If a line of a thousand blind walk along the way, and there is at least one leader amongst them who can see, they are certain to take the right path and not fall in the pits and obstacles, since they are following the sighted one who leads them. But if that person is missing, they are certain to stumble over every hurdle on the way, and will all fall into the pit.

So is the issue before us. If the worshipers of the Creator had, at least, engaged in the internality of the Torah and extended a complete Light from *Ein Sof*, the whole generation would have followed them. And everyone would be certain of their way, that they would not fall. But if even the servants of the Creator have distanced themselves from this wisdom, it is no wonder the whole generation is failing because of them. And because of my great sorrow I cannot elaborate on that!

58) Indeed, I know the reason: it is mainly because faith has generally diminished, specifically faith in the holy men, the wise men of all generations. And the books of Kabbalah and *The Zohar* are filled with corporeal parables. Therefore, people are afraid lest they will lose more than they will gain, since they could easily fail with materializing. And this is what prompted me to compose a sufficient interpretation to the writings of the Ari, and now to the Holy *Zohar*. And I have completely removed that concern, for I have evidently explained and proven the spiritual meaning of everything, that it is abstract and devoid of any corporeal image, above space and above time, as the readers will see, to allow the whole of Israel to study *The Book of Zohar* and be warmed by its sacred Light.

And I have named that commentary *The Sulam* (Ladder) to show that the purpose of my commentary is as the role of any ladder: if you have an attic filled abundantly, then all you need is a ladder to reach it. And then, all the bounty in the world will be in your hands. But the ladder is not a purpose in and of itself, for if you pause on the rungs of the ladder and will not enter the attic, your goal will not be achieved.

And so it is with my commentary on *The Zohar*, because the way to fully clarify these most profound of words has not yet been created. But nonetheless, with my commentary, I have constructed a path and an entrance for any person by which to rise and delve and scrutinize *The Book of Zohar* itself, for only then will my aim with this commentary be completed.

59) And all those who know the ins and outs of the holy *Book of Zohar*, that is, who understand what is written in it, unanimously agree that the holy *Book of Zohar* was written by the Godly Tanna (sage) Rabbi Shimon Bar Yochai. Only some of those who are far from this wisdom doubt this pedigree and tend to say, relying on fabricated tales of opponents of this wisdom, that its author is the Kabbalist Rabbi Moshe De Leon, or others of his contemporaries.

60) And as for me, since the day I have been endowed, by the Light of the Creator, with a glance into this holy book, it has not crossed my mind to question its origin, for the simple reason that the content of the book brings to my heart the merit of the Tanna Rashbi (Rabbi Shimon Bar Yochai) far more than all other sages. And if I were to clearly see that its author is some other name, such as Rabbi Moshe De Leon, than I would praise the merit of Rabbi Moshe De Leon more than all other sages, including Rashbi.

Indeed, judging by the depth of the wisdom in the book, if I were to clearly find that its writer is one of the forty-eight prophets, I would consider it much more acceptable than to relate it to one of the sages. Moreover, if I were to find that Moses himself received it from the Creator Himself on Mount Sinai, then my mind would really be at peace, for such a composition is worthy of him. Hence, since I have been blessed with compiling a sufficient interpretation that enables every examiner to acquire some understanding of what is written in the book, I think I am completely excused from further toil in that examination, for any person who is knowledgeable in *The Zohar* will now settle for no less than the Tanna Rashbi as its writer.

61) Accordingly, the question arises, "Why was *The Zohar* not revealed to the early generations, whose merit was undoubtedly greater than the latter ones, and were more worthy"? We must also ask, "Why was the commentary on *The Book of Zohar* not revealed before the time of the Ari, and not to the Kabbalists that preceded him"? And the most bewildering question, "Why were the commentaries on the words of the Ari and on the words of *The Zohar* not revealed since the days of the Ari through our generation"?

The answer is that the world, during the six thousand years of its existence, is like one *Partzuf* divided into three thirds: *Rosh* (head), *Toch* (interior), *Sof* (end), meaning HBD (*Hochma, Bina, Daat*), HGT (*Hesed, Gevura, Tifferet*), NHY (*Netzah, Hod, Yesod*). This is what our sages wrote, "Two millennia of *Tohu* (chaos), two millennia of Torah, and two millennia of the days of the Messiah" (*Sanhedrin* 97a).

In the first two millennia, considered *Rosh* and HBD, the Lights were very small. They were regarded as *Rosh* without *Guf* (body), having only Lights of *Nefesh*. This is because there is an inverse relation between Lights and vessels: with the *Kelim* (vessels) the rule is that the first *Kelim* grow first in each *Partzuf*; and with the Lights it is the opposite—the smaller Lights dress in the *Partzuf* first.

Thus, as long as only the upper parts are in the *Kelim*, the *Kelim* HBD, only Lights of *Nefesh* dress there, which are the smallest Lights. This is why it is written about the first two millennia that they are considered *Tohu*. And in the second two millennia of the world, which are *Kelim* of HGT, the Light of *Ruach* descends and clothes in the world, which is considered the Torah. This is why it is said about the two middle millennia that they are Torah. And the last two millennia are *Kelim* of NHYM (*Netzah, Hod, Yesod, Malchut*). Therefore, at that time, the Light of *Neshama* dresses in the world, which is the greater Light, hence they are the days of the Messiah.

This is also the conduct in each particular *Partzuf*. In its vessels of *HBD*, *HGT*, through its *Chazeh* (chest), the Lights are covered and do not begin to shine open *Hassadim*, which means that the appearance of the sublime Light of *Hochma* occurs only from the *Chazeh* down, in its *NHYM*. This is the reason that before the *Kelim* of *NHYM* began to show in the *Partzuf* of the world, which are the last two millennia, the wisdom of *The Zohar* in particular and the wisdom of Kabbalah in general were hidden from the world.

But during the time of the Ari, when the time of the completion of the *Kelim* below the *Chazeh* had drawn closer, the Light of the sublime *Hochma* was revealed in the world, through the soul of the Godly Rabbi Isaac Luria (the Ari), who was ready to receive that great Light. Hence, he revealed the essentials in *The Book of Zohar* and the wisdom of Kabbalah, until he overshadowed all his predecessors.

Yet, since these *Kelim* were not yet completed (since he passed away in 1572), the world was not yet worthy of discovering his words, and his holy words were only known only to a chosen few, who were prohibited to tell them to the world.

Now, in our generation, since we are nearing the end of the last two millennia, we are given permission to reveal his words and the words of *The Zohar* throughout the world to a great measure, in such a way that from our generation onwards the words of *The Zohar* will become increasingly revealed in the world, until the full measure is revealed, as the Creator wills it.

63) Now you can understand that there really is no end to the merit of the first generations over the last, as this is the rule in all the *Partzufim* (plural for *Partzuf*) of the worlds and of the souls, that the purer one is the first to be selected into the *Partzuf*.

Therefore, the purer *Kelim*, *HBD*, were selected first in the world and in the souls.

Thus, the souls in the first two millennia were much Higher. Yet, they could not receive the full measure of Light, due to the lack of the lower parts in the world and in themselves, which are *HGT NHYM*.

And afterwards, in the two middle millennia, when the *Kelim* of *HGT* were selected into the world and in the souls, the souls were indeed very pure, in and of themselves. This is because the merit of the *Kelim* of *HGT* is close to that of *HBD*. Yet, the Lights were still concealed in the world, due to the absence of the *Kelim* from the *Chazeh* down, in the world and in the souls.

Thus, in our generation, although the essence of the souls is the worst, which is why they could not be selected for *Kedusha* thus far, they are the ones that complete the *Partzuf* of the world and the *Partzuf* of the souls with respect to the *Kelim*, and the work completed only through them.

This is because now, when the *Kelim* of *NHY* are being completed, and all the *Kelim*, *Rosh*, *Toch*, *Sof* are in the *Partzuf*, full measures of Light, in *Rosh*, *Toch*, *Sof*, are now being extended to all those who are worthy, meaning complete *NRN*. Hence, only after the completion of these lowly souls can the Highest Lights manifest, and not before.

66) Bear in mind that in everything there is internality and externality. In the world in general, Israel, the descendants of Abraham, Isaac and Jacob, are considered the internality of the world, and the seventy nations are considered the externality of the world. Also, there is internality within Israel themselves, which are the wholehearted workers of the Creator, and there is externality—those who do not devote themselves to the work of the Creator. Among the nations of the world, there is internality as well, which are the Righteous of the Nations of the World,

and there is externality, which are the rude and the harmful among them.

Additionally, among the servants of the Creator among the Children of Israel, there is internality, being those rewarded with comprehension of the soul of the internality of the Torah and its secrets, and externality, who merely observe the practical part of the Torah.

Also, there is internality in every person from Israel—the Israel within—which is the point in the heart, and externality—which is the inner Nations of the World, the body itself. But even the inner Nations of the World in that person are considered proselytes, since by cleaving to the internality, they become like proselytes from among the Nations of the World, that came and cleaved to the whole of Israel.

67) When a person from Israel enhances and dignifies one's internality, which is the Israel in that person, over the externality, which are the Nations of the World in him, that is, when one dedicates the majority of one's efforts to enhance and exalt one's internality, to benefit one's soul, and gives minor efforts, the mere necessity, to sustain the Nations of the World in him, meaning the bodily needs, as it is written (Avot, 1), "Make your Torah permanent and your labor temporary," by so doing, one makes the Children of Israel soar upwards in the internality and externality of the world as well, and the Nations of the World, which are the externality, to recognize and acknowledge the value of the Children of Israel.

And if, God forbid, it is to the contrary, and an individual from Israel enhances and appreciates one's externality, which is the Nations of the World in him, more than the inner Israel in him, as it is written (Deuteronomy 28), "The stranger that is in the midst of thee," meaning the externality in that person rises and soars, and you yourself, the internality, the Israel in you, plunges down? With these actions, one causes the externality of the world in general—the Nations of the World—to soar ever higher and overcome Israel, degrading them to the ground, and the Children of Israel, the internality in the world, to plunge deep down.

68) Do not be surprised that one person's actions bring elevation or decline to the whole world, for it is an unbending law that the general and the particular are as equal as two peas in a pod. And all that applies in the general, applies in the particular, as well. Moreover, the parts make what is found in the whole, for the general can appear only after the appearance of the parts in it, according to the quantity and quality of the parts. Evidently, the value of an act of a part elevates or declines the entire whole.

That will clarify to you what is written in *The Zohar*, that by engagement in *The Book of Zohar* and the wisdom of truth, they will be rewarded with complete redemption from exile (*Tikkunim*, end of *Tikkun* No. 6). We might ask, what has the study of *The Zohar* to do with the redemption of Israel from among the nations?

69) From the above we can thoroughly understand that the Torah, too, contains internality and externality, as does the entire world. Therefore, one who engages in the Torah has these two degrees, as well. When one increases one's toil in the internality of the Torah and its secrets, to that extent, one makes the virtue of the internality of the world—which are Israel—soar high above the externality of the world, which are the Nations of the World. And all the nations will acknowledge and recognize Israel's merit over them, until the realization of the words, "And the people shall take them, and bring them to their place: and the house of Israel shall possess them in the land of the Lord" (Isaiah 14, 2), and also "Thus says the Lord God, Behold, I will lift up my hand to the nations, and set up my standard to the peoples: and

they shall bring thy sons in their arms, and thy daughters shall be carried on their shoulders" (Isaiah 49, 22).

But if, God forbid, it is to the contrary, and a person from Israel degrades the virtue of the internality of the Torah and its secrets, which deals with the conduct of our souls and their degrees, and the perception and the tastes of the *Mitzvot* with regard to the advantage of the externality of the Torah, which deals only with the practical part? Also, even if one does occasionally engage in the internality of the Torah, and dedicates a little of one's time to it, when it is neither night nor day, as though it were redundant, by that one dishonors and degrades the internality of the world, which are the Children of Israel, and enhances the externality of the world—meaning the Nations of the World—over them. They will humiliate and disgrace the Children of Israel, and regard Israel as superfluous, as though the world has no need for them, God forbid.

Furthermore, by that, they make even the externality in the Nations of the World overpower their own internality, for the worst among the Nations of the World, the harmful and the destructors of the world, rise above their internality, which are the Righteous of the Nations of the World. And then they make all the ruin and the heinous slaughter our generation had witnessed, may God protect us from here on.

Thus you see that The redemption of Israel and the whole of Israel's merit depend on the study of *The Zohar* and the internality of the Torah. And vise versa, all the destruction and the decline of the Children of Israel are because they have abandoned the internality of the Torah. They have degraded its merit and made it seemingly redundant.

70) This is what is written in the *Tikkunim* (corrections) of *The Zohar* (*Tikkun* 30): "Awaken and rise for the Holy Divinity, for you have an empty heart, without the understanding to know

and to attain it, although it is within you." The meaning of it is, as it is written (Isaiah 40), that a voice pounds in the heart of each and every one of Israel, to cry and to pray for raising the Holy Divinity, which is the collection of all the souls of Israel. But Divinity says, "I have no strength to raise myself off the dust, for 'all flesh is grass,' they are all like beasts, eating hay and grass." This means that they keep the Mitzvot mindlessly, like beasts, "and all the goodliness thereof is as the flower of the field, all the good deeds that they do, they do for themselves."

That means that with the Mitzvot they perform, they have no intention of doing them in order to bring contentment to their Maker. Rather, they keep the Mitzvot only for their own benefit, and even the best among them, who dedicate all their time to engagement in the Torah, do it only to benefit their own bodies, without the desirable aim—to bring contentment to their Maker.

It is said about the generation of that time: "A spirit leaves and will not return to the world," meaning the spirit of the Messiah, who must deliver Israel from all their troubles until the complete redemption, to keep the words, 'for the earth shall be full of the knowledge of the Lord.' That spirit had left and does not shine in the world.

Woe unto them that make the spirit of Messiah leave and depart from the world, and cannot return to the world. They are the ones that make the Torah dry, without any moisture of comprehension and reason. They confine themselves to the practical part of the Torah, and do not wish to try to understand the wisdom of Kabbalah, to know and to understand the secrets of the Torah and the flavors of Mitzva. Woe unto them, for with these actions they bring about the existence of poverty, ruin, and robbery, looting, killing, and destructions in the world.

71) The reason for their words is, as we have explained, that when all those who engage in the Torah degrade their own internality

and the internality of the Torah, leaving it as though it were redundant in the world, and engage in it only at a time that is neither day nor night, and in this regard, they are like blind searching the wall, by that, they intensify their own externality, the benefit of their own bodies. Also, they consider the externality of the Torah higher than the internality of the Torah. And with these actions they cause all the forms of externality in the world to overpower all the internal parts in the world, each according to its essence.

This is so because the externality in the whole of Israel, meaning the Nations of the World in them, overpowers and revokes the internality in the whole of Israel, which are those who are great in the Torah. Also, the externality in the Nations of the World—the destructors among them—intensify and revoke the internality among them, which are the Righteous of the Nations of the World. Additionally, the externality of the entire world, being the Nations of the World, intensify and revoke the Children of Israel—the internality of the world.

In such a generation, all the destructors among the Nations of the World raise their heads and wish primarily to destroy and to kill the Children of Israel, as it is written (*Yevamot* 63), "No calamity comes to the world but for Israel." This means, as it is written in the above corrections, that they cause poverty, ruin, robbery, killing, and destruction in the whole world.

And through our many faults, we have witnessed to all that is said in the above-mentioned *Tikkunim*, and moreover, the judgment struck the very best of us, as our sages said (*Baba Kama* 60), "And it start with the righteous first." And of all the glory Israel had had in the countries of Poland and Lithuania, etc., there remains but the relics in our holy land. Now it is upon us, relics, to correct that dreadful wrong. Each of us remainders should take upon himself, heart and soul, to henceforth intensify the internality of the Torah, and give it its rightful place, according to its merit over the externality of the Torah.

And then, each and every one of us will be rewarded with intensifying his own internality, meaning the Israel within us, which is the needs of the soul over our own externality, which is the Nations of the World within us, that is, the needs of the body. That force will come to the whole of Israel, until the Nations of the World within us recognize and acknowledge the merit of the great sages of Israel over them, and will listen to them and obey them.

Also, the internality of the Nations of the World, the Righteous of the Nations of the World, will overpower and submit their externality, which are the destructors. And the internality of the world, too, which are Israel, shall rise in all their merit and virtue over the externality of the world, which are the nations. Then, all the nations of the world will recognize and acknowledge Israel's merit over them.

And they shall follow the words (Isaiah 14, 2), "And the people shall take them, and bring them to their place: and the house of Israel shall possess them in the land of the Lord." And also (Isaiah 49, 22), "And they shall bring thy sons in their arms, and thy daughters shall be carried on their shoulders." That is what is written in *The Zohar* (*Nasoh*, p 124b), "through this composition," which is *The Book of Zohar*, "they will be delivered from exile with mercy." Amen, would that be so.

PREFACE
TO THE BOOK OF ZOHAR

1) The depth of wisdom in the holy *Book of Zohar* is enclosed and caged behind a thousand locks, and our human tongue too poor to provide us with sufficient, reliable expressions to interpret one thing in this book to its end. Also, the interpretation I have made is but a ladder to help the examiner rise to the height of the matters and examine the words of the book itself. Hence, I have found it necessary to prepare the reader and give him a route and an inlet in reliable definitions concerning how one should contemplate and study the book.

2) First, you must know that all that is said in *The Book of Zohar*, and even in its legends, is denominations of the ten *Sefirot*, called KHB (*Keter, Hochma, Bina*), HGT (*Hesed, Gevura, Tifferet*), NHYM (*Netzah, Hod, Yesod, Malchut*), and their permutations. Just as the twenty-two letters of the spoken language, whose permutations suffice to uncover every object and every concept, the concepts, and permutations of concepts, in the ten *Sefirot* suffice to disclose all the wisdom in the book of Heaven. However, there are three boundaries that one must be very prudent with, and not exceed them while studying the words of the book.

3) First boundary: There are four categories in the conduct of learning, called "Matter," "Form in Matter," "Abstract Form," and "Essence." It is the same in the ten *Sefirot*. Know that *The Book of Zohar* does not engage at all in the Essence and the Abstract Form in the ten *Sefirot*, but only in the Matter in them, or in the Form in them, while clothed in Matter4) Second boundary: We distinguish three discernments in the comprehensive, Godly reality concerning the creation of the souls and the conduct of their existence:

- *Ein Sof* (Infinity);
- The world of *Atzilut*;
- The three worlds called *Beria, Yetzira*, and *Assiya*.

You should know that *The Zohar* engages only in the worlds, BYA (*Beria, Yetzira, Assiya*), and in *Ein Sof* and the world of *Atzilut*, to the extent that BYA receive from them. However, *The Book of Zohar* does not engage in *Ein Sof* and the world of *Atzilut* themselves at all.

5) Third boundary: There are three discernments in each of the worlds, BYA:

- The ten *Sefirot*, which are the Godliness that shines in that world;
- *Neshamot* (Souls), *Ruchot* (spirits), and *Nefashot* (life)[1] of people;
- The rest of reality in it, called "angels," "clothes," and "palaces," whose elements are innumerable.

Bear in mind that although *The Zohar* elucidates extensively on the details in each world, you should still know that the essence of the words of *The Zohar* always focuses on the souls of people in that world. It explains other discernments only to know the measure that the souls receive from them. *The Zohar* does not mention even a single word of what does not relate to the reception of the souls. Hence, you should learn everything presented in *The Book of Zohar* only in relation to the reception of the soul. [...]

11) Here we should study these four manners of perception, presented above in the first boundary:

- Matter;
- Form Clothed in Matter;
- Abstract Form;
- Essence.

Yet, I shall first explain them using tangible examples from this world. For example, when you say that a person

---

1 Translator's note: The usual translation for both Neshamot and Nefashot is "souls," but here I had to choose a different word for Nefesh to distinguish it from Neshama.

is strong, truthful, or deceitful, etc., you have the following before you:

- His matter, meaning his body;
- The form that clothes his matter—strong, truthful, or deceitful;
- The abstract form. You can shed the form of strong, truthful, or deceitful from the matter of that person, and study these three forms in and of themselves, unclothed in any matter or body, meaning examine the attributes of strength, truth, and deceitfulness and discern merit or demerit in them, while they are devoid of any substance.
- The person's essence.

12) Know that we have no perception whatsoever in the fourth manner, the essence of the person in itself, without the matter. This is because our five senses and our imaginations offer us only manifestations of the actions of the essence, but not of the essence itself.

For example, the sense of sight offers us only shadows of the visible essence as they are formed opposite the light.

Similarly, the sense of hearing is but a force of striking of some essence on the air. And the air that is rejected by it strikes the drum in our ear, and we hear that there is some essence in our proximity.

The sense of smell is but air that emerges from the essence and strikes our nerves of scent, and we smell. Also, the sense of taste is a result of the contact of some essence with our nerves of taste.

Thus, all that these four senses offer us are manifestations of the operations that stem from some essence, and nothing of the essence itself.

Even the sense of touch, the strongest of the senses, separating hot from cold, and solid from soft, all these are but manifestations of operations within the essence; they are but incidents of the essence. This is so because the hot can be chilled; the cold can be heated; the solid can be turned to liquid through chemical operations, and the liquid into air, meaning only gas, where any discernment in our five senses has been expired. Yet, the essence still exists in it, since you can turn the air into liquid once more, and the liquid into solid.

Evidently, the five senses do not reveal to us any essence at all, but only incidents and manifestations of operations from the essence. It is known that what we cannot sense, we cannot imagine; and what we cannot imagine, will never appear in our thoughts, and we have no way to perceive it.

Thus, the thought has no perception whatsoever in the essence. Moreover, we do not even know our own essence. I feel and I know that I take up space in the world, that I am solid, warm, and that I think, and other such manifestations of the operations of my essence. But if you ask me about my own essence, from which all these manifestations stem, I do not know what to reply to you.

You therefore see that Providence has prevented us from attaining any essence. We attain only manifestations and images of operations that stem from the essences.

13) We do have full perception in the first manner, which is **Matter**, meaning the manifestations of operations that manifest from each essence. This is because they quite sufficiently explain to us the essence that dwells in the substance in such a way that we do not suffer at all from the lack of attainment in the essence itself.

We do not miss it just as we do not miss a sixth finger in our hand. The attainment of the matter, meaning the manifestation of the operations of the essence, is quite sufficient for our every need and learning, both for attaining our own being and for attaining the all that exists outside of us.

14) The second manner, **Form clothed in Matter**, is a satisfactory and clear attainment, too, since we acquire it through practical and real experiments we find in the behavior of any matter. All our higher, reliable knowledge stems from this discernment.

15) The third manner is **Abstract Form**. Once the form has been revealed, while clothed in some matter, our imaginations can abstract it from any matter altogether and perceive it regardless of any substance. Such as that are the virtues and the good qualities that appear in moral books, where we speak of properties of truth and falsehood, anger, and strength, etc., when they are devoid of any matter. We ascribe them merit or demerit even when they are abstract.

You should know that this third manner is unacceptable to the prudent erudite, since it is impossible to rely on it one hundred percent, since being examined while not clothed in matter, they might err in them.

Take, for example, one with idealistic morals, meaning one who is not religious. Because of his intensive engagement in the merit of truth, while in its abstract form, that person might decide that even if he could save people from death by telling them a lie, he may decide that even if the whole world is doomed, he will not utter a deliberate lie. This is not the view of Torah, since nothing is more important than saving lives (*Yoma*, 82a).

Indeed, had one learned the forms of truth and falsehood when they are clothed in matter, he would comprehend only with respect to their benefit or harm to matter.

In other words, after the many ordeals the world has been through, having seen the multitude of ruin and harm that deceitful people have caused with their lies, and the great benefit that truthful people have brought by restricting themselves to saying only words of truth, they have agreed that no merit is more important than the quality of truth, and there is no such disgrace as the quality of falsehood.

And if the idealist had understood that, he would certainly agree to the view of Torah, and would find that falsehood that saves even one person from death is far more important than the entire merit and praise of the abstract quality of truth. Thus, **there is no certainty at all in those concepts** of the third manner, which are abstract forms, much less with abstract forms that have never clothed in any substance. Such concepts are nothing but a waste of time.

16) Now you have thoroughly learned these four manners—Matter, Form in Matter, Abstract Form, and Essence—in tangible things. It has been clarified that we have no perception whatsoever in the fourth manner, the essence, and the third manner is a concept that might mislead. Only the first manner, which is Matter, and the second manner, which is Form Clothed in Matter, are given to us by the Upper Governance for clear and sufficient attainment.

Through them, you will also be able to perceive the existence of spiritual objects, meaning the Upper Worlds *ABYA*, since there is not a tiny detail in them that is not divided by the four above manners. If, for example, you take a certain element in the world of *Beria*, there are *Kelim* there, which are of red color, through which the Light of *Beria* traverses to the dwellers of *Beria*. Thus, the *Kli* in *Beria*, which is the color red, is considered Matter, or object, meaning the first manner.

And even though it is only a color, which is an occurrence and manifestation of an operation in the object, we have already said that we have no attainment in the Essence itself, but only in the manifestation of an operation from the Essence. And we refer to that manifestation as Essence, or Matter, or body, or a *Kli*.

And the Godly Light, which travels and clothes through the red color, is the form clothed in the object, meaning the second manner. For this reason, the Light itself seems red, indicating its clothing and illumination through the object, considered the body and the substance, meaning the red color.

And if you want to remove the Godly Light from the object—the red color—and discuss it in and of itself, without clothing in an object, this already belongs to the third manner—Form removed from the Matter—which might be subject to errors. For this reason, it is strictly forbidden in studying the Upper Worlds, and no genuine Kabbalist would engage in that, much less the authors of *The Zohar*.

It is even more so with regards to the Essence of an element in *Beria*, since we have no perception whatsoever even in the essence of corporeal objects, all the more so in spiritual objects.

Thus you have before you four manners:

- The *Kli* of *Beria*, which is the red color, considered the object, or the substance of *Beria*;
- The clothing of the Godly Light in the *Kli* of *Beria*, which is the form in the object;
- The Godly Light itself, removed from the object in *Beria*;
- The essence of the item.

Thus, the first boundary has been thoroughly explained, which is that there is not even a single word of the third and fourth manners in the whole of *The Zohar*, but only from the first and second manners.

17) Along with it, the second manner has been clarified. Know that as we have clarified the four manners in a single item in the world of *Beria*, specifically, so are they in the general four worlds ABYA. The three colors—red, green, black—in the three

worlds *BYA*, are considered the substance, or the object. The white color, considered the world of *Atzilut*, is the form clothed in the matter, in the three colors called *BYA*.

Ein Sof in itself is the essence. This is what we said concerning the first manner, that we have no perception in the essence, which is the fourth manner, concealed in all the objects, even in the objects of this world. When the white color is not clothed in the three colors in *BYA*, meaning when the Light of *Hochma* is not clothed in *Bina*, *Tifferet*, and *Malchut*, it is abstract form, which we do not engage in.

The Zohar does not speak in this manner whatsoever, but only in the first manner, being the three colors *BYA*, considered substance, namely the three *Sefirot Bina*, *Tifferet*, and *Malchut*, and in the second manner, which are the illumination of *Atzilut*, clothed in the three colors *BYA*, meaning Light of *Hochma*, clothed in *Bina*, *Tifferet*, and *Malchut*, which are in turn form clothed in matter. These are the two that *The Book of Zohar* is concerned with in all the places.

Hence, if the reader is not vigilant, restricting his thought and understanding to always learn the words of *The Zohar* strictly under the two above-mentioned manners, the matter will be immediately and entirely miscomprehended, for he will take the words out of context.

19) Now we shall explain the third boundary. *The Zohar* engages in the *Sefirot* in each and every world, being the Godliness that shines in that world, as well as in every item of the SVAS (Still, Vegetative, Animate and Speaking), being the creatures in that world. However, *The Zohar* refers primarily to the Speaking in that world.

Let me give you an example from the conducts of this world. It is explained in the "Introduction to the Book of Zohar" (item 42) that the four kinds, Still, Vegetative, Animate and Speaking

in each and every world, even in this world, are the four parts of
the will to receive. Each of them contains these own four kinds of
SVAS. Thus, you find that a person in this world should nurture
and be nourished by the four categories SVAS in this world.

This is so because man's food, too, contains these four
categories, which extend from the four categories SVAS in man's
body. These are a) wanting to receive according to the necessary
measure for one's sustenance; b) wanting more than is necessary
for sustenance, craving luxuries, but restricting oneself solely to
physical desires; c) craving human desires, such as honor and
power; d) craving knowledge.

These extend to the four parts of the will to receive in us:

- Wanting the necessary provision is considered the
  Still of the will to receive.
- Wanting physical lusts is considered the Vegetative
  of the will to receive, since they come only to
  increase and delight one's *Kli* (vessel), which is the
  flesh of the body.
- Wanting human desires is considered the Animate
  in the will to receive, since they magnify one's spirit.

Wanting knowledge is the Speaking in the will to receive.

20) Thus, in the first category—the necessary measure for one's
sustenance—and in the second category—the physical desires that
exceed one's measure for sustenance—one is nourished by things
that are lower than the person: the still, the vegetative, and the
animate. However, in the third category, the human desires such
as power and respect, one receives and is nurtured from his own
species, his equals. And in the fourth category, knowledge, one
receives and is nurtured by a higher category than one's own—
from the actual wisdom and intellect, which are spiritual.

21) You will find it similar in the Upper, Spiritual Worlds,
since the worlds are imprinted from one another from Above

downward. Thus, all the categories of SVAS in the world of *Beria* leave their imprint in the world of *Yetzira*. And the SVAS of *Assiya* are imprinted from the SVAS of *Yetzira*. Lastly, the SVAS in this world is imprinted from the SVAS of the world of *Assiya*.

It has been explained in "Introduction to the Book of Zohar" (Item 42) that the still in the spiritual worlds are called *Heichalot* (Palaces), the vegetative is called *Levushim* (Clothes or Dresses), the animate is named *Mala'achim* (Angels), and the speaking is considered the *Neshamot* (Souls) of people in that world. And the Ten *Sefirot* in that world are the Godliness.

The souls of people are the center in each world, which are nourished by the spiritual reality in that world, as the corporeal speaking feeds on the entire corporeal reality in this world. Thus, the first category, which is the will to receive one's necessary sustenance, is received from the illumination of *Heichalot* and *Levushim* there. The second category, the animate surplus that increases one's body, is received from the category of *Mala'achim* there, which are spiritual illuminations beyond one's necessary measure for sustenance, to magnify the spiritual *Kelim* that his soul clothes in.

Thus, one receives the first category and the second category from lower categories than one's own, which are the *Heichalot*, *Levushim*, and the *Mala'achim* there, which are lower than human *Neshamot* (souls). The third category, which is human desires that increase one's spirit, is received in this world from one's own species. It follows that one receives from one's own species too, from all the *Neshamot* in that world. Through them, one increases the illumination of *Ruach* of his soul.

The fourth category of the desire, for knowledge, is received there from the *Sefirot* in that world. From them, one receives the HBD to one's soul.

It follows that man's soul, which is present in every single world, should grow and be completed with all the categories that exist in that world. This is the third boundary we have mentioned.

One must know that all the words of *The Zohar*, in every item of the Upper Worlds that are dealt with, the *Sefirot*, the *Neshamot*, and the *Mala'achim*, the *Levushim*, and the *Heichalot*, although it engages in them as they are for themselves, the examiner must know that they are spoken primarily with respect to the measure by which the human soul there receives from them and is nourished by them. Thus, all their words pertain to the needs of the soul. And if you learn everything according to that line, you will understand, and your path will be successful.

23) To understand that, you must remember the explained above, in Item 17. It explains that a necessary object is an essence that we have no perception of, even in the corporeal essences, and even in our own essence, all the more so in The Necessary One.

The world of *Atzilut* is a Form and the three worlds *BYA* are Matter. The illumination of *Atzilut* in *BYA* is Form clothed in Matter. Hence, you see that the name, *Ein Sof*, is not at all a name for the essence of The Necessary One, since what we do not attain, how can we define it by name or word?

Since the imagination and the five senses offer us nothing with respect to the essence, even in corporeality, how can there be a thought and a word in it, much less in The Necessary One Himself? Instead, we must understand the name, *Ein Sof*, as defined for us in the third boundary, that all that *The Book of Zohar* speaks of pertains precisely to the souls (Item 21).

Thus, the name, *Ein Sof*, is not at all The Necessary One Himself, but pertains to all the worlds and all the souls being included in Him, in the Thought of Creation, by way of "The end of an act is in the preliminary thought." Thus, *Ein Sof* is the name of the connection that the whole of Creation is connected in, until the end of correction.

This is what we name "the First State of the souls" ("Introduction to the Book of Zohar," Item 13), since all the souls exist in Him, filled with all the pleasure and the gentleness, at the final Height they will actually receive at the end of correction.

24) Let me give you an example from the conduct of this world: A person wants to build a handsome house. In the first thought, he sees before him an elegant house with all its rooms and details, as it will be when its building is finished.

Afterwards, he designs the plan of execution to its every detail. In due time, he will explain every detail to the workers: the wood, the bricks, the iron, and so on. Then he will begin the actual building of the house to its end, as it was arranged before him in the preliminary thought.

Know, that *Ein Sof* pertains to that first thought, in which the whole of Creation was already pictured before Him in utter completeness. However, the lesson is not quite like the example because in Him, the future and the present are equals. In Him, the thought completes, and He does not need tools of action, as do we. Hence, in Him, it is actual reality.

The world of *Atzilut* is like the details of the thought-out plan, which will later need to manifest when the building of the house actually begins. Know that in these two, the preliminary thought, which is *Ein Sof*, and the contemplated design of the details of the execution in its due time, there is still not even a trace of the creatures, since this is still in potential, not in actual fact.

It is likewise in humans: even though they calculate all the details—the wood, the bricks, and the metal—that will be required for carrying out the plan, it is essentially a mere conceptual matter. There is not even a trace of any actual wood or bricks in it. The only difference is that in a person, the contemplated design is not considered an actual reality. But in the Godly Thought, it is a far more actual reality than the actual, real creatures.

Thus, we have explained the meaning of *Ein Sof* and the world of *Atzilut*, that how all that is said about them is only with respect to the creation of the creatures. However, they are still in potential and their essence has not been revealed whatsoever, as with our allegory about the person who designed the blueprint, which does not contain any wood, and bricks, and metal.

25) The three worlds *BYA*, and this world, are considered the execution from potential to actual, such as one who builds one's house in actual fact and brings the wood, the bricks, and the workers until the house is complete. [...]

26) In the above allegory, you find how the three discernments of one who contemplates building a house are interconnected by way of cause and consequence. The root of them all is the first thought, since no item appears in the planned blueprint except according to the end of the act, which emerged before him in the preliminary thought.

Also, one does not execute anything during the building, but only according to the details arranged before him in the blueprint. Thus you see, concerning the worlds, that there is not a tiny generation in the worlds that does not extend from *Ein Sof*, from the first state of the souls, which are there in their ultimate perfection of the end of correction, as in "The end of an act is in the preliminary thought." Thus, all that will manifest through the end of correction is included there.

In the beginning, it extends from *Ein Sof* to the world of *Atzilut*, as in the allegory, where the blueprint extends from the first thought. Each and every element extends from the world of *Atzilut* to the worlds *BYA*, as in the allegory, where all the details stem from the blueprint when they are actually executed during the building of the house.

Thus, there is not a single, tiny item, generated in this world, that does not extend from *Ein Sof*, from the first state of the souls. And from *Ein Sof*, it extends to the world of *Atzilut*, meaning specifically associated to the thing actually being generated in this world. And from the world of *Atzilut*, the generation extends to the three worlds BYA, where the generation appears in actual fact, where it stops being Godliness and becomes a creature, and to *Yetzira* and *Assiya*, until it extends to the lower one in this world.

It follows that there is no generation in the world, which does not extend from its general root in *Ein Sof*, and from its private root in *Atzilut*. Afterwards, it travels through BYA and adopts the form of a creature, and then it is made in this world.

31) [...]Yet, since the Thought of Creation was to delight His creatures, it teaches us that He has a desire to bestow. We find in this world, that the givers' contentment grows when the receivers from Him multiply, and He wishes to proliferate the receivers. Hence, in this respect, we say that the Lights in *Atzilut* grow when the lower ones are given the bestowal of *Atzilut*, or that they nurture it. Conversely, when there are no lower ones worthy of receiving His abundance, the Lights diminish to that extent, meaning there is no one to receive from them.

32) You might compare it to a candle. If you light a thousand candles from it, or if you light none, you will not find that it caused any changes induced in the candle itself. It is also like *Adam HaRishon*: if he had progeny of thousands of offspring like us today, or if he had no progeny at all, it would not induce any change at all on *Adam HaRishon* himself.

Likewise, there is no change at all in the world *Atzilut* itself, whether the lower ones receive its great abundance lushly, or receive nothing at all. The above-mentioned greatness lies solely on the lower ones.

33) Thus, why did the authors of *The Zohar* have to describe all those changes in the world of *Atzilut* itself? They should have spoken explicitly only with respect to the receivers in *BYA*, and not speak so elaborately of *Atzilut*, forcing us to provide answers.

Indeed, there is a very trenchant secret here: this is the meaning of, "and by the ministry of the prophets have I used similitudes" (Hosea 12). The truth is that there is a Godly will here, that these similitudes, which operate only in the souls of the receivers, will appear to the souls as He Himself participates in them to greatly increase the attainment of the souls.

It is like a father who constrains himself to show his little darling child a face of sadness and a face of contentment, although there is neither sadness nor contentment in him. He only does this to impress his darling child and expand his understanding, so as to play with him.

Only when he grows will he learn and know that all that his father did was no more real than mere playing with him. So is the matter before us: all these images and changes begin and end only with the impression of the souls. Yet, by the will of God, they appear as though they are in Him Himself. He does that to enhance and expand the attainment of the souls to the utmost, in accordance with the Thought of Creation, to delight His creatures.

34) Let it not surprise you that you find such a conduct in our corporeal perception, too. Take our sense of sight, for example: we see a wide world before us, wondrously filled. But in fact, we see all that only in our own interior. In other words, there is a sort of a photographic machine in our hindbrain, which portrays everything that appears to us and nothing outside of us.

For that, He has made for us there, in our brain, a kind of polished mirror that inverts everything seen there, so we will see it outside our brain, in front of our face. Yet, what we see outside us is not a real thing. Nonetheless, we should be so grateful to His Providence for having created that polished mirror in our brains, enabling us to see and perceive everything outside of us. This is because by that, He has given us the power to perceive everything with clear knowledge and attainment, and measure everything from within and from without.

Without it, we would lose most of our perception. The same holds true with the Godly will, concerning Godly perceptions. Even though all these changes unfold in the interior of the receiving souls, they nevertheless see it all in the Giver Himself, since only in this manner are they awarded all the perceptions and all the pleasantness in the Thought of Creation.

You can also deduce that from the above parable. Even though we see everything as actually being in front of us, every reasonable person knows for certain that all that we see is only within our own brains.

So are the souls: Although they see all the images in the Giver, they still have no doubt that all these are only in their own interior, and not at all in the Giver.

40) He named Himself *El*, *Elokim*, *Shadai*, *Tzvaot*, and *Ekie*, so that every single attribute in Him would be known. The ten names in the Torah that are not to be erased pertain to the ten *Sefirot*, as it is written in *The Zohar* (*Vayikra*, item 168):

- The *Sefira Keter* is called *Ekie*;
- The *Sefira Hochma* is called *Koh*;
- And the *Sefira Bina* is called *HaVaYaH* (punctuated *Elokim*);
- The *Sefira Hesed* is called *Kel*;
- The *Sefira Gevura* is called *Elokim*;

- The *Sefira Tifferet* is called *HaVaYaH*;
- The two *Sefirot Netzah* and *Hod* are called *Tzvaot*;
- The *Sefira Yesod* is called *El Hay*;
- And the *Sefira Malchut* is called *Adni*.

41) Had His Light not expanded on all creations by seemingly clothing in these holy *Sefirot*, how would the creatures come to know Him? And how would they keep the verse, "the whole earth is full of His glory"? In other words, by that it explains the Godly desire to appear to the souls as if all these changes in the *Sefirot* are in Him. It is in order to give the souls room for sufficient knowledge and attainment in Him, for then the verse, "the whole earth is full of His glory" shall come true.

INTRODUCTION
TO THE PREFACE
TO THE WISDOM OF KABBALAH

1) It is written in *The Zohar, Vayikra, Parashat Tazria*, p 40, "Come and see, all that exists in the world, exists for man, and everything exists for him, as it is written, 'Then the Lord God formed man,' with a full name, as we have established, that he is the whole of everything and contains everything, and all that is Above and below, etc., is included in that image."

Thus, it explains that all the worlds, Upper and lower, are included in man. And also, the whole of reality within those worlds is only for man.

ACRONYMS
USED IN THIS APPENDIX

ABYA – Atzilut, Beria, Yetzira, Assiya

AK – Adam Kadmon

BYA – Beria, Yetzira, Assiya

SVAS (Still, Vegetative, Animate, and Speaking)

HaVaYaH – Yod, Hey, Vav, Hey

HBD – Hochma, Bina, Daat

HGT – Hesed, Gevura, Tifferet

KHB – Keter, Hochma, Bina

KHBTM – Keter, Hochma, Bina, Tifferet, and *Malchut*

NHY – Netzah, Hod, Yesod

NHYM – Netzah, Hod, Yesod, Malchut

NRN – Nefesh, Ruach, Neshama

NRNHY – Nefesh, Ruach, Neshama, Haya, Yechida

YHNRN – Yechida, Haya, Neshama, Ruach, Nefesh

Appendix 3

Zohar for All

Selected Excerpts

CONTENTS

ABRAHAM

AWAKENING AND DESIRE

Lech Lecha [Go Forth]

28) Since the Creator saw his awakening and his desire, He immediately revealed Himself to him and told him, "Go forth," to know yourself and to correct yourself.

223) "Who has aroused one from the east" is Abraham, who took the awakening to the Creator only from the east because when he saw the sun rising in the morning from the east, he took an awakening for himself, which is the Creator. He said about the sun, "This is the King who created me," and he worshipped the sun the whole day. In the evening, he saw that the sun was setting and the moon rose. He said about the moon, "This one must be ruling the worship that he was worshipping the whole of that day, the sun, since the sun had darkened before the moon and does not shine." Thus, he worshipped the moon the whole of that night.

224) In the morning, he saw that the moon darkened and the east illuminated. He said, "There must be a king and a ruler over all those, who leads them." When the Creator saw Abraham's desire, He appeared before him and spoke to him, as it is written, "He calls in righteousness to His feet." Righteousness is the Creator, who called him and spoke to him and appeared before him.

AND ABRAM TOOK SARAI

Lech Lecha [Go Forth]

58) "And Abram took Sarai his wife." This is extension in good things because man is forbidden to take his wife out to another land against her will. It is also written, "Take Aaron," meaning take

the Levites. This is why "And Abram took" is extension in things, and he alerted her how evil were the ways of the people of the generation. This is why it writes, "And Abram took Sarai his wife."

59) "And Lot his nephew." Why did Abraham see fit to attach Lot to himself? It was because he saw in the spirit of holiness that David was destined to come out of him.

"And the souls that they had made in Haran" are the converted men and women who corrected their souls. Abraham would convert the men, and Sarah would convert the women, and this is why the writing speaks about them as though they had made them.

ABRAHAM AND SARAH
PURIFYING THE PEOPLE OF THE WORLD

VaYaera [And the Lord Appeared]

106) Abraham and Sarah were setting up *Tevila* for every person—he for the men and she for the women. The reason why Abraham engaged in purifying people is that he was pure and he was called "pure," as it is written, "Who can bring a clean thing out of an unclean? not one," and Abraham is pure who came out of Terah, who was unclean.

107) This is why Abraham engaged in *Tevila*, to correct the degree of Abraham. And his degree is water, *Hassadim*, for which he was made to purify all the people in the world with water.

BEER SHEBA

New *Zohar, Toldot* [Generations]

28) Abraham named that well of water, *Malchut*, Beer Sheba...

31) Abraham dug that well. He established it because he taught all the people of the world to serve the Creator. And since he dug it, it put forth living waters that never end.

AN INCARNATION OF ADAM HARISHON

BaHar [On Mount Sinai]

69) Adam's sin was that he broke the Creator's commandment. But there are no commandments except on idol worshipping. He transgressed with idol worshipping, and He put him, meaning incarnated him in the seed of Terah, in which he fumed, meaning angered the Creator and broke the commandment of idol worshipping, for Terah was an idol worshipper. And he came out of the seed of Abraham, who was an incarnation of *Adam HaRishon*. Abraham repented and broke the statutes of idol worshipping and all the foods that were placed before them. He corrected what Adam and Terah sinned, and broke the sin and the evil structure that he built, the structure of the *Klipot* that Adam caused by his sin, and enthroned the Creator and His Divinity over the whole world.

GIFTS TO THE SONS OF THE CONCUBINES

Chayei Sarah [The Life of Sarah]

262) "But unto the sons of the concubines... gifts." What are gifts? Those are lower degrees of holiness, which are uncorrected. They are names of types of spirits of impurity. He gave it to them to complete the degrees, so they would purify them and complement the degrees of holiness. And Isaac rose above all of them in the high faith, which is *Bina*.

263) "The sons of the concubines" are the sons of Keturah. She is called "concubines" since she was a concubine before he sent her away. And she is a concubine now since he took her again. "And he sent them away from Isaac his son," so they would not rule over Isaac. "While he was still alive," while Abraham still lived and exited in the world, so they would not quarrel with him later, and so that Isaac would be corrected in the side of the harsh, high *Din*,

to prevail over all of them. And they all surrendered before him. "Eastward" means to the land in the east since there are various kinds of witchcraft and impurity there.

264) It is written, "And Solomon's wisdom excelled the wisdom of all the children of the east," meaning all those who were from the sons of Abraham's concubines. And in those mountains of the east are those who teach wizardry to people. And Laban, Beor, and Balaam, his son, and all the wizards came from that land in the east.

BOOK OF WISDOM OF THE PREDECESSORS

VaYaera [And the Lord Appeared]

80) Rabbi Aba said, "One day, I came across a city that was one of those that were in the east, and I was told of that wisdom that they knew since the old days. They found their books of wisdom and presented me with such a book."

88) I told them, "My sons, the words in the book are close to words of Torah. But you must stay away from these books lest they will divert your hearts to these works and to all those sides it mentions here. You might stray from the work of the Creator."

89) This is so because all those books mislead people, since the sons of the east were wise and inherited this wisdom from Abraham, who gave to the sons of the maidservants, as it is written, 'But unto the sons of the concubines that Abraham had, Abraham gave gifts,' and afterwards they were drawn in this wisdom to several directions.

90) But the seed of Isaac, the share of Jacob, is not so, as it is written, "And Abraham gave all that he had unto Isaac." This is the holy share of the faith to which Abraham adhered, and it is from this lot and from this side that Jacob came. It is written about it, "And behold, the Lord stood above him," and it is written, "But you... My servant, Jacob."

THESE ARE THE GENERATIONS OF THE HEAVEN AND THE EARTH WHEN THEY WERE CREATED

Lech Lecha [Go Forth]

225) "Speak righteousness and declare things that are right." All of the Creator's words are true. "And declare things that are right" because when the Creator created the world, the world did not stand, but collapsed to this side and to that side. The Creator said to the world, "Why are you falling?" It told Him, "Dear Lord, I cannot stand because I have no foundation [Yesod] on which to stand."

226) The Creator told it, "Thus, I will place a righteous one within you, Abraham, who will love Me." And the world immediately stood and existed. It is written, "These are the generations of the heaven and the earth when they were created." Do not read it, BeHibar'am [when they were created], but BeAvraham [in Abraham, same letters in Hebrew], since the world existed in Abraham.

227) The world replied to the Creator, "Abraham is destined to beget sons who will destroy the Temple and burn the Torah." The Creator told it, "One man will come out of him, Jacob, and twelve tribes will come out of him, all of which are righteous." Promptly, the world existed for him.

BOOK OF CREATION

New Zohar, Yitro [Jethro]

309) Certainly, Jacob had the book of Adam HaRishon, as well as the book Enoch, and The Book of Creation by Abraham the patriarch. They commented that Masechet Avodah Zarah [the treatise Idolatry] by Abraham the patriarch constituted 400 chapters.

From all those books, Jacob the patriarch, the whole man, living in tents, learned much wisdom. And the beauty and lines of Jacob were as the lines of Adam HaRishon.

ABRAHAM, SARAH, ISAAC, AND REBECCA

Lech Lecha [Go Forth]

76) The Creator implies to upper *Hochma*, in Abraham and Isaac. Abraham is *Neshama* to *Neshama*, light of *Haya*. *Neshama* is Sarah. Lot is the serpent, *SAM's* mate. The spirit of holiness is Isaac. The holy *Nefesh* is Rebecca, and the evil inclination is the spirit of the beast. In his wisdom, Solomon says about him, "Who knows the spirit of man, whether it goes upward, and the spirit of the beast, whether it goes downward to the earth?" The spirit of the beast is a *Nefesh* from the side of the evil inclination.

77) *Neshama* to *Neshama* comes to man from the *Sefira* of *Hochma*, with fear and with wisdom. The *Neshama* comes to man in *Bina*, as it is written, "Behold, the fear of the Lord is wisdom." Hence, *Neshama* to *Neshama* comes only through fear and wisdom. But the *Neshama* comes to a person through repentance, which is called *Bina*, and is called "Sarah." *Ruach* [spirit/wind] is called "voice," and it is called *Daat*, and it extends to a man who raises his voice in Torah. The *Ruach* is also called "Written Torah." The good deeds extend from the *Nefesh* of the mind.

Neshama to *Neshama* and NRN extend from *HBD*:

- The *Neshama* to *Neshama*, Abraham, extends from the *Sefira* of *Hochma*.
- The *Neshama*, Sarah, extends from the *Sefira* of *Bina*.
- The *Ruach*, Isaac, extends from the *Sefira* of *Daat*; it is the right of the *Daat*.
- The *Nefesh*, Rebecca, extends from the *Sefira* of *Daat*, which is the left of the *Daat*.

78) Similarly, the Creator created the body out of four basic elements: Fire, wind, dust, and water, similar to *Neshama* to

Neshama, *Neshama*, *Ruach*, and *Nefesh*. *Neshama* to *Neshama* is Water; *Neshama* is fire; *Ruach* is wind; and *Nefesh* is dust.

Water is male, like *Neshama* to *Neshama*, which comes from *Hochma*. This is sweet water of *Kedusha*, and opposite that is the water that causes a curse, which are the evil inclination, SAM.

There is a holy fire, female, like the *Neshama* that comes from *Bina*. Opposite it is the strange fire, of which it is written, "That he shall not enter at any time into the holy place," which is the *Nukva* from the side of the evil inclination, the serpent, the *Nukva* of SAM.

The holy *Ruach* is male, like the wind that comes from the *Sefira* of *Daat*. Opposite it is an impure *Ruach*, the evil inclination. It is said about it, "Out of the serpent's root shall come forth a basilisk," meaning the spirit of the beast, which is called "a basilisk," which is an offspring of the serpent of impurity, from the impure *Bina*.

And there is holy dust, like the *Nefesh* that comes from the left of *Daat*. Opposite it is the impure dust, the beastly *Nefesh* from the side of the evil inclination.

79) Hence, the *Neshama*, which is repentance, *Bina*, assails that serpent to break it by the power of enslavement of the penance, drawing him to the assembly houses and seminaries.

LOVE

MAY HE KISS ME WITH THE KISSES OF HIS MOUTH

Teruma [Donation]

371) Why made King Solomon, who brought words of love between the upper world, *Zeir Anpin*, and the lower world, *Malchut*, and the beginning of the praise of the improvement of love that he introduced between them, "May he kiss me." Indeed, there is love of *Dvekut* [adhesion] of spirit to spirit only in a kiss, and a kiss on the mouth, the outlet of the spirit and its outlet. When they kiss each other, these spirits cleave to one another and become one, and then it is one love.

372) The kiss of love spreads to the four directions, and the four directions cleave together, and they are inside the faith, *Malchut*. And the four spirits rise by four letters, which are the names upon which the holy name depends, and upon which the upper and lower depend. The praise of the Song of Songs depends on them, and they are the four letters of *Ahava* ["love," *Aleph-Hey-Bet-Hey*]. They are the upper *Merkava* [chariot/assembly], HG TM (*Hesed* and *Gevura*, *Tifferet* and *Malchut*), and they are bonding and *Dvekut*, and the wholeness of everything.

SEE LIFE WITH THE WOMAN WHOM YOU LOVE

Miketz [At the End]

70) "See life with the woman whom you love." This verse is a sublime secret. "Enjoy life" is life of the next world, for happy is the man who is rewarded with it, as it should be.

71) "With the woman whom you love" is the assembly of Israel, which is the *Nukva*, since it is about her that love is written, as it is

written, "I have loved you with an everlasting love." When? When the right side clings to her, as it is written, "Therefore with mercy have I drawn you," and mercy [*Hesed*] is the right side.

HALL OF LOVE

VaEtchanan [I Pleaded]

145) The righteous have several sections above sections in that world. The highest among those sections is for those to whom love is their Master is connected, since their section ties to the palace that rises above all because by that, the Creator is enriched with love.

146) This palace, the highest of all, is called "love," and everything stands on love, as it is written, "Many waters cannot quench the love." Everything stands with love because the holy name, *HaVaYaH*, is so. The upper tip, *Keter* of *Yod* of *HaVaYaH*, *Hochma*, never parts from it because the *Keter* is on it with love, and they never part from one another. Likewise is the *Hey* of *HaVaYaH*, as it is written, "And a river, *Bina*, comes out of Eden, *Hochma*." *Bina* always comes out of *Hochma*, and they forever cling with love.

147) When *Vav-Hey*, *Zeir Anpin* and *Malchut*, cling to one another, they cling together in love, the groom with the bride, whose way is always in love. It follows that *Yod* with *Hey*, *Hey* with *Vav*, and *Vav* with the last *Hey* always connect to one another with love, and everything is called "love." Hence, one who loves the King becomes tied to that love, and for this reason, "Love the Lord your God."

LOVE IS THE WHOLE OF THE GRATITUDE

VaEtchanan [I Pleaded]

138) "And you shall love the Lord your God." "And you shall love" means that one should connect to Him with sublime love, that any work that one should do for the Creator should be

done with love, as there is no work like the love of the Creator. These words, love, are the whole of the Torah, since the ten commandments in the Torah are included here.

139) There is nothing more favorable in the eyes of the Creator than one who loves Him properly, as it is written, "With all your heart." What does "With all" mean? It should have said "With all your heart," as well as "With all your soul," and "With all your might"; what is "With all your heart"? It comes to include both hearts—one good and one bad. "With all your soul" means with two souls—one good and one bad. "With all your might" means whether one comes into wealth by inheritance or whether he has earned it.

140) One who loves the Creator is crowned with *Hesed* [grace/ mercy] from all sides. He does *Hesed* to all and has no concern for his own body or wealth. From where do we know that? From Abraham, who had no mercy on his heart, his soul, and his wealth because of his love for his Master.

141) "On his heart" means that Abraham did not look after his own will for his love for his Master. "On his soul" means that he had no mercy for his son and his wife for his love for his Master. "On his wealth" means that he stood at a crossroads and offered food to the whole world. This is the reason why he was crowned with a crown of the *Sefira Hesed*, as it is written, "Mercy to Abraham."

One who is tied with the love of his Master is rewarded with it, and moreover, all the worlds are blessed for him. This is the meaning of what is written, "And Your pious ones shall bless You." Do not pronounce it "Shall bless You," but "Shall bless *Koh*," since the pious ones, those who have been rewarded with the *Sefira* of *Hesed*, will bless Divinity, who is called *Koh*. Thus, even Divinity is blessed because of them.

LOVE IS AS STRONG AS DEATH; JEALOUSY IS AS HARSH AS THE NETHERWORLD

VaYechi [Jacob Lived]

730) "Set me as a seal upon your heart... its flashes are flashes of fire." The assembly of Israel, *Nukva*, has complete desire and craving for the Creator only through the souls of the righteous, who awaken the springing of the lower water in the *Nukva*, opposite the upper water of ZA, which raise MAN to the *Nukva*. This is so because at that time, the complete desire and craving are in adhesion, to bear fruits.

731) And once ZON are clung to one another and she receives a desire for ZA, she says, "Set me as a seal upon thy heart." It is the conduct of a seal that once it is attached to a place, it leaves its imprint there although it is removed from there. Thus, she does not move from him, and all of his impression and form remain there. Thus said the assembly of Israel, the *Nukva*: "Behold, I have clung unto you. And even though I will depart you and go into exile, set me as a seal upon your heart, so that my whole shape will remain in you," like a seal that leaves its whole shape in the place where it had been attached.

732) "For love is as strong as death." It is as strong as the separation of the spirit from the body. When a person's time to depart the world arrives, and he has seen what he has seen, the spirit goes to all the organs in the body and raises its waves, as though sailing in a ship at sea without oars, futilely rising and falling, coming and seeking to bid farewell from all the organs of the body. There is nothing harder than the day when the spirit departs the body. Such is the power of the love of the assembly of Israel to the Creator, as the power of death at the time when the spirit wishes to depart the body.

733) "Jealousy is as harsh as the netherworld." Any person who loves, and jealousy is not tied to it, his love is not love, since jealousy completes the love. From this we learn that a man must

be envious for his wife, so he will connect with her in complete love, since as a result, he does not look at another woman. "Jealousy is as harsh as the netherworld." As the netherworld is harsh in the eyes of the wicked—to go down it, jealousy is harsh in the eyes of the envious lover—to part from the love.

734) When the wicked are brought down to the netherworld, they are told why they are being brought down, and it is harsh for them. Thus, one who is envious demands for sins and thinks how many suspicious deeds she has done, and then a tie of love is tied in him.

735) "Its flashes are flashes of fire, the flame of the Lord." "The flame of the Lord" is a burning flame that emerges from the *Shofar* [a ram's horn], *Yesod Ima*, called *Koh* [*Yod-Hey*], which has awakened and burns. It is the left line of *Ima*, as it is written, "Let his left be under my head." This burns the flame of love of the assembly of Israel, Divinity, for the Creator.

736) For this reason, much water will not be able to quench the love, since when the right—water, *Hesed*—comes, it adds to the burning of the love and does not quench the flame of the left, as it is written, "And his right shall embrace me." This is so because during the illumination of *Hochma* in the left line of *Ima* to the *Nukva*, it is a burning fire, as it is without *Hassadim*. And when the right line comes with its *Hassadim*, called "water," to quench the fire, it does not quench the illumination of *Hochma* by that. On the contrary, it adds and complements her illumination because it clothes the *Hochma* with *Hassadim*, and the *Hochma* shines in complete perfection.

739) In all the places, the male chases the *Nukva* and awakens the love toward her. But here it turns out that she awakens the love and chases him, as it is written, "Set me as a seal upon your heart." Usually, however, it is not to the *Nukva's* credit to chase the male. Indeed, this is an unclear matter and a sublime thing, hidden in the treasures of the King.

LOVE OF FRIENDS

FROM WAR TO BROTHERLY LOVE

Aharei Mot [After the Death]

65) How good and how pleasant. These are the friends, as they sit together inseparably. At first, they seem like people at war, wishing to kill each other. Then they revert back to a state of brotherly love. The Creator, what does He say about them? "How good and how pleasant it is for brothers to dwell together in unity." The word, "together" indicates the presence of Divinity with them. Moreover, the Creator listens to their words and He is pleased and content with them. This is the meaning of the words, "Then those who feared the Lord spoke to one another, and the Lord listened and heard it, and a book of remembrance was written before Him."

66) And you, the friends who are here, as you were in fondness and love before, you will not part henceforth, until the Creator rejoices with you and summons peace upon you. And by your merit, there will be peace in the world. This is the meaning of the words, "For the sake of my brothers and my friends let me say, 'Let peace be in you.'"

LOVE OF FRIENDS

Ki Tissa [When You Take]

54) All those friends, who do not love each other, depart the world before their time. All the friends in Rashbi's time had love of soul and love of spirit among them. This is why in his generation, the secrets of Torah were revealed. Rabbi Shimon would say, "All the friends who do not love each other cause themselves to stray from the right path. Moreover, they put a

blemish in the Torah, since there is love, brotherhood, and truth in the Torah. Abraham loved Isaac; Isaac loved Abraham; and they were embraced. And they were both gripping Jacob with love and brotherhood, and were giving their spirits in one another. The friends should be like them, and not blemish them, for if love is lacking in them, they will blemish their value above, that is, Abraham, Isaac, and Jacob, which are *HGT*."

New *Zohar, Hukot* [statutes]

107) "How good and how pleasant it is for brothers to dwell together." Dwelling together means bonding of the brother, *Zeir Anpin*, with *Tzedek* [justice], *Malchut*. "Also" [the word appears only in the Hebrew text] comes to include Israel, who are the assembly for this unification.

REVEALING THE SECRETS OF TORAH—TO FRIENDS

Pinhas

709) These words are unclear and need to be explained for the friends, for one who closes before them the secrets of the Torah pains them. For the wicked, the lights of the secrets become darkness to them.

This is like concealed money. For one who digs until he finds it, and it is not his, it turns in his mind into darkness and gloom. But for the one that it is his, it shines. This is the reason why one should reveal the hidden secrets of Torah to the friends.

DWELLING IN A PLACE OF MEN OF ACTION

Bo [Come unto Pharaoh]

138) For this reason, one should always dwell only in a place where men of action dwell, since woe unto one who dwells among the wicked, for he is caught for their transgression. And if one dwells among the righteous, he is rewarded for their merit.

PARTING FROM THE WICKED

VaEra [And I Appeared]

176) When the friends are on the way, they should go with one heart. If there are wicked ones walking among them or people who are not from the King's palace, they should part them, as it is written, "But My servant Caleb, because he had another spirit with him," meaning that he separated from the spies, as it is written, "And they went up into the South, and came unto Hebron." It should have said "came" in plural form. But because he parted with the spies and came to Hebron alone to visit the graves of the fathers, it writes "came" in singular form.

DRILLING A HOLE IN THE BOAT

Nasso [Take]

18) Anyone who clings to the Creator and keeps the commandments of the Torah seemingly sustains the worlds—the world above and the world below, as it is written, "And do them."

19) And anyone who breaches the commandments of the Torah seemingly blemishes above, blemishes below, blemishes himself, and blemishes all the worlds. There is an allegory about sailors who were sailing in a boat. One fool among them rose and wished to puncture the boat. His friend told him, "Why are you puncturing the boat?" He replied, "Why should you care? I am drilling under me!" He told him, "But we are both drowning in the boat together!"

FRIENDS WHO ENGAGE IN TORAH ARE PROTECTED

VaEtchanan [I Pleaded]

32) In all of one's actions, he should see the Creator before him. Anyone who is walking along the road, who fears robbers, should

aim for three things—a gift, a prayer, and a war—as did Jacob when he feared Esau. However, the most important of them is the prayer. But even though prayer is the most important, two or three friends engaging in words of Torah is the most important of all, for they do not fear robbers because Divinity is connected to them, for they are engaged in Torah.

LIGHT

SHINES GRADUALLY BRIGHTER UNTIL THE DAY IS SET

VaYishlach [Jacob Sent]

90) When the Creator erects Israel and delivers them from exile, a very small and thin vent of light shall open to them. And then another, a little bigger opening will open for them, until the Creator opens for them the upper gates that are open to the four directions of the world. It is so that their salvation will not appear at once, but like the dawn, which shines gradually brighter until the day is set.

91) And all that the Creator does to Israel and to the righteous among them, when He delivers them bit by bit and not all at once, is like a person who is in the dark and has always been in the dark. When you want to give him light, you first need to light a small light, like the eye of a needle, and then a little bigger. Thus, every time some more until all the light properly shines for him.

92) Such are Israel. And also, one who is healed is not healed at once. Rather, it comes bit by bit until he is healed. But for Esau, it shone at once, and gradually waned, until Israel grow strong and blot him out from the whole of this world and from the next world. And because the day lit up for him at once, he had ruin from everything. But the light of Israel gradually increases until they gain strength and the Creator shines for them forever.

NEFESH, RUACH, NESHAMA (NRN)

Lech Lecha [Go Forth]

158) *Nefesh* is a low awakening that clings to the *Guf*, like candlelight, whose bottom light is black, clings to the wick, does

not depart it, and is corrected only in it. And when the black light is corrected and grips to the wick, it becomes a throne to the white light atop it, for it hovers over the black light. And that white light corresponds to the light of *Ruach*.

159) Once they are both corrected, the black light and the white light atop it, the white light becomes a throne to a hidden light, and it is not seen or known that it hovers over the white light. It corresponds to the light of *Neshama*, and then it is a complete light. Thus, there are three lights one atop the other in a candlelight: 1) The black light that clings to the wick, below all the others; 2) the white light over the black light; and 3) the hidden, unknown light over the white light.

Similarly, a man who is complete in everything has three lights one atop the other, NRN, as with the candlelight. And then a man is called "holy," as it is written, "As for the holy that are in the earth."

THE HIDDEN LIGHT IN WHICH THE WORLD EXISTS

Emor [Speak]

3) "How great is Your goodness, which You have stored up for those who fear You." "How great is Your goodness," meaning how sublime and precious is the Upper Light called, "good," as it is written, "And God saw the light, that it was good." This is the hidden light, with which the Creator does good in the world. He does not deny it every day, for in it is the world sustained, and upon it does it stand.

"...which You have stored up for those who fear You." The Creator made the Upper Light when He created the world, and hid it for the righteous in the future, as it is written, "...which You have stored up for those who fear You, which You have wrought for those who take refuge in You." There are two kinds of light: 1) the hidden light for the righteous in the future, which does not shine in the world; 2) the light that is called "good," which extends from the hidden light and shines in the world every day, and which sustains the world.

EIN SOF—HAVING NO END

Pekudei [Accounts]

360) Their *Dvekut* [adhesion] rises up to *Ein Sof*. This is so because every connection and unity and perfection is to hide and conceal that which is unattainable and unknown, that the desire of all desires is for him, meaning *Ein Sof*. *Ein Sof* is neither about to be known nor to become a *Sof* [end], nor to become a *Rosh* [head/beginning]. It is also not like the first absence, *Keter*, which educed *Rosh* and *Sof*—*Rosh* being the uppermost point. This is the concealed head of everything, and stands within the thought, *Hochma*, since *Hochma* emerged from *Keter*, as it is written, "But wisdom, where shall it be found?" It made an end, called "the end of the matter," *Malchut*, the end of all the lights. But there, in *Ein Sof*, there is no end.

LETTERS

CREATION OF THE WORLD WITH LETTERS

VaYigash [Then Judah Approached]

2) Everything was created in the Torah, and everything was perfected in the Torah. And as the Torah begins with *Bet*, the world was created in *Bet*. This is so because before the Creator created the world, the *Nukva*, all the letters came before Him and entered one at a time in reverse order, in the order of *Tav-Shin-Reish-Kof* and not in the order of *Aleph-Bet-Gimel-Dalet*.

3) The letter *Tav* came before Him and said, "You wish to create the world with me." The Creator replied, "I do not, since many righteous are destined to die in you. It is written about it, 'And set a mark [Hebrew: *Tav*] upon the foreheads of the men,' and it is written, 'And begin at My sanctuary'; do not pronounce, 'At My sanctuary,' but rather, 'At My sanctified,' who are the righteous. This is why the world will not be created in you."

4) The three letters, *Shin-Kof-Reish*, approached each on his own. The Creator told them, "You are unfit for the world to be created in you for you are the letters used for reading *Sheker* [deceit/falsehood], and a lie is unworthy of rising before Me."

5) The letters *Peh* and *Tzadik* approached, and so did all of them until they reached the letter *Chaf*. When the *Chaf* descended from the *Keter* [*Keter* written with *Chaf* in Hebrew], the upper ones and the lower ones were shaken, until everything came to exist in the letter *Bet*, which is the sign for *Beracha* [blessing], and in it, the world was perfected and created.

6) But the *Aleph* is the head of all the letters, so should the world not have been created with it? Yes, indeed, but since *Arur* [cursed] is read with it, the world was not created in it. Thus, although *Aleph* is a letter from above, the world was not created in it so as

to not give strength and fortification to the *Sitra Achra*, who is called "cursed," hence the world was not created in her. Instead, the world was perfected and created in *Bet*.

THE LETTER *BET*

Shmini [On the Eighth Day]

4) Why is the letter *Bet* [ב] open on one side and closed on the other side? When a person comes to join with the Torah, it is open to receive him and partake with him. And when a person shuts his eyes to her and goes by another way, she is blocked from the other side, like the *Bet*, as it is written, "If you forsake me for one day, I will forsake you for two days," and he will not find the opening until he reconnects with the Torah face-to-face and will not depart it. Hence, the Torah opens, calling upon people and declaring and summoning them, "To you, O men, I call."

5) *Bet* has a shape of two roofs and one line that connects them. One roof points up, toward the heaven, and this is ZA, and one roof points down toward the earth, and this is *Malchut*. And the Creator, *Yesod*, grips them and receives them.

6) The three upper lights, three lines, which are clung together are the whole of the Torah, and they open doors to all. They open doors and impart upon faith, meaning *Malchut*, and they are home to all. This is why they are called, "house," since they are the three lines in the *Bet*, implying the three lines of ZA, which are a house. And this is why the Torah begins with *Bet*, since she is the Torah, and the cure for the world.

FIVE OUTLETS OF THE MOUTH

Lech Lecha [Go Forth]

79) ...And those four elements, which are four *Behinot* [discernments], *Hochma*, *Bina*, *Tifferet*, and *Malchut*, spread

into twenty-two letters that come out of the five outlets of the mouth: *Aleph-Het-Hey-Ayin* from the throat; *Bet-Vav-Mem-Peh* from the lips; *Gimel-Yod-Chaf-Kof* from the palate; *Dalet-Tet-Lamed-Nun-Tav* from the tongue; and *Zayin-Samech-Shin-Reish-Tzadik* from the teeth.

Those five outlets correspond to *Keter*. *HB* and *TM* are the four elements—water, fire, wind, and dust. The four elements are the five outlets of the mouth, in which the twenty-two letters spread.

LETTERS—MALES AND FEMALES

VaYetze [Jacob Went Out]

261) All twenty-seven letters in the [Hebrew] alphabet are male and female, included in one another as one. The letters that belong to the right and to the left are males and those that belong to the middle line are females. The male letters impart upper water, and the female letters raise *MAN*, and everything bonds and becomes one. This is the complete unification. Hence, one who knows how to make those unifications and is cautious with aiming them, happy is he in this world and in the next world because this is the essence of the complete unification as it should be.

MEN AND WOMEN

A CANDLE IS A MITZVA AND TORAH IS LIGHT

Teruma [Donation]

729) A candle is a *Mitzva* [correction/good deed]. A candle is a *Mitzva* with which women are rewarded. It is a Sabbath candle. Although women are not rewarded with the Torah, since the men are rewarded with the Torah, they illuminate for that candle, which the women correct with this *Mitzva*. The women with the correction of this candle, the men with the Torah, to light and to illuminate this candle, which is a correction of a *Mitzva* to which women are obliged.

A WOMAN IS THE LORD'S FIRE

Beresheet [Genesis]

218) "The man said, 'This is now bone of my bones, and flesh of my flesh; she shall be called 'Woman.'" The meaning is that it is her of whom there is none other like her; she is the glory of the house. Compared to her, all the women are as a monkey compared to a man, but she shall be called "woman," this one and not another.

The name *Isha* [woman] implies *Esh H* [fire of the Creator], meaning the wholeness of the illumination of the left, called *Esh* [*Aleph-Shin*, but also "fire"], which is connected to the letter *Hey*, which is the *Nukva*. This is the meaning of his praising her, "She shall be called 'Woman.'" Because of the illumination of *Hochma* that shines in her after she has been included in her husband's *Hassadim*, she was given the name "woman," which is illumination of *Hochma*, which is called *Esh* [fire], as it is written, "And the light of the Lord shall become fire." And the name *Isha* is because *Esh* is connected to the *Hey*.

HIS WIFE IS THE ESSENCE OF THE HOUSE

Beresheet [Genesis]

231) His wife is the essence of the house, since Divinity does not depart his house by merit of his wife. It is as we learned that it is written, "And Isaac brought her into the tent of his mother Sarah." The candle was relit, as it was at the time of Sarah, his mother, since Divinity came to the house thanks to Rebecca. Thus, Divinity is in the house by merit of his wife.

232) Upper *Ima*, *Bina*, is with the male, *Zeir Anpin*, only when the house is corrected and male and female, ZON, are connected. At that time, upper *Ima* imparts blessings to bless ZON. Similarly, lower *Ima*, Divinity, is with the male, meaning with a man below, only when the house is corrected and the male comes to the *Nukva* and they conjoin. At that time, lower *Ima*, Divinity, imparts blessings to bless them.

THE CAMP OF ISRAEL

VaYikahel [Assembled]

35) It is written, "So is the way of an adulterous woman." But, "So is the way of an adulterous woman" is the angel of death. "She eats and wipes her mouth," for it burns the world with its flames and puts people to death before their time. And she says, "I have done no evil," for he sought judgment for them and they were caught in their iniquity and died by true judgment.

36) And when Israel had made the calf and all those multitudes died, the angel of death was among the women, inside the camp of Israel. Since Moses saw that the angel of death is among the women and the camp of Israel was among them, he immediately gathered all the men separately, as it is written, "Then Moses assembled all the congregation of the sons of Israel." These were the men that he had congregated and separated to themselves.

37) And the angel of death was not separated from the women until the Temple was built.

THE FLAME OF THE SWORD
THAT TURNS EVERY WAY

VaYikra [The Lord Called]

325) On the day when Adam was born, they were commanded in regards to the tree of knowledge and broke their Master's commandment. And since the woman sinned first and the serpent came upon her, as it is written, "And he shall rule over you," henceforth, whenever men are guilty before the Creator, the women from the side of harsh *Din* will rule over them, as it is written, "As for My people, a babe is their master, and women rule over them."

326) And those women are called, "The flaming sword that turns every way." Yet, it is not that they are the turning sword. Rather, they are a flame from that sword, which is called, "A sword ... that shall execute the vengeance of the covenant," "The sword of the Lord is filled with blood." And that flaming sword that turns every way is sometimes men and sometimes females.

327)...When the prophet of Israel saw that Israel were twisting their ways and performing iniquities before their Master, he said, "Women that are at ease, why do you keep quiet? Why do you sit and not awaken in the world? Rise up and take governance over the men."

DEBORAH AND HANNAH

VaYikra [The Lord Called]

329) There were two women in the world, and they praised the Creator like all the men in the world will not. Those are Deborah and Hannah. Hannah said, "There is none holy as the Lord, for

there is none besides You," and all the writings that follow. She opened the door to faith in the world.

THE HALLS OF THE FEMALE SOULS

Shlach Lecha [Send Forth]

195) ...They showed me six palaces with several pleasures and delights in the place where the curtain is spread out in the garden, since from that curtain onward, males do not enter at all.

196) In one palace, there is Batiah, daughter of Pharaoh, several tens of thousands of righteous women with her. Each of them has places of lights and delights without any pressure. Three times a day, the heralds call out, "Behold, the form of Moses, the loyal prophet, is coming," and Batiah goes out to a place where there is one partition and sees the form of Moses. She bows before him and says, "Happy I am for having raised that light." This is her most special pleasure.

197) Batiah returns to the women and engages in the *Mitzvot* of the Torah. all of them are in the forms that they had in this world, clothed in light, like the clothes of the males, except that they do not shine as much as the male garments. They engage in the flavors and *Mitzvot* of the Torah that they were not rewarded with keeping in that world, and all those women who sit in the same hall with Batiah, daughter of Pharaoh, are called "tranquil women," for they were not afflicted at all by the affliction of Hell.

198) In another hall, there is Serah, daughter of Asher, and several tens of thousands and thousands of women are with her. Three times a day, it is declared before her, "Behold, here comes the form of the righteous Joseph." She rejoices and comes out to one partition that she has, and sees the light of the form of Joseph. She is happy and bows to him, and says, "Happy is that

day when I awoke the word of you to my old man." Afterwards, she returns to the rest of the women and engages in praises of the Master of the world and to thank His name. And each and every one has several places and joy, and then they return to engaging in the commandments of the Torah and their flavors.

199) In another hall, there is Yoheved, the mother of Moses, the loyal prophet, with several thousands and tens of thousands with her. In that hall, there are no declarations at all. Rather, three times a day, she thanks and praises the Creator, she and all those women with her. They sing the song of the sea each day, and she alone begins from here. "Miriam the prophetess, Aaron's sister, took the timbrel in her hand," and all those righteous in the Garden of Eden listen to the voice of her singing, and several holy angels thank and praise the holy name with her.

200) In another hall, there is Prophetess Deborah. Here, too, all the women who are with her thank and chant in singing that she said in this world. Who has seen the joy of the righteous and righteous women who serve the Creator? There are four hidden palaces of the holy mothers who were not given to exile before those palaces, and there is none to see them. Each day t201) Each night, they all gather together because the time for Zivug [coupling] is midnight, whether in this world or in that world. The Zivug of that world is the adhering of soul to soul, of light to light.

The Zivug of this world is of body to body, and all is as it should be, a kind with its kind, a Zivug by Zivug. A body by body is in this world. The Zivug of that world is light by light. The halls of the four mothers are called "halls of trusting daughters," and I have not been rewarded with looking into them. Happy are the righteous, men and females, who follow on the right path in this world and are rewarded with all the pleasures of that world.

202) The *Zivug* in that world produces more fruits than a *Zivug* that is done in this world. In their *Zivug*—in the *Zivug* of that world, in their desire as one, when the souls cling to one another—they bear fruit and lights come out of them and become candles. These are the souls of the proselytes who convert.

BLESSING FOR THE WOMEN IS THROUGH THE MEN

VaYechi [Jacob Lived]

494)... "He will bless—He will bless the house of Israel." Why does it write, "Bless," twice? "The Lord has been mindful of us, He will bless" are the men, and "He will bless the house of Israel" are the women. This is so because the males need to be blessed first, and then the women, for women are blessed only by the blessing of the males. And when the males are blessed, the women are blessed, as it is written, "And made atonement for himself, and for his house." Thus, one needs to make atonement for oneself first, and then for one's home, since the male comes before the female so that she will be blessed from him.

495) Women are blessed only by males, when they are blessed first. And they are blessed from this blessing of the males. They do not need a special blessing of their own. Then why does the verse say, "Will bless the house of Israel," if the women do not need a special blessing? Indeed, the Creator gives an additional blessing to a male who is married to a woman so that his wife will be blessed from him.

Similarly, in all places, the Creator gives additional blessing to a male who has married a woman so she will be blessed by this addition. And since a man marries a woman, He gives him two shares, one for himself and one for his wife. And he receives everything, his own share and his wife's. This is why a special blessing is written for the women, "Will bless the house of Israel," for this is their share. However, the males receive their share, as well, and give it to them later.

ONE WHO DID NOT MARRY A WIFE IS FLAWED

VaYikra [The Lord Called]

63) "When any man of you brings an offering," excluding one who did not marry a wife, since his offering is not an offering and blessings are not present in him, neither above nor below. This means that the verse, "When any man of you brings an offering" is different, for his is not a man and is not included among man, and Divinity is not over him, for he is flawed and he is called, "maimed," and the maimed are removed from everything, all the more so from the altar, from offering a sacrifice.

64) Nadab and Abihu prove that the words, "Then fire came out from before the Lord" was because they were not married. This is why it is written, "When any man of you brings an offering to the Lord." A man with male and female is worthy of making this sacrifice, and no other.

65) Although we spoke of Nadab and Abihu in a different way, it is certainly because they were not married, but incense is the highest of all the offerings in the world, for which the upper and lower are blessed. And they were not worthy of offering this offering, which is above all sacrifices, since they were unmarried. Hence, they were unfit to offer a sacrifice, all the more so such sublime things as incense, for they are not worthy of making the world blessed by them.

66) "Then fire came out from before the Lord and consumed them." Why were they punished so harshly? It is like a man who comes to the queen to tell her that the king has come to her house to be with her and to rejoice with her. The man came before the king and the king saw that the man was crippled.

The king said, "It is dishonorable to me that I will come to the queen through this crippled man." In the meantime, the queen had fixed the house for the king, and since she saw that the king was ready to come to her, and that man caused the king to depart her, she commanded that this man would be put to death.

67) Similarly, when Nadab and Abihu entered with the incense in their hands, the queen (*Malchut*) was glad and fixed herself to receive the king's face (ZA). When the king saw that these men were flawed, the king did not wish to come to be with the queen through them, and the king departed her. When the queen saw that the king had left because of them, promptly, "Then fire came out from before the Lord and consumed them."

68) And all this is because one who is not married is flawed. He is maimed before the king, and the sanctity of the king departs him and does not remain in the flaw. It is written about that, "When any man of you brings an offering," meaning those who are called "men" will bring an offering and those who are not called "men," the unmarried, will not bring an offering.

MAN CONSISTS OF MALE AND FEMALE TOGETHER

Nasso [Take]

141) Man is an inclusion of male and female, since one in whom male and female have conjoined is called, "a man," and then he is God-fearing. Moreover, there is humility in him. And still more, there is *Hesed* in him.

And one who does not have male and female, there is no fear in him, no humility, and no piousness. This is why man is regarded as including everything. And since he is called, "Adam" [man], there is *Hesed* in him, as it is written, "I have said, 'Mercy will be built up forever.'" But the world cannot be built without a male and a female.

142) It is written, "But the mercy of the Lord is from everlasting to everlasting on those who fear Him." "Those who fear Him" are the whole of man, male and female, for otherwise there is no fear in him. "But the mercy of the Lord is from everlasting to everlasting" are the priests that come from the side of *Hesed*. And they inherit this lot, which comes from the upper world, ZA, to the lower world, *Malchut*. "On those who fear Him" means the priests below, who contain male and female, to be inclusive, as in man, which is male and female. "And His righteousness to children's children," since he has been rewarded with children's children.

A MALE SOUL AND A FEMALE SOUL

Ki Tazria [When a Woman Delivers]

9) "A woman who inseminates first, delivers a male child." The Creator sentences whether a drop is male or female, and you say, "A woman who inseminates first, delivers a male child." Thus, the Creator's sentence is redundant. Indeed, it is certainly the Creator who decides between a drop of male and a drop of female. And because He has discerned it, He sentences whether it is to be a male or a female.

There are three partners to a man: the Creator, his father, and his mother. His father gives the white in him; his mother—the red in him; and the Creator gives the soul. If the drop is a male, the Creator gives the soul of a male. If it is a female, the Creator gives the soul of a female. It turns out that when the woman first inseminated, the drop has not become a male yet, if the Creator had not sent within her a soul of a male.

This discernment that the Creator discerns in a drop—that it is fit for a soul of a male or a female—is considered "the sentencing of the Creator." Had He not discerned it and did not send a soul of a male, the drop would not have become a male. Thus, the two statements do not contradict one another.

10) And since she inseminates, does she deliver? After all, this requires pregnancy. It should have said, "If a woman is impregnated, she delivers a male child." What is, "If she inseminates, she delivers"? Since the day of insemination and conception to the day of delivery, a woman has not a word in her mouth except her offspring, whether it will be a male. This is why it is written, "If a woman inseminates, she delivers a male child."

TO BE REWARDED WITH SONS

VaYeshev [And Jacob Sat]

163) Even if a man engages in the Torah day in and day out, but his origin and springing are in vain, for he does not bear sons, he has no place being in the presence of the Creator. If a spring does not enter a well of water, it is not a well, for the well and the origin are one, and one who has no sons is as one whose origin did not enter him and is not acting within him.

177) "Come to your brother's wife." He did not have to tell him that, since Judah and all the tribes knew it. But the main reason why he told him, "...and raise a seed," is that that seed was needed for that thing to be corrected... Even though man has been sentenced to death, which separates him from the eternal root, he is still not completely separated, for he remains attached to his eternal root through the sons that each one has, since every son is a part of the father's body. Thus, each person is like a link in the chain of life, which begins with *Adam ha Rishon* [the first man] and continues through the revival of the dead, forever and ever. And as long as man's chain of life continues, for he leaves a son behind him, death does not separate him from eternity at all, and he is seemingly still alive.

188) Hence, it is written, "Behold, children are a heritage of the Lord." It is the soul's bundle of life, as it is written, "Yet the soul of my lord shall be bound in the bundle of life," considered the next world.

This is what the text calls, "heritage" [can also mean land in Hebrew]. And who awards man with coming to this land? Sons. The sons award him with the land of the Lord; hence, happy is the man who has been rewarded with sons, to teach them the ways of Torah.

EXILE AND REDEMPTION

ON MY BED AT NIGHT
Ki Tazria [When a Woman Delivers]

1) "On my bed night after night I sought him whom my soul loves." The assembly of Israel spoke before the Creator and asked Him about the exile, since she is seated among the rest of the nations with her children, and she lies in the dust. And because she is lying in another land, impure one, she said, "I ask on my bed, for I am lying in exile," and exile is called "nights." Hence, "I sought him whom my soul loves," to deliver me from it.

2) "I sought him but did not find him," since it is not His way to mate in me, but only in His palace, and not in exile. "I called him but he did not answer me," for I was dwelling among other nations, who do not hear his voice, but only His sons. "Did ever a people hear the voice of God?"

3) "On my bed night after night," said the assembly of Israel, Divinity. "On my bed I was angered before Him, asking Him to mate with me to delight me—from the left line—and to bless me—from the right line—with complete joy—from the middle line." When the king, ZA, mates with the assembly of Israel, several righteous inherit inheritance of a holy legacy, upper *Mochin*, and several blessings are found in the world.

EXILE OF DIVINITY

VaYikra [The Lord Called]

344) On the day when the Temple was ruined below and Israel went into exile with millstone round their necks and their hands tied behind them, the assembly of Israel, Divinity, was expelled from the King's house, to follow them into exile. And when

252

Divinity came down she said, "First, I will go and weep for my abode, the Temple, for my sons, Israel, and for my husband, ZA," who has drifted from her. When she came down she saw that her place was destroyed and all the blood of the followers that was shed in it, and the Holy Palace and the House were burnt in fire.

345) Then she raised her voice in weeping, and the upper and lower were moved, and the voice reached up to the place where the King, ZA, resides. But the King wished to return the world into chaos until several battalions and several camps of angels came down to comfort her, but she turned down their comforting. It is written about that, "A voice is heard in Ramah, lamentation, and bitter weeping, Rachel is weeping for her children, she refuses to be comforted for her children," since she did not receive comforting from them. "Because He is gone" means because the holy King went up and is not inside her.

346) "Rachel is weeping for her children." It should have said that Divinity is weeping for her children. Rachel is the assembly of Israel, Divinity, Jacob's wife, the wife of ZA, as it is written, "And Jacob loved Rachel." It is also written, "but Rachel was barren," and also, "Who makes the barren woman dwell in her house as a joyful mother of children." All these verses relate to Divinity.

347) Another interpretation: "He is gone" means "none," that is, there are none who are greater than Me in this house. "Gone," since the Creator departed above and was removed from everything. "He is gone" means He is not in a Zivug with her. "Gone" means that His name, Divinity, is not His great Name. Rather, she is in exile.

348) From which place did Divinity begin to be disclosed? From the Temple, where she was present. Afterwards, she roamed the whole of the land of Israel. Then, when she departed the land, she stood inside the desert and sat there three days, leading the

masses, the camps, and the residents from the King's house, from Jerusalem, and calling about her, "How lonely sits the city."

349) They were not exiled from the land of Israel and the Temple was not ruined before all of Israel were guilty before the King, and before all the leaders of the world were found guilty first, as it is written, "O My people! Those who guide you lead you astray and confuse the direction of your paths." And when the heads of the people went with evil, the whole people followed suit.

FOUR EXILES

Ki Tetze [If You Go Forth]

63) There were four exiles: three corresponding the three *Klipot* of the nut. The first is *Tohu*, a green line, the green shell of the nut. The second is *Bohu*, moist stones, strong rocks, from which the authors of the Mishnah sentenced several sentences, and they grip to them to bring out the waters of Torah. And this is why they are called "moist stones," since water comes out of them. The third *Klipa* [shell] is the thin shell of the nut, the small third exile. This is "And darkness." The fourth exile is the great deep, the hollow of the nut, "And darkness was over the face of the deep."

64) The fourth *Klipa*, the deep, is called "a pit where an ox fell," as it is written about Joseph, "The firstborn of his ox, majesty is his." It is written, "And threw him into the pit," the evil *Nukva* of the *Klipa*. The empty pit is the male of the *Klipa*. Empty means without Torah, which is called "water."

However, there were serpents and scorpions there, and this is the fourth exile, which is empty, without Torah, a generation of wicked, filled with serpents and scorpions, meaning that they are as deceitful as serpents and scorpions because they have uprooted the words of sages and judge falsely. It is said about them, "Her adversaries became the head."

65) "And he looked this way and that, and when he saw there was no one" from Israel among those wicked in that generation. Instead, they were mixed multitude. This will come about at the end of the exile, and for this reason, the end of redemption is stated as the great deep, which is the fourth exile. And Moses, you went down there. The deep [Tehom] is death [HaMavet] with the letters inverted, and there is no death but poverty, poverty of reason. But this was sorted above, before the Tannaim and the Amoraim, who all went down to the deep in the fourth exile because of her, to help you.

HURRY, MY BELOVED, AND BE LIKE A GAZELLE OR A YOUNG HART
Shemot [Exodus]

235) "Hurry, my beloved, and be like a gazelle or a young hart." Every yearning that Israel yearned for the Creator is the yearning of Israel that the Creator will not go and will not walk away, but run like a gazelle or a young hart.

236) No other animal in the world does what the gazelle or the hart does. When it runs, it turns its head slightly to the place from which it came. It always turns its head back. This is what Israel said, "God Almighty, if we cause You to depart from among us, may it be that You will run like the gazelle or the young hart." This is because it runs and turns its head to the place it had left, the place where it was before and left it and fled from there.

This is the meaning of the words, "Yet in spite of this, when they are in the land of their enemies, I will not reject them, nor will I so abhor them as to destroy them, breaking My covenant with them." Another thing: The gazelle sleeps with one eye and is awake with the other eye. This is what Israel said to the Creator, "Do as the gazelle does, for He who keeps Israel will neither slumber nor sleep."

AND I WILL SET MY TABERNACLE AMONG YOU

BeHukotai [In My Statutes]

30) "And I will set My tabernacle among you." My tabernacle is Divinity, My pawn, Divinity, was mortgaged by the iniquities of Israel because she goes into exile with them. There is an allegory about a man who loved his friend. He told him, "Certainly, because of the sublime love that I have for you, I wish to dwell with you." His friend replied, "How will I know that you will dwell with me?" He went and took all the good things in his home and brought them to him and said, "My pawn is with you, so I will never part from you."

31) So is the Creator. He wished to dwell with Israel. He took His treasure, Divinity, and lowered it down to Israel. He told them, "Israel, here is My pawn with you, so I will never part from you." And although the Creator was removed from us, He left the pawn in our hands because Divinity is with us in exile and we keep His treasure. And when He asks for His pawn, He will come to dwell with us. This is why it is written, "And I will set My tabernacle among you." "I will give you a pawn so I will dwell with you." And even though Israel is in exile now, the Creator's mortgage is with them and they have never left it.

32) "And My soul shall not abhor you." This is similar to a man who loves his friend and wishes to dwell with him. What did he do? He took his bed and brought it to his house. He said, "Here, my bed is in your house, so I will not draw far from you, from your bed and from your vessels." Thus said the Creator, "And I will set My tabernacle among you, and My soul shall not abhor you." Thus, My bed, Divinity, is in your home. "And since My bed is with you, know that I will never part from you." And for this reason, "My soul shall not abhor you," I will not part from you.

33) "And I will walk among you, and will be your God." Since my pawn is with you, you should know for certain that I am going with you, as it is written, "For the Lord your God walks in the midst of your camp, to deliver you, and to give up your enemies before you; therefore shall your camp be holy."

LENGTH OF THE EXILE

Ki Tissa [When You Take]

21) We see, and so can the strong ones in the world, meaning the nations, that the exile is continuing and the Son of David has not come. So it is, but what makes Israel suffer this exile? It is all the promises that the Creator had promised them. They enter synagogues and seminaries and see all the comforts in the holy books, and in their hearts they are happy to suffer all that comes upon them. Had it not been for that, they would not have been able to withstand.

22) Everything depends on repentance. But they cannot all awaken to repentance together because it is written, "So it shall be when all of these things have come upon you." It is also written, "And you call them to mind in all nations where the Lord your God has banished you." Also, it is written, "And you shall return to the Lord your God." And then, if the One who banished you will be at the end of the sky, from there will He gather you. And before all these things come true, they cannot be awakened by them for repentance.

23) O how You have sealed all the trails and paths from the children of the exile, and have left no possibility for them to speak, for they did not delve in redemption every single generation, did not suffer the exile, did not seek reward, departed the rules of Torah, and mingled with the rest of the nations24) "As the pregnant woman approaches the time to give birth, she writhes and cries out in her birth pangs," since it is the nature of a pregnant woman to wait

nine whole months. But there are quite a few in the world who go through only one or two days of the ninth month, while all the pains and pangs of the pregnant woman are on the ninth. Hence, even if she only went through one day of the ninth month, it is considered as though the whole of the ninth month had passed for her. So are Israel: since they tasted the taste of exile, if they repent, it is considered for them as though they had experienced all the troubles that are written in the Torah, especially that they had experienced several pangs since the beginning of the exile.

IN ITS TIME, I WILL HASTEN IT

VaYera [The Lord Appeared]

454) How long should we be in exile until that time? The Creator made redemption completely dependent on whether they repent. Thus, they will be rewarded or not rewarded with redemption by whether or not they repent, as it is written, "I the Lord will hasten it in its time." If they merit, they will repent, and "I will hasten it." If they do not merit, they will not repent, and "in its time."

THE ALLEGORY OF THE KING AND THE QUEEN

VaYikra [The Lord Called]

78) In all of Israel's exiles, He set a time and an end to all of them. And in all of them, Israel return to the Creator, and the virgin of Israel, *Malchut*, returns to her place at the set time. But now, in the last exile, it is not so. She will not return as in the other exiles. This verse teaches, "She has fallen; she will not rise again—the virgin of Israel," and it does not say, "She has fallen and I will not raise her again."

79) It is like a king who was angry with the queen and expelled her from her palace for a certain period of time. When that time was through, the queen would immediately come and return

before the king. This was so once, twice, and thrice. But on the last time, she became remote from the king's palace and the king expelled her from his palace for a long time. The king said, "This time is not as like the other times, when she came before me. Instead, I and all my household will go and seek her."

80) When he reached her, he saw that she was lying in the dust. Who saw the glory of the queen at that time, and the king's requests of her? Finally, the king held her in his arms, raised her, and brought her to his palace. And he swore to her that he would never part from her again and will never be far from her.

81) It is similar with the Creator: every time the assembly of Israel were in exile, she would come and return before the King. But now, in this exile, it is not so. Rather, the Creator will hold her by the hand and will raise her, appease her, and bring her back to His palace.

TO THE EXTENT OF CONCEALMENT, THE EXTENT OF DISCLOSURE

VaYera [The Lord Appeared]

453) *Vav* and everything appears in it, for everything appears by the perfection of the *Vav*. This is so because in everything that is concealed, He reveals all that is hidden, and one who is revealed will not come and reveal what is concealed.

Man is created in utter wickedness and lowliness, as it is written, "When a wild ass's foal is born a man." And all the vessels in one's body, meaning the senses and the qualities, and especially the thought serve him only wickedness and nothingness all day. And for one who is rewarded with adhering unto Him, the Creator does not create other tools instead, to be worthy and suitable for reception of the eternal spiritual abundance intended for him. Rather, the same lowly vessels that have thus far been used in a filthy and loathsome way are inverted to become vessels of reception of all the pleasantness and eternal gentleness.

Moreover, each *Kli* whose deficiencies had been the greatest has now become the most important. In other words, the measure that they reveal is the greatest. It is so much so that if he had a *Kli* in his body that had no deficiencies, it has now become seemingly redundant, for it does not serve him in any way. It is like a vessel of wood or clay: the greater its deficiency, meaning its carving, the greater its capacity and the greater its importance.

And this applies in the upper worlds, as well, since no revelation is dispensed upon the worlds except through concealed discernments. And by the measure of concealment in a degree, so is the measure of revelations in it, which is given to the world. If there is no concealment in it, it cannot bestow a thing.

This is the meaning of the *Vav* in the name, *HaVaYaH*. It is ZA, whose *Mochin* are always in covered *Hassadim* and are concealed from the illumination of *Hochma*. This is why it will reveal the complete redemption, as it is written, "The *Vav* will raise the *Hey*." This is so because the measure of concealment and covering in it will determine the measure of its revealing in the future. And the bottom *Hey* of *HaVaYaH*, the *Nukva*, where the *Hassadim* appear, and all the discernments of disclosure of *Hochma* in the worlds come only from her. And since there is no concealment in her, she cannot reveal what is concealed, meaning redemption. And although there are other concealments in the *Nukva*, they are nonetheless insufficient for this great disclosure of the complete redemption, since by the measure of this revelation, so must be the measure of the concealment.

THE DARKNESS BEFORE REDEMPTION

Beresheet [Genesis]

308) As they were walking, they saw that the dawn has paled and then the light rose. Rabbi Hizkiya said to Rabbi Yosi, "Come and I will show you that so is Israel's redemption: When the sun of redemption shines for them, trouble after trouble will come upon them, and darkness after darkness. And when the light of the Creator shines upon them, as it is said, 'His going forth is as sure as the dawn,' it is written, 'But the sun or righteousness will rise for you who fear My name, with healing in its wings.'"

309) At that time, wars will awaken in the world—nation against nation, and city against city—and many troubles will surface over the enemies of Israel until their faces are darkened like the sides of a caldron. After that, their redemption will appear over them out of the roar of their pressure and stress.

BEIT LECHEM [BETHLEHEM]

VaYechi [Jacob Lived]

87) And why is this holy place called "bread," since the writing says that Ephrat is *Beit Lechem* [House of Bread]? This is because it is from the name of the Creator, for they will die there in fighting for His name, "The hand upon the throne of *Koh* [Yod-Hey]: the Lord will have war against Amalek." This means that they will die there to complement the name *Yod-Hey*. This is so because the name is not complete with *HaVaYaH* until the memory of Amalek is blotted out, and this is why the war is to complement the name *Yod-Hey* with *Vav-Hey*. This is why the name is called *Lechem*, from the word *Milchamah* [war], since he fought in exile because he came to complement the name of the Creator.

WITH *THE ZOHAR*, WE WILL COME OUT OF EXILE

Nasso [Take]

89) Such as that will be done, testing Israel in the last exile, as it is written, "Many will be purged, purified and refined," which are from the side of the good, enduring the trial. "But the wicked will act wickedly," from the side of the evil, and the verse, "Nor will they enter the land of Israel," will come true in them, and he kills them.

90) The wise will understand, for they are from the side of *Bina*, the tree of life. It was for them that *The Book of Zohar* said, "And the wise will shine like the radiance of the firmament," from the radiance of Upper *Ima*, who is called, "repentance." These do not require testing, and because Israel are destined to taste of the tree of life, which is this *Book of Zohar*, they will be delivered from the exile with mercy through it.

NATURE

EARTH IS ROUND

New *Zohar, Beresheet* [Genesis]

619) The world is as round as a ball. When the sun comes out in the east, it goes in a circle until it reaches below the earth, and then it becomes evening. At that time, it gradually descends by circles of certain steps, descending and circling the whole earth and the whole world.

620) When the sun comes down and is covered by it, it grows dark upon us and lights up to those who are dwelling below us, those who are on the other side of the earth, below our feet. And so it grows dark on one side and shines on the other side, below it, following the world and circle of the earth, round and round.

621) And similarly, its light gradually descends and separates between the water below the water of the ocean and the water for those who go above, separating in the middle of the waters of the sea, detaining a pipe of water that comes out of Hell from passing through and harming people. For this reason, the sun is not called *Shemesh* [sun], but *LeShamesh* [to serve] people, as this is why it is called *Shemesh*, that is, *MeShamesh* [serving], for it serves everyone.

Had the light of the sun not bathed itself in the sea of the ocean, it would have burned and lit up the whole world.

CHANGES IN THE AIR

VaYikra [The Lord Called]

141) The whole world revolves in a circle like a ball, some are above and some are below. The people all around the earth stand opposite each other and the seven parts in the ball are the

seven lands. And all the people in the six lands differ in their appearances according to the different air in each place. And they persist as the rest of the people.

THE EARTH QUAKES

Shemot [Exodus]

306) Rabbi Isaac came across a mountain and saw a man sleeping under a tree. Rabbi Isaac sat there. While he was sitting, he saw that the earth was quaking and that tree broke and fell, and he saw crevices and holes in the ground, and the ground was rising and falling.

307) That man awoke, yelled toward Rabbi Isaac and told him, "Jew, Jew, weep and wail, for a minister is being raised in the firmament, an appointee, a high governor, and he is destined to inflict much harm upon you. This quake of the earth was for you, since every time the earth quakes, it is because an appointee who will harm you rises in the firmament."

WHEN PEOPLE CORRUPT THEIR WAYS

Noah

39) Why was the earth corrupted? Is the earth punishable? It is because every flesh corrupted its way. When people are righteous and keep the commandments of the Torah, the earth is strengthened and every joy is in it because Divinity is upon the earth. At that time, the upper ones and lower ones are all in joy.

40) When people corrupt their way, do not keep the commandments of the Torah, and sin before their Master, they seemingly repel Divinity from the world and the earth remains corrupted. Thus, Divinity is repelled from it and is not present on it, and then she is corrupted. At that time, it is corrupted because another spirit is over it, which corrupts the world.

THE GENERATION OF THE FLOOD

Noah

58) Why does the Creator sentence the world—the generation of the flood—with water and not with fire or with something else? It is because they corrupted their ways by the upper water and lower water, not connecting male and female properly. This is so because anyone who corrupts his way, corrupts female and male waters, that is, he blemishes the upper MAD and MAN and causes them to not unite, hence they are sentenced in water, in what they sinned.

59) And the water was boiling and they stripped the skin off them, as though they had corrupted their ways with boiling water. Judgment for judgment means that he avenged them an eye for an eye. "All the fountains of the great deep burst open" is the lower water, and "The windows of heaven opened" is the upper water. Thus, they were afflicted by the upper water and the lower water.

THE STARS

Pinhas

384) What do comets—stars that a tail of light stretches behind them, which run back and forth—imply?

385) The Creator created all the stars in the firmament, great and small, and all thank and praise the Creator. When their time to praise arrives, the Creator calls them by name, as it is written, "He calls them all by name." Then, they run and stretch a tail of light to go and praise their Master in that place where they were counted, as it is written, "Raise up your eyes and see who created these?"

All the degrees in GAR (first three) are called "stars" or "stars of heaven." No illumination of *Hochma* can be elicited from them, which is called numbering and counting from above to below. This is the meaning of the words, "Look now toward the heaven and count the stars, if you can count them." Indeed, the Creator Himself reveals the number and calculation in them in their own place. This is illumination of *Hochma*, but they shine from below to above, and it counts the number of stars because the Creator Himself counts the number.

"He calls them all by name." "By name" means attainment, as what we do not attain, we do not call by name. And when the Creator assembles them to disclose the number in them, then for all the light, they bring back *Ohr Hozer* [reflected light] from below to above, and this is considered a tail. It is that that the comets imply in the earth.

THE RITE OF THE SUN

Ki Tissa [When You Take]

7) When the face of the east shines, all the sons of the east, of the mountains of light, bow before the light that shines instead of the sun, before it emerges over the face of the earth, and worship it. This is so because how many worship the sun after the sun comes out? They are those who worship this light of the illumination of the dawn, who call this light, "The God of the illuminating jewel." And they swear by the God of the illuminating jewel.

8) And should you say that this work is in vain, then since the ancient days, they knew wisdom when the sun was shining, before it came out over the face of the earth, at which time that appointee that was appointed over the sun comes out with holy

letters of the Upper Name written on his head. And by the power of these letters, he opens all the windows of the heavens, strikes them, and passes. And that appointee enters that radiance, which shines around the sun before it comes out and he is there until the sun comes out and spreads through the world.

9) And that appointee is appointed over gold and red jewels, and they worship that form which is in the light of the sun, which is the appointee. Then, in points and in signs that they inherited from the first, from ancient days, they walk and know the points of the sun, to find the places of gold and jewels. But how much longer will there be these many labors in the world? After all, the lie has no pillars to support it for its existence.

MAN'S EYES

VaYehi [Jacob Lived]

341) Because the view of the world is seen in a man's eyes, and all the colors are in them, too, and the white color in them is like the great ocean that surrounds the world from all sides, the other color in them is like the land that the waters brought out, and the land stands between the waters. Similarly, this color stands between the waters, in this white color, which implies to the ocean water.

342) The other, third color, is in the middle of the eye. This is Jerusalem, the middle of the world. The fourth color in the eye— the black in the eye—is where all the power to see in the whole of the eye is found. It is called "pupil," and in that pupil, the face is seen. And the most precious vision of all is Zion, the point in the middle of everything. The vision of the whole world is seen there, and Divinity—the beauty of everything and the view of everything—is present there. This eye is the inheritance of the world. For this reason, the one who dies leaves it and his son takes it and inherits it.

MAN IS A SMALL WORLD

Lech Lecha [Go Forth]

330) How great are the deeds of the Creator? The art and painting of a man are like the artisanship and the depiction of the world. In other words, man comprises the entire deed of the world, and he is called "a small world."

ZIVUG [COUPLING]

THE CREATOR MAKES ZIVUGIM

Lech Lecha [Go Forth]

346) All the souls that are destined to come into the world stand in *Zivugim, Zivugim* [*Zivugim*—plural of *Zivug* (coupling)] before Him. Each divides into male and female, and when they come into this world, the Creator makes *Zivugim*, as it is written, "The daughter of so and so with so and so."

347) What does it mean when it says that the Creator says, "The daughter of so and so with so and so"? After all, it is written, "There is nothing new under the sun," and all has already been done in the act of creation. Can it be that the matter of *Zivugim* is a new thing in each *Zivug*, that there is a need to declare, "The daughter of so and so with so and so"? Indeed, it is written, "There is nothing new under the sun." However, above the sun there is news. So why does He declare here, "The daughter of so and so with so and so," if it is said that at the very same time when one is born into the world, his mate is made ready for him?

348) Happy are the righteous, whose souls are crowned before the holy King before they come to the world to clothe in a body. At the time when the Creator elicits the souls to the world, all those spirits and souls consist of male and female, which conjoin.

349) They are given into the hands of that appointee, the emissary, who has been appointed over the impregnation of people, and whose name is "Night." When they come down to the world and are given into the hands of that appointee, they part from one another. Sometimes, one comes down before the other and descends and clothes in people.

350) When their time to mate arrives, the Creator, who knows the males and females of those spirits and souls, brings them together as they were in the beginning, before they came to the world, and declares about them, "The daughter of so and so with so and so." And when they unite, they become one body and one soul, and they are right and left, as it should be. The male is the right of the body and the soul, and the female is the left part in them.

For this reason, there is nothing new under the sun. Even though the Creator declares, "The daughter of so and so with so and so," it is still nothing new but a return to how they were prior to their arrival in the world. And since it is known only to the Creator, He declares them.

351) But we learn that a person is given a mate according to his deeds and ways. Indeed, if his deeds are upright, he is rewarded with uniting with his mate as they were united at the time when they departed from the Creator, before they were clothed in a body.

352) Where will one whose deeds are upright seek his mate? It is written, "One should always sell all that he has and marry the daughter of a wise disciple." This is so because the wise disciple has the deposit of his Master trusted in his hands, and he will certainly find his mate with him.

353) All those souls that come through reincarnation and have no mate can hurry their mate with mercy by hurrying and taking the mate of another person. The friends commented on that and said, "One does not wed a woman on a festival, but one does sanctify, lest another will come before him with mercy." They also made a precision about "another," that the one who incarnated without a mate, it is because he descended and became *Achoraim* [posterior], who is himself regarded as a *Nukva* [female]. This is why he has no

mate. Hence, this incarnated one is called "another," to indicate that he comes from *Achoraim*, and this is why the conduct about him is that he takes the mate of another.

This is why the *Zivugim* are difficult for the Creator, since because the mating male and female are two parts of one soul and they divided even before they came into the world, why is it said that man's *Zivug* before the Creator is difficult? After all, it is only a repetition of something that was done before. However, from what has been explained, that there are incarnated souls that have no mate, who rush and take the mate of another through mercy, then afterwards, if his friend is rewarded through his actions with his mate being given back to him, the Creator must take from one and give to the other. And this is hard for Him—to reject one before the other. And yet, "The ways of the Lord are right," for certain, and all that the Creator does is good and just.

354) Those who come by reincarnation and have no mate, where will they take their mate? The story of the sons of Benjamin proves that the incarnated souls must hurry with mercy and take their mate from another. This is why the writing says, "Lest another will precede him with mer355) Certainly, the *Zivugim* are hard for the Creator because He must take from one and give to the other. Happy are Israel, for the Torah teaches them the ways of the Creator and all the secrets that are hidden and concealed before Him.

356) "The law of the Lord is perfect" because it contains everything. Happy are those who engage in the Torah and do not part from it, for anyone who is separated from the Torah for even an hour, it is as though he has parted from life in the world. And it is written, "For it is your life and the length of your days," and it is written, "For length of days, and years of life, and peace, will they add to you."

CRAVING

Lech Lecha [Go Forth]

205) The female's craving for the male makes a soul. And also, the male's craving for the female and his adhesion with her produces a soul, which includes the soul from the craving of the female and takes it. Thus, the craving of the lower one, the female, is included in the craving of the upper one, the male, and the two souls become one, without separation.

206) And then the female contains everything, taking both souls and becoming impregnated by the male in them. The craving of the both of them becomes attached and they become as one. Hence, everything is mingled with each other and when the souls come out, male and female are mingled in them as one.

207) Afterwards, when they descend to the world, the male and female separate from one another; one turns this way and the other turns that way, and later, the Creator mates them. But the key for the *Zivug* is given to none other than the Creator, for only He knows how to mate them, to unite them properly so they become male and female of the same soul.

ONE—THE COMPLETE ZIVUG

VaYikra [The Lord Called]

101) How does the word, "one," indicate the complete *Zivug*? It is written, "Hear O Israel, the Lord our God, the Lord is One." "One" is the assembly of Israel united with the Creator, ZA. The *Zivug* of male and female is called "one," since a place where the *Nukva* is present is called "one," for a male without a female is called "a half body," and a half is not one. But when two half bodies unite, they become one body and they are called "one."

ENVY, LUST, LOVE

Noah

154) The awakening of the male to the female is when he envies for her. When there is a righteous in the world, Divinity does not depart from him and her desire is for him. At that time, the upper lust, from Zeir Anpin, is awakened toward her with love, as a male's lust toward the female when he envies for her, as it is written, "And I will set up My covenant with you." That is, the lust has awakened in Me because of you, as it is written, "And I will establish My covenant with Isaac," for it is because of Isaac, as with Noah.

Everything is extended to the world through the Nukva, whether corrections or corruptions, as it is written, "And His kingdom rules over all." When bestowal is corrected, it extends from a Zivug of Zeir Anpin and Nukva. When bestowal is corrupted, it extends from Zivug Zeir Anpin and Nukva of Tuma'a [impurity], which are called "another god," which clings to Nukva de Zeir Anpin and draws toward it the abundance of Kedusha [holiness], turning it into Tuma'a and corruptions. This is the envy that Zeir Anpin envies for the Nukva, so another god will not cling to her.

And when there is a righteous in the world, due to the great desire of the Nukva to bestow upon the righteous, she stays far from another god and the love of Zeir Anpin to mate with Divinity, to bestow upon the righteous, grows extensively, as the love of a man for his wife grows when he is envious for her and fears that she will hide with another. Similarly, Zeir Anpin was afraid that she would cling to bestow upon another god.

I WASHED MY LEGS

New Zohar, Beresheet [Genesis]

107) When the Creator confers with the Malchut and Israel are unfit to be a wick unto her, to shine, when they are unfit to raise

MAN for the *Zivug* of *Zeir Anpin* and *Malchut*, it is written, "I have taken off my gown, how can I wear it again? I have washed my feet, how can I dirty them again?"

"I have taken off my gown" are the monikers, which are *Netzah* and *Hod*, the garments. When they all join, they are regarded as the Creator's gown. When He confers with her, He is devoid of all those garments so as to bond with her. This is why the Creator said, "I have taken off my gown," to be corrected and ready to benefit you, and you are not properly corrected. Now, "How can I wear it again," how shall I put these garments back on, for they illuminate only in *Achoraim*, from afar, and by that I will depart from you once more?

108) "I have washed my feet, how can I dirty them again?" I have washed My feet from that filth. And what is it? When I was set up and made for you, I moved the other side, the impure one, from before My feet. Now, how shall I put that filth back on, covering the Temple, since you are not ready with your corrections to be corrected toward Me? We learn from this that when the spirit of impurity passes from the world, everything grows from above and below. For this reason, "I have washed my feet, how can I dirty them again," as before?

When wishing to repel the *Sitra Achra* and correct the *Malchut* into being worthy of a *Zivug* with *Zeir Anpin*, an obstacle must be placed before the *Sitra Achra*, as it is written, "I will put hooks in your cheeks." That is, first it is given a grip unto *Kedusha* [holiness], and by that it is later failed completely.

This is the meaning of what is written, "I have washed My feet from that filth," when I was being corrected and made ready for you, meaning when *Malchut* was corrected into being fit for a *Zivug*. "I moved the other side, the impure one, from before My feet," by first giving it a grip unto *Kedusha*, by which He later failed him and removed him completely. "Now, how shall I put that filth back on, covering the Temple," should she drift away from Him again, and I will have to correct it once again. Thus, I will have to give the *Sitra Achra* a grip on the Temple once again in order to fail it, since that prior gripping is considered the dirtying of the feet.

AS AN APPLE TREE
AMONG THE TREES OF THE WOOD

Aharei Mot [After the Death]

317) "As an apple tree among the trees of the forest, so is my beloved among the young men." How fond is the Creator of the Assembly of Israel, for she praises Him with this verse. And why does she praise Him with an apple and not with something else, or with something that has color or fragrance or flavor?

318) Because it writes an apple, it follows that she praises Him with everything: colors, fragrance, and flavor. This is so because as an apple is a cure for everything, the Creator is the cure for everything. As the apple is colorful, for there are white, red, and green in it, the Creator has the upper colors, *Hesed*, *Gevura*, *Tifferet*, which are white, red, and green. As an apple has a finer scent than all other trees, the Creator smells like the Lebanon. As an apple is tasty and sweet, the Creator is sweet to the palate.

GOOD AND EVIL

Tetzaveh [Command]

86) Moreover, words of Torah settle in only there, since there is no light except for that which comes out of that darkness. This is so because when that side surrenders, the Creator rises above and His glory grows. Also, the work of the Creator is only out of darkness, and there is no good except from within the bad. And when one enters a bad way and leaves it, the Creator rises in his glory. Hence, the perfection of everything is good and bad together, and to later depart to the good. And there is no good except for that which comes out of the bad. And in that good, the glory of the Creator increases, and this is complete work.

NOTHING IS SUPERFLUOUS

Aharei Mot [After the Death]

136) Ben Zoma was asked if it is permitted to castrate a dog. He replied, "Neither shall ye do thus in your land." That is, anything that is in your land, you will not do, not even a dog, since as the world needs this, the world also needs that. This means that there is nothing superfluous in the land. This is why we learned, "And behold, it was very good" is the angel of death, who must not be revoked from the world because the world needs him. And even though it is written about the angel of death, "And the dogs are greedy, they are not satisfied," it is not good that they will be revoked from the world. Everything is needed, both good and bad.

THE JOY OF STUDYING

Toldot [Generations]

57) The evil inclination is needed in the world like the rain is needed in the world. Without the evil inclination there would be no joy of studying in the world.

AND BEHOLD, IT WAS VERY GOOD

Emor [Speak]

328) "And God saw all that He had made, and behold, it was very good." "And God saw all that He had made" was said generally, to include even snakes, scorpions and mosquitoes, and even those that are seen as the harm-doers of the world. About all of them, it is written, "And behold, it was very good." They all serve the world, the leaders of the world, and people do not know.

329) While they were walking, they saw a serpent walking ahead of them. Rabbi Shimon said, "This one is going to make a miracle for us, for certain." That serpent ran before then and was tied to an adder [extremely venomous snake] in the middle of the road. They fought each other and died. When they came to them, they saw them lying on the road. Rabbi Shimon said, "Blessed be the merciful One who made a miracle for us, for anyone who looks at that adder when it is alive—or if it looks at a person—is certain to not be saved from it, especially if it is close to him." He called upon it, "No harm shall come to you and affliction shall not come near your tent. The Creator does His mission through everything, and we must not be contemptuous of anything that He has done. This is why it is written, 'The Lord is good to all, and His mercies are over all His works,' and 'All Your works shall give thanks to You, O Lord.'"

EVERYTHING IS REQUIRED IN THE WORLD

Yitro [Jethro]

29) Everything that the Creator does above and below is true, and His work is true. There is nothing in the world that one should reject or despise, since they are all true works, and everything is needed in the world.

30) It is written, "If the serpent bites before being charmed." The serpent does not bite people until it is whispered to from above. It is told, "Go and kill this or that person."

31) Sometimes—as it does that—so it saves people from other things. Through it, the Creator works miracles to people; it all depends on the Creator; it is all the work of His hands. But the world needs them. If it did not need them, the Creator would not make them. Hence one need not be contemptuous toward things in the world, and certainly not toward the words and deeds of the Creator.

32) "And God saw all that He had done, and behold, it was very good." "And God saw" is the living God, *Bina*. "Saw" means that He looked, to illuminate for them and to watch over them. "All that He had done" means it is all included as one, above and below. "And behold, it was very good" is the right side. "Very" is the left side, "Good" is the angel of life. "Very" is the angel of death, and it is all one matter for those who observe the wisdom.

DAYS OF THE MESSIAH

CHILDREN OF ISHMAEL

VaEra [And I Appeared]

201) Four hundred years, the appointee of the sons of Ishmael stood and asked before the Creator. He told him, "Do those who were circumcised have a part in Your name?" The Creator told him, "Yes." He told him, "But Ishmael was circumcised, why has he no share in you like Isaac?" He replied, "One was circumcised properly and with his corrections, and the other was not. Moreover, they adhere to Me properly for eight days, and the others are as far as several days away from Me." The appointed minister told him, "And yet, since he was circumcised, will he not have a good reward for it?"

202) Woe unto that time when Ishmael was born in the world and was circumcised. What did the Creator do with regards to the complaint of Ishmael's minister? He removed the sons of Ishmael from adhesion with the upper one and gave them a part in the holy land below, because of the circumcision in them.

203) And the children of Ishmael are destined to rule over the holy land for a long time, when it is empty of everything, as their circumcision is empty without perfection. And they will detain the children of Israel from returning to their places until the merit of the sons of Ishmael is complemented.

204) And the children of Ishmael are destined to evoke great wars in the world. And the children of Edom will gather against them and will wage war on them—one at sea, one on land, and one near Jerusalem. And they will rule over each other but the holy land will not be given to the children of Edom.

205) At that time, a nation will awaken against evil Rome from the end of the world and will wage war against it for three months. Nations will gather there and will fall into their hands until all the children of Edom gather to it from all corners of the world.

Then the Creator will awaken upon them, as it is written, "For the Lord has a sacrifice in Bozrah." And what does it say afterwards? "That it might take hold of the ends of the earth," and obliterate the children of Ishmael from the land and break all the forces above, and no force will remain above over the nations of the world, which is Israel, except the force of Israel, as it is written, "The Lord is your shade upon your right hand."

206) Because the Holy Name is in the right, and the Torah is in the right, everything depends on the right, and we must raise the right above the left, as it is written, "At His right hand was a fiery law." And in the future, "Save with Your right hand and answer me," "For then will I turn to the peoples a pure language, that they may all call upon the name of the Lord, to serve Him with one consent," and it is written, "In that day shall the Lord be One, and His name One."

THE COMING OF THE MESSIAH

Shemot [Exodus]

96) Rabbi Shimon raised his hands and wept. He said, "Woe unto he who will be at that time, and happy is he who will be and can be present at that time." "Woe unto he who will be at that time" because when the Creator comes to visit the deer, meaning Divinity, He will look to see who are the ones that are standing with her, He will observe all the deeds of each and every one of those who are with her, and no righteous shall be found. It is written about that, "And I looked, and there was none to help." At that time, many troubles will come over Israel.

97) "Happy is he who will be and will be present at that time." This is because one who is in faith at that time will be rewarded with that light of the King's joy. It is written about that time, "And [I] will refine them as silver is refined, and will try them as gold is tried."

98) After these troubles awaken upon Israel, all the nations and their kings will seek counsel together against them. They will awaken several evil sentences, unite against them, and trouble after trouble will come, and the last makes the first forgotten. Then the pillar of fire that stands from above downwards will be seen for forty days and all the nations in the world will see it.

99) At that time, the Messiah King will awaken to come out of the Garden of Eden, from the place called "the bird's nest," and will appear in the land of the Galilee. And on the day when the Messiah goes out there, the whole world will be angered and all the people in the world will hide in caves and in crevices in stones and they will not know how to be saved. It is written about that time, "And men shall go into the caves of the rocks, and into the holes of the earth, from before the terror of the Lord, and from the glory of His majesty, when He arises to shake mightily the earth."

100) "Before the terror of the Lord" is the angering of the whole world. "And from the glory of His majesty" is the Messiah. "When He arises to shake mightily the earth" is when the Messiah rises and will appear in the land of the Galilee, since this is the first place that was ruined in the Holy Land by Assyria. For this reason, he will appear there before all other places, and from there he will evoke wars upon the entire world.

101) After forty days, when the pillar rises from earth to heaven in the eyes of the whole world and the Messiah has appeared, a star will rise up on the east, blazing in all colors, and seven other stars will surround that star. And they will wage war on it from

all sides, three times a day for seventy days, and all the people in the world will see.

102) And that star will make war with them with torches of blazing fire, sparkling in every direction, and it will strike them until it swallows them every single night. And at daytime, it lets them out again. They will make the war before the whole world repeatedly for seventy days. After seventy days, that star will be hidden and the Messiah will be hidden for twelve months, the pillar of fire will return as before, the Messiah will be hidden in it, and that pillar will not be seen.

103) After twelve months, the Messiah will be raised inside that pillar into the firmament, where he will receive strength and the crown of kingship. And when he descends to the earth, that pillar of fire will be seen again as before, in the eyes of the whole world. Afterwards, the Messiah will appear and many nations will gather unto him, and he will make wars throughout the world. At that time, the Creator will awaken all the peoples of the world with His might, the Messiah King will be known throughout the world, and all the kings in the world will awaken and unite to wage war against him.

104) Several rulers in Israel will revert and return to the gentiles and will come with them to wage war against the Messiah King. Then, the whole world will darken for fifteen days and many from the people of Israel will die in that darkness. This is why it is written, "For, behold, darkness shall cover the earth."

THE MESSIAH KING—THE NUKVA

VaYechi [Jacob Lived]

589) The Messiah King will be called "poor" because he has nothing of his own, for he is the *Nukva de ZA*, and she is called "the Messiah King." However, this is the holy moon above, *Nukva*

de ZA, who has no light of her own, except what she receives from the sun, ZA. This is why she is considered poor.

590) The Messiah King, the *Nukva*, will reign in His dominion, will unite in His place above. And then, as it is written, "Your king shall come to you," precisely "King," since he contains the *Nukva* above and the Messiah King below.

If below, he is poor, the moon, the upper *Nukva*, since it is discerned as the moon, which is the upper *Nukva*, since the Messiah King below extends from the *Nukva* and is therefore called, "poor," like her. And if above, which is the *Nukva* herself, she is poor, since she is a mirror that does not shine by itself, but from ZA. For this reason, she is called, "bread of affliction." Yet, the Messiah is riding on a donkey and a foal, the stronghold of the idol worshipping nations, to subdue them under him. And the Creator, the *Nukva*, will strengthen in His place above, for the words, "Your king shall come to you" contain them both.

SIGNS OF THE MESSIAH

VaYera [The Lord Appeared]

476) "Then will I remember My covenant with Jacob." Why is Jacob spelled with a *Vav* [in Hebrew] when they are absent from the exile, in the *Vav*, in the sixth millennium, it implies that Jacob, the children of Israel, will be redeemed in the *Vav*.

477) The commandment concerning the *Vav* is six and a half minutes. And at the sixtieth year to the bar of the door, in the sixth millennium—the *Vav*, *Tifferet*, is the middle bar that bolts inside the boards from one end to the other, hence its name, "the door-bolt,"—the God of heaven will raise a count for the daughter of Jacob. And it will take six and a half years from that time until she has remembering. This is the length of time of the count. And from that time, it will take six other years, which is

the length of time of remembering, and they are seventy-two and a half years.

This is so because each illumination appears in *Katnut* and in *Gadlut*. It begins in *Katnut*—VAK, which shines only from below upwards—female light, and this is the time of the count. Subsequently, the *Gadlut* appears, light of GAR, which shines from above downwards. This revelation is called, "remembering," "male light."

Your indication is that the female's face turns upwards, and the male's face turns downwards. This is why the birth of Isaac begins with the words, "Then the Lord took note of Sarah," which is female light, called "counting," when she was still unfit for delivery, until the remembering was extended to her. This is why it is written a second time, "And the Lord did for Sarah as He had promised," which is the remembering. This is so because it mentions action here, and action is considered male, since there is no action in female light because a woman is the ground of the world.

Also, in the future redemption, when the *Vav* raises the *Hey* in the complete and great light, as it is written, "And the light of the moon shall be as the light of the sun," the count of this great light will appear first, and then the remembering. The count, which extends in the form of *Vav*, will shine for only six minutes, HGT NHY, which shine in her by mingling with the male while with respect to herself she has only half a time, meaning half the *Malchut*, called, "time," that is, only from the *Chazeh* up in her, and not from the *Chazeh* down. This is so because she is still in the form of counting, which is female light, which does not shine from above downwards; hence, half a moment is missing in her, meaning from the *Chazeh* down.

And for this reason, the years of the count will be six and a half years, from sixty years to sixty-five and a half. Then the light of remembering, the male light, will appear from the *Vav*, and then the Messiah King will appear, which is male and *Vav*, and his illumination will last six other years.

478) In sixty-six years will the Messiah King be revealed in the land of the Galilee, and it is the Messiah Son of Joseph. Hence, the place of his revelation is the Galilee, the lot of Joseph. And when a star on the east will swallow seven stars on the north, and a blaze of black fire will be hanging in the firmament for sixty days, wars will awaken in the world on the north side, and two kings will fall in these wars. And all the peoples will come together over the daughter of Jacob, to repel her from the world. It is written about that time, "it is a time of trouble unto Jacob, but he will be saved from it." At that time, all the souls will perish from the body and will need to return and be renewed. And your sign is, "All the souls belonging to Jacob that came into Egypt," all sixty six souls.

This is so because prior to the complete redemption, there were redemptions from Egypt and from Babylon by the force of the lights and *Kelim de Ima* [vessels of *Ima*]. But *Malchut* herself had had no redemption yet, in and of herself. This is the rainbow, in which only three colors shine—white, red, and green—while her black color does not shine, since *Malchut* has nothing of her own. Instead, she needs to receive from ZA, her husband, who gives her from the lights and *Kelim de Ima*. But complete redemption means that *Malchut* herself will be built with her own *Kelim* and lights, and will no longer need to receive the lights and *Kelim de Ima* from ZA, as it is written, "And the light of the moon will be as the light of the sun."

As in *Malchut's* previous redemptions, *Malchut* is built in three lines, and then she herself is built—the vessel of reception of the three lines. Similarly, in the future redemption, the light of redemption must correct the *Malchut* one at a time in three lines, and then her own self, which receives from three lines. Subsequently, she will have all the perfection suitable for the complete *Zivug*, which are the five discernments of correction.

This leads to an order of times:

- First correction—from sixty years to sixty-six and a half, only the right line in her will be corrected in the light of counting.
- Second correction—from sixty-six to seventy-three years, the left line in her will be corrected in the light of remembering. Hence, at that time, the Messiah Son of Joseph will appear in the land of the Galilee. All the signs at that time come from the *Dinim* [judgments], which apply during the illumination of the left.
- Third correction—from seventy-three years to 100 years, corrects the middle line in her, by which the Messiah Son of David will appear.
- Fourth correction—her self, to receive all that there is in the three lines, from 100 years to the end of the sixth millennium, in a *Zivug* of the *Vav* in the *Hey*. And all the old souls that came out since the days of the creation of the world through the end of the sixth millennium will then receive complete renewal.
- The fifth correction—the seventh millennium, when *Malchut* is completed in its entirety, and it will be one day for the Creator, for one *Zivug* for begetting new souls, which have never existed since the day of the creation of the world through the seventh millennium.

He said that on the 66th, the Messiah King will appear in the land of the Galilee, and it is the Messiah, Son of Joseph, who appears in his domain, and his time is seven years through seventy-three years. This is so because he comes to correct with the light of remembering, the half of *Malchut* that is still missing in the light of counting, whose time is six and a half years, since it is light of *VAK*. And now that the light of remembering—which is *GAR*—has arrived, the Messiah, Son of Joseph, appeared first, to correct the whole of the left line—seven years. This indicates that the *Malchut* has been completely corrected, even from the *Chazeh* down, since in the previous redemptions, her left line was corrected only by the force of her ascension to *Ima*, which received the left line of *Ima*. But now, her own left line will be corrected in her place below, and she no longer needs the left line of *Ima*.

It was said, "And one star from the east will swallow seven stars from the north." This is so because of the four winds—*HB TM*—*Bina* is on the north and *Tifferet* is on the east. Remembering is the light of the *Vav*, *Tifferet*, the star on the east, which will correct the *Malchut* in the left line herself. Thus, by that it revokes the left side of *Ima*, the north side, which was in the structure of *Malchut* thus far. It is perceived as swallowing the seven stars of *Bina* within it, and the seven stars are the seven *Sefirot*, *HGT NHYM*, that are included in the left line.

It was said, "And a blaze of black fire will be hanging in the firmament for sixty days." *Dinim* that come to the world by the illumination of the left are called, "a blaze of fire." Thus far, the blaze was a red-color fire, from *Bina* and not from *Malchut*. This is because the four colors—white, red, green, and black—are *HB TM*, where red is *Bina*. But now that the *Malchut* has obtained lights and *Kelim* from her own self, and the left line extends to her in her own *Kelim*, which is the color black, the blaze of fire that comes by the illumination of the left is of the color black. This is why he says that a black fire will be hanging in the firmament. And the number sixty days is sixty heroes, for it is called, "illumination of the left," where even though it is the light of *GAR*, it is still only *GAR* in *VAK*, where each tip consists of ten, and they are sixty. Also, days are *Sefirot*.

It was said, "And wars will awaken in the world on the north side, and two kings will fall in these wars." By the force of the *Dinim* in the illumination of the left, wars will be extended to the world. And because the east will then swallow the north, the *Dinim* will stretch from the east to the north, as well. "And two kings will fall in these wars," one from the nations of the world and one from Israel, which is the Messiah Son of Joseph.

It is written, "And all the peoples will come together, over the daughter of Jacob, to repel her from the world." This is because after the fall of the Messiah Son of Joseph, the nations will greatly intensify and will want to repel Israel from the world, as it is written, "It is a time of trouble unto Jacob, but he will be saved from it." This means that those *Dinim* and troubles will not come as punishments, but so as to afterwards become *Kelim* for the complete salvation. This is the meaning of, "He will be saved from it."

It is written, "At that time, all the souls will perish from the body," where by the *Dinim* and the troubles that they will suffer at that time, the power of the souls that were once in a body will be emptied, and not only the souls from that generation, but the souls from all the generations that were once in a body since the day of the creation of the world. All of them will weaken and their force will run out, until, "And will need to return and be renewed," meaning that they will need to (and must) be renewed.

480) In seventy-three years, seven years after the disclosure of the Messiah Son of Joseph, all the kings of the world will gather in the big city, Rome, and the Creator will awaken upon them fire and hail and crystal stones, and they will perish from the world. And only those kings that did not come to Rome will remain in the world and will later return to wage other wars. At that time,

the Messiah King will awaken throughout the world, and several nations and several armies will gather to him from the world over, and all the children of Israel will gather in their places.

Interpretation: Here is where the middle line is established, which is about the subjugation of the left so as to be included in the right line, as well as the right in the left. Then the degree is completed on all sides. This is the meaning of, "In seventy-three years... all the kings of the world," all those whose strength is from the left will gather in the big city, Rome, which is the head of all the forces of the left. "And the Creator will awaken upon them... and they will perish from the world." This is so because through the illumination of the middle line, all the *Dinim* [judgments] will be cancelled and the forces of the left will perish from the world. "And only those kings that did not come to Rome," those who extend from the *Klipot* of the right, who did not come to Rome, which is left, "Will later return to wage other wars," since during the fourth correction, there will be a time for the forces of the right to fight Israel, as is written below.

"At that time, the Messiah King will awaken,"—the Messiah Son of David—who extends from the middle line, and hence his time to appear has come, along with his correction. "And all the children of Israel will gather in their places," to go to Jerusalem, for then begins the ingathering of the exiles and they will gather in their places to go to Jerusalem. But they will not go before the arrival of the fourth correction, which is the correction of the *Malchut* that will receive the illumination of the three lines within her. And then all of Israel will gather and come to Jerusalem.

481) Until the years were completed and came to 100 years in the sixth millennium. Then the *Vav* will bond with the *Hey*, bestowing the corrections of the three lines upon the *Hey*,

Malchut, meaning the fourth correction. "Then they shall bring all your brothers from all the nations as an offering to the Lord," and then will be the ingathering of the exiles. And the children of Ishmael—the head of all the forces of the *Klipot* from the right (as is Rome with the forces of the left)—will awaken at that time along with all the peoples of the world who did not come to Rome, to come to Jerusalem for war, as it is written, "For I will gather all nations against Jerusalem to battle." And it is also written, "The kings of the earth stand up," and also, "He who sits in the heavens will laugh."

482) After all the forces of the *Sitra Achra* on the right and on the left are gone, the small *Vav* will awaken, *Yesod de ZA*, to unite with the *Hey* and to renew the old souls, meaning all those who were in a body since the time of the creation of the world until then, so as to renew the world, *Malchut*, as it is written, "Let the Lord rejoice in His works." It is also written, "May the glory of the Lord endure forever," so the *Hey* will properly bond with the *Vav*, as it should be. "Let the Lord rejoice in His works," to bring down His deeds, which are the renewed souls to the world, so they will all be new creations and all the worlds will unite as one.

483) Happy are all those who will remain in the world at the end of the sixth millennium, to enter the Sabbath, which is the seventh millennium. This is because then it is one day, for the Lord alone, to properly mate with the *Hey* and to assemble new souls to bestow upon the world, meaning souls that have never been to the world. They will be in the world along with the old souls that remained from the beginning and were renewed, as it is written, "And it shall come to pass that he that is left in Zion, and he that remains in Jerusalem shall be called 'holy,' even every one that is written unto life in Jerusalem."

THE SECRETS OF THE TORAH ARE REVEALED IN THE DAYS OF THE MESSIAH

VaYikra [The Lord Called]

387) After Moses died, it is written, "And this people will rise up, and go astray." Woe unto the world when Rabbi Shimon departs it, when the fountains of wisdom are blocked in the world and a man seeks a word of wisdom, but none shall be found to speak. And the whole world will be erring in the Torah and there will be no one to evoke in the wisdom.

It is written about that time, "And if the whole congregation of Israel shall err," meaning if they err in the Torah and do not know her ways and what they are because "and the matter is hidden from the eyes of the assembly," meaning that there is none who knows how to reveal the depth of the Torah and her ways, woe unto those generations that will be in the world at that time.

388) At the time of the Messiah, the Creator will reveal profound secrets in the Torah, "For the earth shall be full of the knowledge of the Lord, as the waters cover the sea." It is written, "And they shall teach no more every man his neighbor, and every man his brother, saying, 'Know the Lord'; for they shall all know Me, from the least of them unto the greatest of them."

THE APPEARANCE OF THE WISDOM TO ALL THE NATIONS

VaYera [The Lord Appeared]

460) When it is near the days of the Messiah, even infants in the world will find the secrets of the wisdom and know the ends and calculations of redemption in it. And at that time, it will be revealed to all. This is the meaning of the verse, "For then will I turn to the peoples." What is "Then"? It is the time when the Assembly of Israel rises from the dust. When the Creator raises her, "Then will I turn to the peoples a pure language, that they may all call upon the name of the Lord, to serve Him shoulder to shoulder."

EXODUS FROM EGYPT

AS A LILY AMONG THORNS

Ki Tissa [When You Take]

31) "As a lily among thorns, so is my love among the daughters." The Creator wished to make Israel similar to what is above, so there would be one lily in the earth that is like the lily above, *Malchut*. And the fragrant lily, better than all the lilies in the world is only one who has grown among the thorns. This one smells as it should. Hence, He sowed seventy pairs, which are seventy souls, and brought them among the thorns, the Egyptians. And as soon as these thorns came, those pairs out there grew branches and leaves and dominated the world. Then the lily blossomed among them.

32) Since the Creator wished to take out the lily from among them, the thorns dried out and were thrown away and were corrupted until they were regarded as nothing. When He went to collect the lily, to bring out his firstborn son, the King went within several armies, ministers, and rulers with waved banners. He took out his firstborn son with several mighty ones and brought him to His palace to sit in the King's house, as it should be.

OPEN FOR ME, MY SISTER, MY WIFE

Emor [Speak]

128) "I am asleep but my heart is awake; A sound, my beloved is knocking." The assembly of Israel said, "I sleep in the exile in Egypt." This is because the exile was due to the domination of the left over the right, and the *Mochin* of *Malchut*, which are sleep, move away from the *Dinim* of the left. My sons were in

harsh enslavement, and my heart is awake so as to keep them so they will not perish in the exile. "A sound, my beloved is knocking" is the Creator, who said, "And I have remembered My covenant."

129) Open for me an opening like the tip of a needle, and I will open the high gates for you. Open for me, my sister, because the door for my entrance is in you. My sons can enter only in you. If you do not open your door, then I am locked; I will not be found. Hence, "Open for me." Certainly, open for me. This is why when David wished to come into the King, he said, "Open to me the gates of righteousness ... This is the gate of the Lord." The gates of righteousness is *Malchut*; it is the way to enter the King. "This is the gate of the Lord," to find Him and to adhere to Him. Hence, "Open to me, my sister, my love," to mate with you and forever be at peace with you.

For itself, ZA is in *Hassadim* covered from *Hochma*. And *Malchut* in and of herself is in *Hochma* without *Hassadim*. She is called "night" because *Hochma* does not shine without *Hassadim*. Hence, there is complete abundance for the redemption of Israel only through *Zivug* of ZA and *Malchut*. This is because then the *Hassadim* of ZA are mingled with the *Hochma* of *Malchut*, and Israel receive the complete abundance from GAR.

UNLEAVENED BREAD AND MATZA

Tetzaveh [Command]

74) It is like a king who had an only son, who was sickened. One day, he wished to eat. They said, "Let the king's son eat this medicine, and before he eats it, let no other food be in the house." And so they did. When he ate that medicine he said,

"Henceforth, let him eat whatever he chooses; it will not be able to harm him."

75) Similarly, when Israel came out of Egypt, they did not know the meaning and the foundation of the faith. The Creator said, "Let Israel taste the cure, and as long as they eat that medicine let no other food be seen by them," meaning leaven. When they ate the *Matza*, which is the medicine to come and to know the meaning of faith, which is *Malchut*, the Creator said, "Henceforth, they are fit for leaven. Let them eat it for it can no longer harm them." And on the day of *Shavuot*, the high bread of ZA was found, meaning complete healing.

76) This is why leaven is offered, meaning the evil inclination, to be burnt at the altar through the sacrifices that are offered at the altar, and the two other breads are offered by waving them together. Two other breads means besides the sacrifices. The leaven, the evil inclination, is burned in the fire of the altar through the sacrifices and cannot rule and harm Israel. This is why the holy Israel adhere to the Creator on this day with the healing of the Torah.

THE CROSSING OF THE RED SEA AND THE DOE THAT MUST GIVE BIRTH

BeShalach [When Pharaoh Sent]

178) When Israel camped by the sea they saw several multitudes, several soldiers, and several camps above and below, and they all gathered over Israel. In their plight, Israel began to pray.

179) At that time, Israel saw adversity on all sides. The sea with its mounting waves was before them, behind them were all the appointees, all the camps of Egypt, and above them were several slanderers. They began to cry out to the Creator.

182) There is a doe [female deer] in the land and the Creator does a lot for her. When she cries out, the Creator hears her

plight and accepts her voice. And when the world needs mercy for water, she makes a sound and the Creator hears her voice, and then the Creator has mercy over the world, as it is written, "As the deer craves for the water brooks."

183) And when she needs to deliver, she is blocked from all sides. She places her head between her knees and cries out in a loud voice. Then the Creator has pity on her and sends her a serpent who bites her pudendum and opens her, tearing that place in her, and delivers her immediately. In this, do not ask or try the Creator.

THE COMMANDMENT OF TELLING THE STORY OF THE EXODUS

Bo [Come unto Pharaoh]

179) The commandment that follows is to speak in the praise of the exodus from Egypt, which is mandatory for man for all time. Every man who tells the story of the exodus from Egypt and delights in that story will rejoice with Divinity (which is joy from all sides) in the next world. This is a man who is delighted with his master, and the Creator is delighted with that story of his.

180) When the Creator brings his company together and tells them, "Go and listen to the story of My praise, which my children tell, and rejoice in My redemption," they all come and gather and bond with Israel, and listen to the story of the praise, that they are happy with the delight of redemption from their master, and come and thank the Creator for these miracles and mighty deeds, and thank Him for the holy nation that He has in the land. And they are happy with the joy of redemption of their Lord.

181) Then more power and might is added to him above. And with that story, Israel give strength to their Master, like a king who is given further power and might when his strength is praised and he is thanked, and all fear him and his honor rises above all. For this reason, this story and praise must be

told. Similarly, man must always speak before the Creator and publicize the miracle with all those miracles that He had done.

182) But why is it a must to speak of the miracles? After all, the Creator knows everything—what came before and what will come after. So why the publication before Him of what He had done and knew? Indeed, man must make the miracle known and speak before Him of all that He had done because these words rise and the whole of the household of above gathers and sees them and thanks the Creator, and His honor rises in their eyes above and below.

THE DESTINED REDEMPTION

Ki Tazria [When a Woman Delivers]

186) "As in the days when you came out from the land of Egypt, I will show you miracles." The Creator is destined to show redemption to His sons, such as in the days when the Creator sent to deliver Israel from Egypt. And He showed these plagues on the Egyptians and struck them for Israel.

What is the difference between the redemption at the end of days and the redemption from Egypt? The redemption from Egypt was in one king and in one kingdom, while here it is in all the kings in the world. At that time, the Creator will be honored throughout the world and everyone will know the reign of the Creator, and everyone will be struck by blows from above, twice for one, since they will all refuse to let Israel go.

187) Then will the reign of the Creator appear, as it is written, "And the Lord shall be King over all the earth." And then the nations will volunteer to bring Israel to the Creator, as it is written, "And they shall bring all your brothers." Then the patriarchs will be revived in joy to see the redemption of their sons as in the beginning, as it is written, "As in the days when you came out from the land of Egypt, I will show you miracles."

THE EVIL INCLINATION AND
THE GOOD INCLINATION

AT FIRST, THE EVIL INCLINATION IS LIKE A GUEST

VaEtchanan [And I Pleaded]

150) What is the evil inclination similar to? When it comes to bond with a person, it is as iron before it is placed in fire. After it is heated, it is brought back entirely like fire.

151) When the evil inclination comes to bind with a person, it is like a person who sees the opening and sees that there is no one to stop him. He enters the house and becomes a guest there, and he sees that there is no one to stop him from leaving there to go on his way. Since he entered the house and there was no one to stop him, he became appointed over the house and became the landlord of the house, until he finds that the whole of the house is in his possession.

HOW THE EVIL INCLINATION SEDUCES A PERSON

VaYera [The Lord Appeared]

339) It is written that the leech has two daughters, Hav, Hav [give, give]. Those are the two daughters of the evil inclination, who evoke the evil inclination to rule over the body. One is a soul that always grows in the body, and one is a soul that craves evil lusts and all the ill desires in this world. This is the senior one, and the first one is the younger one.

340) The evil inclination bonds only to those two souls, to seduce people so they believe in him and he will lead them to a place where they throw arrows of death at them that pierce them, as it is written, "Until an arrow pierces through his liver."

297

341) It is similar to robbers who rob in the mountains and hide themselves in a terrible place in the mountains, and know that people avoid going to those places. What did they do? They fled from them. He who is wittier than all, who knows how to seduce people, who departed them and sat on the right path, where all the people in the world go—once he comes to the people of the world he begins to connect with them there until he lures them into his net. He brings them to a terrible place where there are robbers who kill them. Such is the way of the evil inclination: it lures the people in the world until they believe it and then brings them to a place of death-arrows.

COPING WITH THE EVIL INCLINATION

Miketz [At the End]

195) One should always anger the good inclination over the evil inclination and exert after it. If it parts with him, good. If not, let him engage in Torah, since nothing breaks the evil inclination except the Torah. If it leaves, good. If not, let him remind it of the day of death, to break it.

196) We should observe here. After all, this is the evil inclination, the angel of death. Will the angel of death break before the day of death? He kills people, which means that his joy is to put people to death which is why he always fools them, to lure them toward death.

197) Indeed, one should remind him of the day of death to break the heart of man, for the evil inclination is present only in a place where there is joy of wine and pride. And when man's spirit is broken, it parts with him and is not over him. This is why one should remind it of the day of death, so his body will break and it will depart.

198) The good inclination needs the joy of Torah, and the evil inclination needs the joy of wine, adultery, and pride. This is why man needs to always anger it from that great day, judgment

day, the day of account, when all that protects a person are the good deeds that he does in this world so they will protect him at that time.

TWO ANGELS

Ve'Eleh Toldot Itzhak [These Are the Generations of Isaac]

170) "When a man's ways please the Lord, He makes even his enemies be at peace with him." There are two angels for a person, emissaries from above to unite with him, one to the right and one to the left. And they testify to a person, and they are present in everything he does. Their names are "the good inclination" and "the evil inclination."

171) When a man comes to be purified and to exert in the Mitzvot of the Torah, that good inclination that has become connected to him has already prevailed over the evil inclination and reconciled with it, and the evil inclination has become a servant to the good inclination. And when a person comes to be defiled, that evil inclination intensifies and overcomes the good inclination.

When that person comes to be purified, he needs to overcome several intensifications. And when the good inclination prevails, his enemies, too, make peace with him, since the evil inclination, which is his enemy, surrenders before the good inclination. When a person goes by the Mitzvot of the Torah, his enemies make peace with him, meaning the evil inclination and all who come from his side make peace with him.

WITH ALL YOUR HEART

Teruma [Donation]

668) The love of the Creator, when a person loves Him, he awakens only from the heart, since the heart is the place of the awakening, to evoke love toward Him...

669) "With all your heart [with a double *Bet* in "heart" in Hebrew]," that is, with two hearts, which are two inclinations, the good inclination and the evil inclination. Each is called "a heart"—one is called "a good heart" and the other is called "a bad heart." This is why it was said "With all your heart," and does not say "With all your heart [with a single *Bet*]," for it implies two, which are the good inclination and the evil inclination.

671) The evil inclination, how can one love the Creator with it? After all, the evil inclination slanders so one will not approach the work of the Creator, so how can one love the Creator with it? However, the work of the Creator is more important when this evil inclination surrenders to Him and the person breaks it. This is the love of the Creator, for one knows how to bring the evil inclination into the work of the Creator.

672) This is the secret for those who know the *Din* [judgment]: Anything that the Creator does above and below is only to show His glory, and everything is to serve Him. And anyone who has seen a slave slandering his master becomes a slanderer so as to not do his master's will in anything that is his master's will. The Creator's will is for people to always serve Him and to walk by the path of truth, to reward them with great good. And since this is the Creator's will, how can a bad servant come and slander his master's will, deflecting people toward the bad path and deviating them from the good path, making them not do their master's will and deflecting people to the bad path?

673) Indeed, he certainly does his master's will. It is like a king who had an only son, whom he loved dearly. For his love, he commanded him to stay away from an evil woman because anyone who comes near her is unworthy of entering the king's palace. That son promised to do his father's will with love.

675) And at the king's house, on the outside, there was a harlot—beautiful to look at and beautiful in form. One day, the king said,

"I wish to see my son's desire toward me." He summoned that harlot and told her, "Go seduce my son, to see his desire toward me." The harlot followed the king's son and began to embrace him and kiss him and seduce him with all sorts of seductions. If that son is decent and keeps his father's commandment, he rebukes her, does not listen to her, and repels her from him. Then his father is happy with his son and brings him into his palace, giving gifts and presents and great honor. And who caused all that good to that son? It is that harlot.

675) Does that harlot get any praise for all that or not? Of course she is praised in every way: 1) For having done as the king commanded; 2) for having caused all that good to that son, all that love of the king toward him. This is why it is written, "And behold, it was very good." "It was good" is the angel of life. "Very" is the angel of death, who is the evil inclination, who is certainly very good for one who keeps his master's commandment. Were it not for that slanderer, the righteous would not have inherited those high treasures that they are destined to inherit in the next world.

A TALL MOUNTAIN OR A HAIR'S BREADTH

VaYeshev [And Jacob Sat]

240) In the future, the righteous will see the evil inclination as a tall mountain. They will wonder and say, "How could we have conquered such a tall mountain?" Also in the future, the wicked will see the evil inclination as thin as a hair's breadth. And they will wonder and say, "How could we not conquer this hair's breadth thread?" These cry and those cry, and the Creator will uproot them from the world and He will slaughter them before their eyes, and it will no longer govern the world. Then the righteous will see and rejoice, as it is written, "Only the righteous will give thanks to Your name."

RIDING THE DONKEY

Pinhas

485) The *Yod* of *Shadai* is the letter of the covenant, a ring from a chain on the demon's neck, meaning the evil inclination. This is so because *Shadai* has the letters of *Shad* and *Yod* [*Shed* means demon in Hebrew]. who will not harm a person. David said about him, "Deliver my soul from the sword, my only one from the dog," since the evil inclination is a serpent, a dog, a lion. David said about it, "He lurks in a hiding place as a lion in his lair," and the prophet called it "a bear," as it is written, "He is to me like a bear lying in wait, a lion in secret places." It is compared to beasts, compared to all the prey animals, and it is compared to every person, to the extent of his iniquities, for according to the iniquity is one named "Lion" or "Bear," etc..

486) The evil inclination is a God, a serpent, and a braying donkey on which the soul is placed. As soon as it is known that that rider upon it is wicked, it is written about it, "And his rider falls backward," for one who falls off it shall fall. This is why Job said, "I am not inferior to you [in Hebrew, *Noffel* means both "inferior" and "fallen."]," and the righteous who rides it ties it with a knot of the strap of the *Tefillin*, the token of the *Tefillin*, the *Yod* of *Shadai*, the ring on its neck. The *Shin* of the *Tefillin* is the chain on its neck.

487) Elijah rose with it to the heaven, as it is written, "And Elijah went up by a whirlwind to heaven." In it, "The Lord answered Job out of the whirlwind," and this is why they said about it, "Who is a hero? He who conquers his inclination." Some become a donkey to it, not afflicting its rider, and they are the ones who exert in all the more so. This is why it was said regarding Abraham, "And saddled his donkey," and this is why it was said about the Messiah, "A poor one, riding a donkey.".

This is so because the evil inclination receives its strength to harm and to deflect people from the left line. Through his times, the wicked increases the power of the left over the right, by which he falls into the authority of the evil inclination, which is called by many names, according to the substance of man's sin. And one is called by the kind of iniquity that makes a person sin. The *Yod* of *Shadai*, the token of the covenant, is the middle line, in which there is the *Masach de Hirik* that diminishes the GAR of the left, which are the whole power of the evil inclination. And a righteous who guards the covenant ties it so it cannot make one sin. This is similar to one who drops a ring off a chain on one's neck and governs it. Also, the *Shin* [ש] of *Tefillin* indicates three lines.

The evil inclination is given to every person to conquer it and to ride it. If one conquers it, all the perfection comes through the evil inclination, as it is written, "With all your heart," meaning with both your inclinations, the good inclination and the evil inclination. It follows that if one is rewarded and rides over the evil inclination, he is rewarded. The whirlwind is the evil inclination, which he conquered and rode and was rewarded with rising up to heaven.

It is also written, "And the Lord answered Job out of the whirlwind," since he was rewarded with conquering the whirlwind. It is also written, "Who is a hero? He who conquers his inclination," for if he conquers it, he is rewarded with the entire perfection. To one who is rewarded with conquering it partially, the evil inclination becomes a donkey on which to ride, and the evil inclination never afflicts him again, for he keeps the light *Mitzvot* [commandments] as well as the serious ones, and then the evil inclination becomes a donkey to them, for *Homer* [matter/substance] has the letters of *Hamor* [donkey]. It is as written about Abraham, "And he saddled his donkey," a poor man riding a donkey, for they have been rewarded with conquering the evil inclination until it became a donkey for them to ride, to bring them to the perfection.

FEAR

FEAR—THE FIRST COMMANDMENT

Introduction of The Book of Zohar

189) "In the beginning God created." This is the first *Mitzva* (commandment). This *Mitzva* is called "fear of the Creator," called *Resheet* (beginning), as it is written, "Fear of the Lord is the beginning of wisdom." Fear of the Creator is the beginning of knowledge because this fear is called "beginning." And this is the gate that leads to faith. And the whole world exists on this *Mitzva*...

190) Fear is interpreted by three discernments, two of which have no proper root, and one is the root of fear. There is a man who fears the Creator so that his children may live and not die, or fears bodily punishment or punishment through money, hence he always fears Him. It follows that the fear he fears the Creator is not placed as the root because his own benefit is the root, and the fear is a result of it.

And there is a person who fears the Creator because he is afraid of a punishment in that world, and the punishment of Hell. These two fears—the fear of punishment in this world and in the next world—are not the essence of the fear and its root.

191) The real fear is when one fears one's Master because He is great and ruling, the essence and the root of all the worlds, and all else is nothing compared to Him.

THE LORD IS MY LIGHT AND MY SALVATION; WHOM SHALL I FEAR?

BaMidbar [In the Desert]

39) "The Lord is my light and my salvation; whom shall I fear?" Since Adam gazed in the upper light and the Creator shone upon him, he fears neither upper ones nor lower ones, as it is written, "But upon thee the Lord will arise, and His glory shall be seen upon thee." "The Lord is the stronghold of my life." When the Creator holds a person, he does not fear all the litigants in the world.

NO TORAH, NO JERUSALEM

VaYetze [Jacob Went Out]

85) Rabbi Hiya and Rabbi Hizkiyah were sitting under the trees of the field of his strength. Rabbi Hiya dozed, and saw Elijah. Rabbi Hiya said to Elijah, "From my lord's proof of the way, the field—which is the *Nukva*—shines." Elijah said, "I have come to you now, to alert you that Jerusalem is nearing destruction, and all the cities of the sages along with it," since Jerusalem, the *Nukva*, is *Din* [judgment]. It stands on *Din* and is ruined over the *Din* in it. And Sam'el has already been given permission over her and over the heroes of the world.

As long as the Torah awakens from below, when people engage in it, the tree of life will not depart Jerusalem above. The Torah below has stopped, since people have stopped engaging in it, in the tree of life, ZA, the tree of life from the world, the *Nukva*, which is called, "world," as well as "Jerusalem." And we must not say that this refers to the Jerusalem below, for the sages were many years after the ruin of Jerusalem.

86) Hence, as long as the sages rejoice in the practice of Torah, Sam'el cannot prevail over them, for it is written, "The voice is the voice of Jacob, but the hands are the hands of Esau." This is the upper Torah, ZA, called, "the voice of Jacob," and while the voice does not stop, the speech rules and triumphs. Hence, the Torah must not be stopped.

87) One who leans to the left destroys the *Nukva*, since it is written, "Unless the Lord guards the city, the watchman keeps

awake in vain." Those who engage in Torah, who cling to the middle line, called "Torah," the holy city, *Nukva*, stands over them. At that time, *HaVaYaH*, which is the middle pillar, guards the city, and not the strong people of the world, meaning those who cling to the left. This is why it is written, "Unless the Lord," the middle line, "guards the city, the watchman keeps awake in vain," for it will finally be ruined.

BE JOYFUL WITH JERUSALEM

Bamidbar [In the Desert]

21) "Be joyful with Jerusalem and rejoice for her, all you who love her." How favored is the Torah by the Creator because wherever words of Torah are heard, the Creator and all His armies listen to His words. And the Creator comes to dwell with him, as it is written, "In every place where I cause My name to be mentioned." Moreover, those who hate Him fall before him.

23) "Be joyful with Jerusalem," since there is joy only when Israel are in the holy land, where a woman connects with her husband, ZA and *Malchut*. Then it is the joy of everyone, a joy above and below. And when Israel are not in the holy land, one is forbidden to rejoice and to display joy, as it is written, "Be joyful with Jerusalem and rejoice for her." Rejoice for her, when Israel are in h26) "For you shall go out with joy." This is the assembly of Israel. As long as she is in exile and lies in the dust, she is not called "joy," until the Creator comes to her and raises her from the dust, and says, "Shake thyself from the dust; arise," shine and they will bond together. Then she is called "joy," the joy of everyone. And then, "For you shall go out with joy." Then several armies will go out to welcome the mistress for the joy of the King's meal.

WALLS AND GATES

Bo [Come unto Pharaoh]

126) The Creator made Jerusalem below, Malchut, such as Jerusalem above, Bina. And He had made the walls of the holy city and its gates. One who comes does not enter until the gates are opened to him, and one who climbs does not rise until the steps to the walls are fixed.

Who can open the gates of the holy city, and who fixes the high steps? It is Rabbi Shimon Bar-Yochai. He opens the gates to the secrets of the wisdom, and he fixes the high degrees. It is written, "All your males shall appear before the face of the Lord God." Who is, "the face of the Lord God"? It is Rashbi.

ZION

Aharei Mot [After the Death]

175) When the Creator wished to create the lower world, He made it entirely as above. He made Jerusalem the middle of the whole of the earth, and a place on top of it, called Zion, Yesod, and from this place, she is blessed. From this place, Zion, the world began to be built and from it, it was built, as it is written, "God, the Lord, has spoken, and summoned the earth from the rising of the sun to its setting." God appeared from Zion, from the inclusive beauty. God appeared from Zion, who is the perfection of the beauty of the world. Jerusalem, Malchut, was blessed only out of Zion, who is Yesod, and Zion was blessed from above, who is Zeir Anpin. All is tied to one another, Zeir Anpin and Malchut to one another, united by Zion.

JERUSALEM OF ABOVE AND OF BELOW

Chayei Sarah [The Life of Sarah]

113) The whole of the land of Israel is folded under Jerusalem, which is the *Malchut*. And she is above and below. Thus, there is Jerusalem above, which is *Bina*, and there is Jerusalem below, which is *Malchut*, for she is gripped above and she is gripped below. Jerusalem above is gripped by two sides—above and below. And Jerusalem below is gripped by two sides—above and below. This is why she is twofold.

Jerusalem above is *Bina* and Jerusalem below is *Malchut*. It is known that the association of the quality of *Rachamim* in *Din* means that they were mingled in one another. And four discernments emerged out of this mingling—*Bina*, *Malchut* in *Bina*, *Bina*, and *Malchut* in *Malchut*. It turns out that the quality of *Malchut* is twofold, since there is *Malchut* in *Bina* and there is *Malchut* in *Malchut*.

ISRAEL AND THE NATIONS

THE CREATOR OFFERED THE TORAH TO EVERYONE

Balak

140) "The Lord came from Sinai" is as it is written, "Behold, I will come to you in a thick cloud." "[He] came from Sinai" and appeared to them, "And dawned on them from Seir," from what the children of Seir said, that they did not wish to receive. From that, it shone for Israel and added much light and love to them. Similarly, "He shone forth from Mount Paran," from what the children of Paran said, that they did not wish to receive. From that, Israel were given a great addition of love and illumination.

141) By whom was He revealed to them? This is a sublime secret and will be revealed through your question. The Torah came out from a sublime secret, from the head of the hidden king, *Bina*. When He reached the left arm, Isaac, *Gevura*, the Creator saw bad blood in that arm, which was proliferating from there, who is Esau, Sam'el. And the *Sitra Achra* said, "I should sort out and scrutinize this arm, and if I do not shed that bad blood, it will blemish everything. Indeed, every flaw must be cleared out from here."

142) He called to Sam'el, Esau's minister, and told him, "Would you like to have my law?" He replied, "What is written in it?" He said, "You shall not kill." The Creator skipped to show him the right place, He skipped to the place that He knew he would not be able to tolerate. Sam'el said, "God forbid, this law is Yours, and Yours it shall stay. I have no wish for this law." He pleaded with Him once more and said, "Lord of the world, if you give the law to me, all of my governance will be gone, for my whole governance is by killing. If I accept the law, there

will be no wars, while my governance is on planet Mars, which indicates bloodshed. Thus, everything would be cancelled from the world."

143) "Lord of the world, do take Your law and I will have no part of it. But if it pleases You, the people that are the sons of Jacob are worthy of the law." He thought he was slandering them. This is the meaning of "And dawned on them from Seir," meaning that the light came out for Israel from the very Seir [scapegoat], meaning from Sam'el, Seir's minister.

Sam'el said to himself, "If Jacob's children accept the law, they will probably vanish from the world and will never be able to govern." The Creator replied to him several times, "For you are the firstborn and for you should the law be given." He told Him, "But the birthright is his, for it was sold to him and I confessed." The Creator told him, "Since you wish to have no part in the law, move away from it entirely." He said, "Very well."

144) The Creator told him, "Since this is so, advise Me—how should I make Jacob's children accept it, as you say?" Sam'el replied to Him, "Lord of the world, they must be bribed. Take some light from the light of the hosts of heaven and pour it over them. By that they will accept it. And here, I will give of my light first." He took the light that was covering him off himself and gave it to the Creator to give it to Israel, as it is written, "And dawned on them from Seir," actually out of Seir, who is Sam'el, of whom it is written, "The goat shall bear on itself." "On them" means on Israel.

145) Since he uprooted this Sam'el and removed the bad blood from the left arm, Isaac, *Gevura*, He returned to the right arm, Abraham, *Hesed*. In it, too, He saw bad blood—Ishmael. He said, "This arm, too, must be cleaned from bad blood." The Creator summoned Rahav, Ishmael's minister, and told him, "Would you like to have My law?" Rahav replied, "What is written in

it?" He skipped over everything and told him, "You shall not commit adultery." He said, Oh dear, should the Creator inherit me with this inheritance, it is a bad inheritance that will remove all my governance from me, which is based on adultery, for I have taken the blessings of the water, the blessing of the fish of the sea, as it is written, "Be fruitful and multiply." And it is written, "I ... will make him fruitful and will multiply him," and it is written, "And he will be a wild donkey of a man."

146) He began to plead before his Master. He told him, "Lord of the world, two sons came out of Abraham. Here, the children of Isaac, give it to them, it is right for them." The Creator told him, "I cannot, for you are the elder, and the law should be given to you." He began to implore Him and said, "Lord of the world, Let my birthright be his, and that light that I have inherited for the birthright, take it and give it to them." So did the Creator, and this is the meaning of the verse, "He shone forth from Mount Paran..."

148) When the Creator took those gifts to Israel from those ministers that rule over Esau and Ishmael, He came and called upon all the holy tens of thousands of appointees over the rest of the nations, and they, too, replied to him as did Sam'el and Rahav. He took from all of them and received gifts to give to Israel.

WE SHALL DO AND WE SHALL HEAR

Lech Lecha [Go Forth]

315) "Bless the Lord, you His angels... hearing unto the voice of His word." Happier are Israel than all the other nations of the world, for the Creator has chosen them from among all nations, and has made them His share and His lot. Hence, He has given them the holy Torah, since they were all in one desire at Mount Sinai and preceded doing to hearing, as they said, "We shall do and we shall hear."

316) And since they preceded doing to hearing, the Creator called upon the angels and told them: "Thus far, you were the only ones before Me in the world. Henceforth, My children on the earth are your friends in every way. You have no permission to sanctify My name until Israel bond with you in the earth, and all of you together will join to sanctify My name, since they preceded doing to hearing, as the high angels do in the firmament," as it is written, "Bless the Lord, you His angels ... They do His word," first. And then it is written, "Hearing the voice of His word."

317) "Bless the Lord, you His angels" are the righteous in the land. They are as important before the Creator as the high angels in the firmament, since they are mighty and powerful, for they overcome their inclination like a hero who triumphs over his enemies. "Hearing the voice of His word" means being rewarded hearing a voice from above every day and at any time they need.

318) Who can stand with them, these high, holy ones? Happy are they for they can stand before them. Happy are those who can be saved from them. The Creator's guidance is over them each day. How can we stand before them? This is why it is written, "Choose, and bring near, so he may dwell in Your courts," as well as, "Happy is the man whose strength is in You."

MY BELOVED IS FOR ME AND I AM FOR HIM

Noah

108) When the moon is filled with blessings above properly, Israel alone come and suckle from her. This is why it is written, "On the eighth day you shall have an assembly." An assembly is a collection, since no other nations suckle from everything that was collected from the upper blessings but Israel alone. This is why it is written, "You shall have an assembly," you and not other nations, you and not other appointees.

109) For this reason, Israel appease the Creator with water that they pour on the altar, to give to the appointees of the nations a part of the blessings, so they engage in it and do not mingle with Israel's joy when Israel suckle the upper blessings. It is written about that day, "My beloved is for me and I am for him," that no other mingles with us.

110) There is an allegory about a king who invited his loved one to a meal that he was having on a certain day, so that the king's loved one would know that the king favored him. The king said, "Now I wish to be happy alone with my loved one and I fear that while I am at the meal with my loved one, all those officers and appointees will come and sit with us at the table, to dine in the meal of joy along with my loved one."

What did the lover do? He made stews of vegetables and ox meat and offered it for those officers and appointees to eat, and then the king sat with his loved one for a more sublime meal than all the delicacies in the world. And while he was alone with the king, he asked of him for all his needs, and he gave them to him, and the king rejoiced with his loved one alone, and no stranger interfered between them. So are Israel with the Creator, and this is why it is written, "On the eighth day you shall have an assembly."

THE SLANDERERS LOVE ISRAEL AGAIN

Emor [Speak]

273) All those offerings, the seventy oxen, are to give nourishments to the appointees of the rest of the nations, since because the Creator loves His children, He wishes for all the ministers to love them, as it is written, "When a man's ways are pleasing to the Lord, He makes even his enemies make peace with him." This means that even all the upper slanderers become lovers of Israel once again. And when the forces above become lovers of Israel again, it is all the more so with all of them below.

ISRAEL'S ACTIONS DETERMINE EVERYTHING

VaYechi [Jacob Lived]

412) Had Israel gathered good deeds before the Creator, the idol worshipping nations would never have risen against them. But Israel cause the rest of the nations to raise their heads in the world, for if Israel had not sinned before the Creator, the rest of the idol worshipping nations would have surrendered before them.

413) If Israel had not extended bad deeds to the other side in the land of Israel, the rest of the idol worshipping nations would not have ruled in the land of Israel and they would not be exiled from the land. It is written about that, "For we are very poor" because we have no good deeds as we should.

IN EXILE, ISRAEL ARE NOURISHED ON THE REMAINS OF THE NATIONS

Teruma [Donation]

485) And you shall eat and be satisfied, and you shall bless the Lord your God. How happy are Israel because the Creator favored them and brought them near Him from among all other nations. For Israel, He gives His food and satiation to the whole world. Were it not for Israel, the Creator would not have given nourishment to the world. And now that Israel are in exile, it is all the more so: the world receives sevenfold nourishment and satiation so that an extract of that will suffice for Israel.

486) When Israel were in the holy land, nourishments would come down to them from a high place, and they gave an extract to the idol-worshipping nations, and all the nations were feeding on the extract. Now that Israel are in exile, the matter has been turned around in a different way: the food comes to the nations of the world and Israel receive an extract of that.

487) There is an allegory about a king who made a meal for his household. As long as they do his will, they eat at the meal with the king and give the part of the bones for the dogs to chew on. When his household do not do the king's will, he gives the entire meal to the dogs and the bones to his household.

488) As long as Israel do their Master's will, they eat at the King's table and the entire meal is prepared for them. In their joy, they give the bones, which is the extract, to the idol-worshipping nations. And as long as Israel do not do their Master's will, they are exiled and the meal is given to the dogs, while they are given the extract, as it is written, "Thus will the sons of Israel eat their bread unclean among the nations," for they eat the extract of their disgust, their loathsome food. Woe unto a king's son who sits and waits for the servant's table, that what is left of his table is food.

WHEN ISRAEL FALL, THEY ARE THE WORST

VaYechi [Jacob Lived]

196) What is the difference between Israel and the idol worshipping nations? In Israel, when a person dies, he defiles each body and the house is defiled. And the body of an idol worshipper does not defile another, nor is his body impure when he dies.

197) When one of Israel dies, all the sanctities of his master are removed from him, the holy Tzelem [semblance] is removed from him, the holy spirit is removed from him, and his body remains impure.

198) However, an idol worshipper, a foreigner, one who performs idolatry, who is impure in every way during his life, his Tzelem is impure and his Ruach [spirit] is impure, since these impurities are within him. It is forbidden to draw near him. Once he dies, all these impurities come out of him and the body remains without impurity so as to defile.

199) And although their *Guf* [body] is impure both in their lives and in their death, in their lives, all the impurities within them have the power to defile others. In their death, when all the impurities come out of them, they cannot defile. And the *Guf* of Israel can defile others after its death, since all the sanctities have departed it and the other side is on it.

ISRAEL'S PRESENCE IN OTHER NATIONS STRENGTHENS IT

Shemot [Exodus]

75) "And a new king arose over Egypt." All the nations in the world and all the kings in the world were strengthened in their government only because of Israel. Egypt did not rule the whole world until Israel came and entered there in the exile. Then they overcame all the peoples in the world. Babel was stronger than all the peoples in the world only because of Israel, when they were in exile among them. Edom were stronger than all the people in the world only because of Israel, when they were in exile among them. Those peoples were in lowliness among the rest of the nations, and were lower than all of them but grew strong because of Israel.

76) Egypt were lower than all the peoples; they were actually called, "slaves" because they, the Egyptians, were the lowest of all peoples. Babylon were low, as it is written, "Behold, the land of the Chaldeans—this is the people that was not." Edom were lowly, as it is written, "Behold, I make you small among the nations, and greatly despised."

77) They all receive strength only because of Israel, since when Israel are in exile with them, they immediately become stronger than all other nations in the world, since Israel alone are equal to all the nations in the world.

When Israel went into the exile in Egypt, Egypt immediately rose and their government strengthened above all the nations, as it is written, "And a new king arose over Egypt." "Arose" means that they had rising, meaning that the angel appointed over the government of Egypt was strengthened and rose and was given strength and rule over all the appointees of all the other nations.

In the beginning, that appointee above was given governance, and subsequently his people below. And because of that the writing says, "And a new king arose over Egypt." This was their appointee, who was new because until this day he had no governance over all the other nations, and now he was raised to rule over all the peoples in the world. And then the words, "Under three things the earth quakes ... Under a slave when he becomes king" come true, since the Egyptians were slaves.

THE REASON FOR ISRAEL'S AFFLICTION

Pinhas

143) One day, a sage from the nations came to Rabbi Eliezer. He told him, "Old man, old man...

144) "You say that you are closer to the High King than all other nations. One who is close to the King is always happy, without sorrow, fear, or troubles. But you are always afflicted, in trouble, and in more grief than all the people in the world. We, however, no affliction, trouble, or grief come upon us at all. Thus, we are close to the High King and you are far from Him, and this is why you are having sorrow, troubles, mourning, and grief, which we do not..."

152) The question that that gentile asked him was this: We are certainly closer to the High King than all other nations. Indeed, this is so, since Israel were made by the Creator, the heart of the whole world. Hence, so are Israel among the nations, like a heart

among the organs. And as the organs of the body cannot exist even a minute without the heart, all the other nations cannot exist in the world without Israel. And so is Jerusalem among the rest of the countries, like a heart among the organs. Hence, it is in the middle of the whole world, like a heart, which is in the middle of the organs.

153) Also, Israel are lead within the rest of the nations as the heart is within the organs. The heart is soft and weak, and it is the sustenance of all the organs, and all the organs do not feel any sorrow, trouble, and grief, but only the heart, in which there are sustenance and intelligence. Sorrow and grief do not come near the rest of the organs whatsoever because there is no sustenance in them, and they do not know anything. All the other organs are not close to the King, who is wisdom and intelligence that are in the brain, except the heart, while the rest of the organs are far from it and do not know of it at all. So are Israel—close to the holy King, while the rest of the nations are far from Him.

HE WHO SPARES HIS ROD HATES HIS SON

Shemot [Exodus]

304) It is written, "He that spares his rod hates his son." It is also written, "I have loved you, says the Lord," and it is written, "But Esau I hated." "I hated" is as it is written, "He that spares his rod hates his son." I hated him, hence I spared him the rod.

THE ALLEGORY ABOUT
THE QUEEN AND THE MAIDSERVANTS

BeShalach [When Pharaoh Sent]

151) But is it respectable for the King, ZA, that the queen, Malchut, will go and make war and go on a mission? But like a king who mated with the upper queen, the king saw her merit,

that she is above all the other queens in the world. He said, "They are all considered maidservants compared to this queen of Mine; she is above all of them. What shall I do for her? My whole house shall be in her hands The King sent out an announcement: Henceforth, all the words of the King will be conveyed through the queen. And the King placed all His arms in her hands, all the warriors, all the King's gems, and all the King's treasures. He said, "Henceforth, anyone who wishes to speak with Me will not be able to speak with Me before he notifies the queen."

152) Thus, for the Creator's fondness and love for the assembly of Israel, *Malchut*, He placed everything in her possession. He said, "Everything else is considered by her as nothing." He said, "Sixty is *Malchut*, one is My dove, My undefiled. What shall I do for her? Indeed, My whole house will be in her hands." The king sent out an announcement: Henceforth, all the words of the king will be conveyed through the queen. He placed all his arms in her hands, as it is written, "Behold, it is the bed of Solomon, sixty mighty men around it, all are wielders of swords, trained in war."

FEAR NOT, YOU WORM OF JACOB

VaYishlach [Jacob Sent]

250) The Creator placed all the idol worshipping nations in the world under appointed ministers, and they all follow their gods. All shed blood and make war, steal, commit adultery, mingle among all who act to harm, and always increase their strength to harm.

251) Israel do not have the strength and might to defeat them, except with their mouths, with prayer, like a worm, whose only strength and might is in its mouth. But with the mouth, it breaks everything, and this is why Israel are called "a worm."

252) "Fear not, thou worm of Jacob." No other creature in the world is like that silk-weaving worm, from which all the garments of honor come, the attire of kings. And after weaving, she seeds and dies. Afterwards, from that very seed, she is revived as before and lives again. Such are Israel. Like that worm, even when they die, they come back and live in the world as before.

253) It is also said, "as clay in the hands of the potter, so you, the house of Israel, are in My hands." The material is that glass; even though it breaks, it is corrected and can be corrected as before. Such are Israel: even though they die, they relive.

254) Israel is the tree of life, ZA. And because the children of Israel clung to the tree of life, they will have life, and they will rise from the dust and live in the world, and they will become one nation, serving the Creator.

LIFE'S PURPOSE

CONTEMPLATING IN ONE'S HEART

New *Zohar, Beresheet* [Genesis]

741) "I went down to the garden of nuts to see the buds of the valley." See how much there is for man to contemplate and make precisions on each day, to search one's actions, and to scrutinize all of one's matters. One should take it to one's heart that the Creator created him and placed a high soul within them, above the rest of His creations, only to contemplate His work and to adhere to Him, and to not follow vanity.

HARDNESS OF THE HEART

BeHaalotcha [When You Mount]

140) How hard-hearted are people, for they do not watch over the words of that world at all. The evil in the heart, which clings to all organs of the body, does that to them. "There is an evil which I have seen under the sun, and it is heavy upon men." This evil is the force of the evil in the heart that wishes to dominate the worldly matters and does not watch over the matters of that world at all.

EYES TO SEE AND A HEART TO LOOK AFTER

Aharei Mot [After the Death]

30) Rabbi Shimon said, "I wonder about the people in the world: they have neither eyes to see nor hearts to observe, and they do not know and are not attentive regarding their Master's will. They sleep and are not awakening from their slumber before that day comes when darkness and gloom cover them and the lender demands His bill of them.

31) "And the herald calls to them everyday, their soul testifies to them each day and night, and the Torah calls out loud in all directions saying, 'Until when, you fools, will you be loving folly? Whoever is naive, let him turn in here. To him who lacks understanding she says, 'Come, eat of my bread and drink of the wine that I have mixed.' But no one lends an ear and there is no one who awakens his heart."

32) In the last generations that will come, the law will be forgotten from among them. Then wise at heart will gather in their places, and none will be found who will close and open the Torah. Woe unto that generation. Henceforth there will not be as this generation until the arrival of the generation of the Messiah, the knowledge awakens in the world, as it is written, "For they shall all know Me, from the least of them unto the greatest of them."

UPPER WISDOM [HOCHMA]

Toldot [Generations]

189) Everything that the Creator does in the land is with wisdom, and it is all in order to teach people the upper wisdom, so they will learn the secrets of the wisdom from those deeds. And everything is as it should be, and all His deeds are the ways of the Torah, since the ways of the Torah are the ways of the Creator, and there is no small thing that does not have several ways, routes, and secrets of the upper wisdom.

OPENING OF THE EYES

VaEtchanan [I Pleaded]

35) The Creator is destined to open the eyes, for there has never been wisdoms that would gaze upon the upper wisdom and attain what they did not attain in this world, so they would

know their Master. Happy are the righteous who are rewarded with that wisdom, for there is no wisdom like that wisdom, no knowing like that knowing, and no adhesion like that adhesion.

THE WISDOM THAT ONE SHOULD KNOW

New *Zohar*, Song of Songs

482) The wisdom that one should know: to know and to observe the secret of his Master, to know himself, to know who he is, how he was created, where he comes from and where he is going, how the body is corrected, and how he will be judged by the King of All.

483) To know and to observe the secret of the soul. What is the soul within him? Where does it come from and why does it come into this body, which is a foul drop that is here today and in the grave tomorrow? To know the world one is in, and for what the world will be corrected, to gaze upon the sublime secrets of the Upper World, and to know one's Master. And one observes all that from within the secrets of the Torah.

484) Anyone who walks into that world without knowing the secrets of the Torah will be sent out of all the gates of that world, even if he has acquired many good deeds.

485) The soul says to the Creator, "Tell me the secrets of the sublime wisdom, how You lead and govern the Upper World; teach me the secrets of the wisdom that I have not known and not learned thus far, so I will not be shamed among those High Degrees, among which I come."

486) The Creator replies to the soul, "If you know not, O fairest among women," if you have come and did not gaze in the wisdom before you came here, and you do not know the secrets of the Upper World, "go thy way," for you are not worthy of entering here without knowledge. "Go thy way by the footsteps

of the flock," reincarnate in the world and become knowing by these "footsteps of the flock." Those are human beings that people trample with their heels, for they consider them lowly; but they are the ones who know their Master's sublime secrets. From them will you know how to observe and to know, and from them will you learn.

487) Little children in the Temple, studying Torah by the shepherds' tents, more than in those synagogues and seminaries where they study the Higher Wisdom. And even though they do not know, for they are children, you will know and understand from the words of wisdom that they say.

JONAH, WHO WENT DOWN TO THE BOAT

VaYikahel [And Moses Assembled]

81) Jonah, who went down to the boat, is man's soul that comes down to this world to be in man's body. It is called Jonah [Heb: dove] because when it partakes in one's body, it is a dove in this world, meaning it is deceived from the body, which Me'aneh [deceives] it, as it is written, "You shall not deceive one another." Then, a person walks in this world as a ship about to break in the great sea, as it is written, "And the ship was about to break."

82) When a person in this world sins and thinks that he has escaped his Master because his Master is not watching over in this world, the Creator throws in a strong stormy wind, which is the sentence of the Din that always stands before the Creator, asking Him to sentence man. The stormy wind reaches the boat and reminds one's iniquities, to capture him.

83) When one is caught by the storm in the house where he is sick, it is written, "And Jonah went below into the hold of the ship, lain down and fallen asleep." Even when one is in one's house of sickness, the soul does not awaken to repent before its Master to redeem his iniquities.

It is written, "So the captain approached him." the captain is the good inclination that leads everything. "And he said, 'How is it that you are sleeping? Get up, call on your God,'" it is not the time to sleep for you are being sentenced for everything you did in this world. repent from your iniquities.

84) Observe these matters and return to your Master. "What is your occupation," which you were doing in this world? Confess it before your Master, observe where you have come from, from a foul drop, and do not be proud before Him. "What is your country," meaning see that you are a creature from the earth and shall return to the earth. See if you have ancestral merit to protect you.

IF A MAN HIDES HIMSELF IN HIDING PLACES

Noah

194) "'If a man hides himself in hiding places, do I not see him?' Says the Lord..."

195) It is similar to a king who built a palace, and underneath the palace built fortified hideouts. In time, the subjects rebelled against the king and the king surrounded them with his armies. What did they do? They hid themselves in the fortified tunnels. The king said, "I made those hideouts, and they want to use them to hide from me, as it is written, 'If a man hides himself in hiding places, do I not see him?' Says the Lord.' I am the one who made those fortified tunnels, and I made light and darkness. So how can you hide from Me?"

MAN AND BEAST

Shlach Lecha [Send Forth]

21) The fools, who do not know and do not observe with wisdom, say that this world is operating on chance and the Creator is not

watching over them. Rather, man's fate and the fate of the beast are the same.

22) When Solomon looked at those fools who were saying it, he called them "beasts," for they actually make beasts of themselves, by saying these words ... cursed be the spirit of those beasts, those fools, those faithless. Woe unto them and woe unto their souls; it would be better for them had they not been born.

REDEEM EVERY FIRST OFFSPRING OF A DONKEY TO REDEEM ONE'S SOUL

Korah

42) "Every thing that opens the womb, of all flesh which they offer unto the Lord, both of man and beast, shall be yours ... and the firstling of unclean beasts shall you redeem." This *Mitzva* [commandment] is to redeem the firstborn of a beast, to redeem himself for the next world. And if he does not redeem his *Nefesh*, *Ruach*, and *Neshama* in the Torah before he goes to that world, he will reincarnate into this world as before, as it is written, "He returns to the days of his youth," receiving *Nefesh*, and *Ruach*, and *Neshama*.

SOULS

THE SOUL OF ADAM HARISHON

VaEra [And I Appeared]

32) "And I appeared unto Abraham." "Happy is the man for whom the Lord does not count iniquity." How dense are people for not knowing and not observing why they are in the world. After all, when the Creator created the world, He made man in His image and established him with His corrections, to engage in Torah and to walk in His ways.

33) When *Adam ha Rishon* was created, he was established out of the dust of the Temple below, *Malchut*, which is called "dust," but *Malchut* that is mitigated in *Bina*, called "the dust of the Temple below." And the four directions of the world, *HG TM*, connected in that place, called "The Temple," in *Malchut* that was mitigated in *Bina*. And those four directions of the world conjoined in four sides, the foundations of the world—fire, wind, water, and dust—the internality of *HG TM*. The four directions of the world conjoined in the four foundations of the world and the Creator established out of them a single body in the upper correction, which is *Bina*, in which the *Malchut* was mitigated in *Bina*. It turns out that that body was made of two worlds from this bottom world, *Malchut*, and from the upper world, *Bina*. This is the meaning of the two points that were joined together.

PAST, PRESENT AND FUTURE—AT ONCE

Aharei Mot [After the Death]

94) "That which is has been already, and that which will be..." "That which is has been already..." Before the Creator created this world, He created worlds and destroyed them. This is the

breaking of the vessels. Finally, the Creator desired to create this world, and consulted with the Torah, the middle line. Then He was corrected in His corrections, decorated in His decorations, and created this world. And then, everything that exists in this world was before Him at the time of creation, and was established before Him.

95) All the leaders of the world in every generation stand before the Creator in their forms, before they come into the world. Even all the souls of people, before they come to the world, are engraved before Him in the heaven, in the very same form they have in this world. And all that they learn in this world, they know before they come into the world. And we learned that all this is in those who are true righteous.

96) And all those who are not righteous in this world are removed from the Creator even there, above, before they come to the world. They enter the hole of the great abyss and rush to descend to the world. And their soul is as obstinate in this world as it was before it came into the world.

Also, they throw that holy part that the Creator gave them from the side of holiness and wander and roam. They are defiled in that hole of the great abyss and take their share from there, and rush to descend to the world. If one is later rewarded and repents before his Master, he takes his very own piece, the part of holiness he had thrown above, as it is written, "That which is has been already, and that which will be has already been."

This is so because when the souls are created, while they are still above, before they come into this world under time, they are in eternity, above time, where past, present, and future apply at once, as is the nature of eternity. It follows that all the deeds that the souls will do one at a time when they come into this world already exist there all at once, as their actions in this world.

This is so because the whole of the Torah that they will learn in this world during the years of their lives already exists there. And all their bad deeds are already depicted in their souls. And as they will throw the holy part in this world, they will there, too. And if they are destined to first sin and then repent in this world, it is depicted above as all at once, as is the nature of eternity, for this, too, is already pictured there.

And there is a difference between a soul that is destined to be in a righteous and one that is destined to be in a wicked. The one that is destined for the righteous is already there in all its sanctity, and therefore has no desire to come into this world, to the filthy material body, unless by the decree of the Creator. But a soul that is destined to be in a wicked rushes to come and clothe the filthy body, for she craves filth.

THE SOUL COMPRISES
THE CREATOR AND DIVINITY

Teruma [Donation]

590) From the day one inherits the soul, which comprises the Creator and His Divinity, from that time he is called "a son." This is the meaning of what David said in Psalms, "I will tell of the law of the Lord: He said to Me, 'You are My Son, today I have begotten You.'" This applies to every person when one obtains the soul.

MY DOVE, MY UNDEFILED, IS BUT ONE

Chayei Sarah [The Life of Sarah]

141) "My dove, my undefiled, is but one; she is the only one," the Neshama [soul]. Why is it that here, in Song of Songs, we call the soul in feminine form, "My dove, my undefiled," and there, in the Torah, we call it in masculine form, Abraham?

142) In the Torah, the soul is called by masculine form, relating to the body. This is so because with respect to the body, the soul is as a woman toward a man. Also, toward a higher degree than itself, the soul is as a female before a male. And each inherits his merit according to the matter at hand. This is why in *Song of Songs*, when the king that peace is his speaks of the soul, which is a higher degree than her, it is considered a female and he refers to it as a female, "My dove, my undefiled." But the Torah speaks of the soul in and of itself; hence, it refers to it as masculine form, Abraham.

SOUL AND LOVE

VaYechi [Jacob Lived]

744) Thus, the souls are higher from two sides, from ZA and from *Nukva*, and they come from their internality. Therefore, why do they descend to this world and why do they depart it? It is like a king who had a son, whom he sent to some village to raise him until he is grown and to teach him the ways of the king's palace. When the king heard that his son had grown, he sent his mother out of his love for his son and she brought him to his palace, and he rejoiced with his son.

745) Thus the Creator begot a son with its mother, which is the uppermost, holy soul, the generations of ZON. He sent him to atone, that is, to this world, to grow in it and to be taught the conducts of the King's palace. Since the King knew that his son would grow in that village, and the time had arrived to bring him to his palace, out of his love, he sent his mother and she brought him to his palace. The soul does not depart this world until his mother comes for her and brings her to the King's palace, where she sits forever.

746) Yet, it is the nature of the world that the people of the village cry over the departure of the King's son from them. There

was a sage there, who told them, "Why are you crying? Is he not
a prince, who should not be living among you any longer, but in
his father's palace?" So was Moses, who was a sage. He saw that
the people of the village were crying and hence said, "You are
the children of the Lord your God: you shall not cut yourselves."

747) If all the righteous knew that, they would be happy when
their day came to depart from this world. Is it not the highest
honor that the mistress comes for them to lead them to the
King's palace so the King will rejoice in them all day? After all,
the Creator entertains only with the souls of the righteous.

748) The love of the assembly of Israel, the *Nukva*, to the Creator,
ZA, awakens when the souls of the righteous below awaken it,
since they come from the side of the King, ZA, from the male's
side. Thus, this awakening comes to the *Nukva* from the male,
and the love awakens.

It turns out that the male awakens the fondness and love
to the *Nukva* and then the *Nukva* becomes connected with love
to the male. This settles the question that it is not good for the
Nukva to chase after the male. Now it is clear that the souls of the
righteous, which are males, awaken this love for ZA.

749) Similarly, the craving of the *Nukva* to shoot lower waters
opposite upper waters is only in the souls of the righteous.
Happy are the righteous in this world and in the next world, for
the upper and lower stand over them. Hence, "A righteous is the
foundation of the world" can be related to the upper righteous,
Yesod de ZA, and can be related to the souls of the righteous;
both are true.

750) The meaning of all that is that the righteous is the *Yesod*
above, *Yesod de ZA*, and *Yesod* below, in the *Nukva*, and the
souls of the righteous. And the assembly of Israel, the *Nukva*, is
included in the righteous above and below. A righteous from the

side of *Yesod de ZA*, and a righteous from the side of the soul of the righteous below, inherit her, meaning the *Nukva*. This is the meaning of, "The righteous shall inherit the land," the *Nukva*. The righteous, *Yesod de ZA*, inherits the land, *Nukva*, imparts blessings upon her every day, and gives her pleasures and dainties extended from above, from *Bina*, which he draws to.

PEOPLE AND ANGELS

Aharei Mot [After the Death]

220) Since the day the world was created, the souls of the great righteous stand before the Creator and pause before Him. And the Creator gazes upon them until it is time to bring them down to earth to clothe a body. And they govern above and below, as it is written, "As the Lord... lives, before whom I stood." "...I stood," meaning before he came into this world. Afterwards, he returned to his place in heaven and went up to his chamber.

But other souls do not rise to their places until they die because they did not stand before the Creator at the same degree, such as Enoch [*Hanoch*] and Elijah [*Eliyahu*], who were rewarded with rising to their places while they were still alive. This is why Elijah became an emissary and a messenger above, as did Enoch. Also, they adhered to the King more than an angel.

221) All the Holy Spirits above, meaning angels, work as the Creator's emissaries, and they all come from one place. But the souls of the righteous come from two degrees that are included in one; hence, they rise higher than angels, and their degrees are more than those of angels. And all those who were hidden there descended and rose in their lives, like Enoch, in whom there was no death.

Two points are included in *Malchut*—a lock and a key. All the lights extend only through the key, and the point of the lock is concealed in it. And she is called, "The tree of knowledge of good and evil," since the people, who extend from *Malchut*, are good if they are rewarded and do not sin, when the point of the lock does not appear and he is awarded all the lights. And if one is not rewarded, he is evil, and the point of the lock appears on him. At that time, all the lights depart at once and thus, death comes upon man, for Satan, who is the angel of death, awakens the point of the lock upon man, which causes the departure of the light of life.

There is a virtue in angels that does not exist in people: angels do not die. People, however, are made of the point of the lock, as well, and therefore die. But there is a virtue in people that does not exist in angels, since the angels have no burden of correction, as the key needs no correction, since it comes from *Bina* and it comes only to correct the lock. Thus, they always stand at the same degree as when they were created, and there are no ascents and descents in them.

But people, who contain a lock, carry the entire burden of correction; hence, when they are rewarded, they rise and attain degrees that do not exist in the angels. And there are great souls in whom the lock is so deeply hidden that it will never be fit of revealing. But they do not die, since the lock in them is hidden and concealed in their root.

UPS AND DOWNS
ALONG THE WAY

AS LIGHT EXCELS OVER DARKNESS

Ki Tazria [When a Woman Inseminates]

105) "As light excels over darkness." The benefit of the light comes only out of the darkness. The correction of the white is black, for without the black, the white would be pointless. And because there is black, the white is elevated and respected. It is like sweet and bitter. A person cannot know the taste of sweetness before he has tasted bitterness. Thus, what makes it sweet is the bitter.

In things where there are opposites, the one reveals the other, such as in white and black, light and darkness, sick and healthy. If there were no sickness in the world, the term healthy would be unattainable, as it is written, "God has made the one opposite the other." And it is also written, "It is good that you grasp the one, and also not let go of the other."

SHIMON FROM THE MARKET

Beresheet [Genesis]

159) "And God said, 'Let us make man,'" "The secret of the Lord is for those who fear Him." In the verse, "And God said," there is a secret that is revealed only to those who fear Him. The oldest among the elder started and said, "Shimon, Shimon, who is it who said, 'Let us make man,' of whom it is written, 'And God said'? Who is this name Elokim [God]?"

In the meantime, that oldest among the elder fled and no one saw him. And as Rabbi Shimon heard, he called him Shimon, and not Rabbi Shimon. He said to his friends, "This must be the

Creator, of whom it was said, 'And *Atik Yomin* [Ancient of Days] sits.' Thus, now is the time to disclose that secret, for there is a secret here that was not permitted to disclose, and now it means that permission to disclose has been given."

It is known that the secrets that were revealed to the authors of *The Zohar* was by attainments of the lights of the high degrees, by inspiration. Also, there are *Panim* [anterior] and *Achoraim* [posterior] in them, which means concealment and disclosure. And by the measure of the *Panim* in the degree, so is the measure of its *Achoraim*. The instilling of the *Achoraim* is a call and invitation to instill the *Panim*. For this reason, they knew the measure of their destined disclosure according to the measure of the concealment of the *Achoraim* that they had attained.

This is the meaning of what is written, that Rabbi Shimon heard that he called him Shimon and not Rabbi Shimon, which means that the instilling of the *Achoraim*, the call, was so strong that all of his degrees were lost and he became an ordinary person, Shimon from the market. By that, he recognized it as a call and invitation to obtain a very high attainment of *Panim*. For this reason, he promptly said to his friends, "This must be the Creator, of whom it was said, 'And *Atik Yomin* [Ancient of Days] sits,'" since there is no higher degree than Him.

DAY TO DAY POURS FORTH SPEECH, AND NIGHT TO NIGHT REVEALS KNOWLEDGE

Introduction of the Book of the Zohar

140) "Day to day pours forth speech, and night to night reveals knowledge." This means a holy day, from among those upper days of the King, from the *Sefirot de ZA*, which are called "days," praising the friends who engaged in Torah on the night of *Shavuot*... And "Night to night" means that each degree that governs in the night, the *Sefirot* of *Malchut* praises the other, and

that knowledge is that each receives from his friend. And for all the wholeness, they have become friends and lovers...

This is so because prior to the end of correction, before we qualified our vessels of reception to receive only in order to give contentment to our Maker and not to our own benefit, *Malchut* is called "the tree of knowledge of good and evil." This is so because *Malchut* is the guidance of the world by people's actions. And since we are unfit to receive all the delight and pleasure that the Creator had contemplated in our favor in the thought of creation, we must receive the guidance of good and evil from the *Malchut*. This guidance qualifies us to ultimately correct our vessels of reception in order to bestow and to be rewarded with the delight and pleasure He had contemplated in our favor...

Often, the guidance of good and evil causes us ascents and descents, each according to what he is. You should know that for this reason, each ascent is regarded as a separate day because due to the great descent that he had, doubting the beginning, during the ascent he is as a newly born child. Thus, in each ascent, it is as though he begins to serve the Creator anew. This is why each ascent is considered a specific day, and similarly, each descent is considered a specific night.

It is written, "Day to day pours forth speech"...This is so because through the great *Zivug* at the end of correction they will be rewarded with repentance from love, for they will complete the correction of all the vessels of reception, so they will be only in order to bestow contentment upon the Creator. In that *Zivug*, all of the great delight and pleasure of the thought of creation will appear to us.

At that time, we will evidently see that all those punishments from the time of descents, which brought us into doubting the beginning, were the things that purified us and were the direct causes of all the happiness and goodness that have come to us at the time of the end of correction. This is so because were it not for those terrible punishments, we would never have come to this delight and pleasure. Then these sins will be inverted into actual merits...

This is so because all those nights are the descents, the suffering, and the punishments that arrested the *Dvekut* [adhesion] with the Creator until they became many days one after the other. Now, once the night and darkness have become merits and good deeds, as well, the night shines like the day and darkness like light, there are no more arrests, and all 6,000 years unite into a single great day.

Thus, all the *Zivugim* that came out one at a time and disclosed ascents and descents that were separate from one another have now assembled into a level of one, sublime, and transcendent level of *Zivug*, which shines from the end of the world through its end....Thus, they all became one day for the Lord.

When it is said, "And night to night"...This is because all those words and sufferings that are called "nights," for which the degrees became discrete, one at a time, now they, too, shine like the day, since they have all gathered and become a single receptacle for the great knowledge that fills the whole earth with knowledge of the Lord.

It follows that each night for itself would remain in the dark, had it not come into a gathering with all the nights. This is so because each night receives its share in the knowledge only out of the bonding with the rest of the nights... since only all of them together, assembled, became worthy of receiving that great knowledge. This is why it was said, "And for all the wholeness, they have become friends and lovers," for in the great wholeness that they received together, all the nights become loving friends to one another.

AND THERE WAS EVENING, AND THERE WAS MORNING, ONE DAY

Toldot [Generations]

119) "And God called the light Day" is Abraham, who is the light of day, the right line. His light grows stronger by the correction of the day, which is the light of Hassadim. This is why it is written, "Now Abraham was old, advanced in age" [the Hebrew text uses the word "days"], meaning with the shining lights of Hassadim. And he is old, as it is written, "That shines more and more unto the perfect day." This is why it is written about it, "And God called the light Day."

120) "And the darkness He called Night." This is Isaac, who is dark, darkening so as to receive the night within him. Hence, when he grew old, it is written, "And it came to pass that when Isaac was old, and his eyes were dim, so that he could not see," since he was completely darkened. Certainly, he should be completely darkened and properly cling unto his degree.

The day is ZA and the night is the Nukva. At their root, ZA is regarded as being entirely from the right line and the Nukva is regarded as being entirely from the left line. It is known that the left line is Hochma without Hassadim, which cannot shine without mingling with Hassadim. Hence, at that time, it is regarded as darkness.

Also, the left line is in dispute with the right line and does not wish to be mingled with Hassadim whatsoever until the arrival of the middle line, which is the level of Hassadim that emerges on the Masach de Hirik that diminishes the left line. And then it decides between them and the Hochma dresses in Hassadim. At that time, she shines in full and ZA is regarded as including the right line that is mingled with the left, and the Nukva as being the left line that is mingled with the right, and they unite in one another, as it is written, "And there was evening and there was morning, one day."

POOR AND RICH

ALMS FOR THE POOR

BeHukotai [In My Statutes]

20)...Woe unto people who do not know and do not consider the glory of their Master, for who makes the Holy Name every day? One who gives righteousness to the poor.

21) The poor is gripped in *Din* and all his feeding is in *Din*, in a place called "justices," which is *Malchut*, as it is written, "A prayer for the poor when he is weakened." This prayer is the *Tefillin* of the hand, *Malchut*. When she is not in a *Zivug* with ZA, she is poor and she is called "justice," and one who gives *Tzedaka* [alms, but also righteousness in Hebrew] to the poor makes the Holy Name above properly whole, connecting her with ZA, which gives her everything. Because *Tzedaka* is the tree of life, ZA, and *Tzedaka* gives and bestows upon justice, *Malchut*, when she gives to justice, ZA and *Malchut* connect with one another and the Holy Name is complete.

One who evokes that awakening below, who gives *Tzedaka*, it is certainly as though he performed the work of the Creator in completeness. As one does below, so it awakens above. This is why it is written, "Happy are they that keep justice, that do righteousness at all times." The one who does righteousness is the Creator, as though he made Him.

22) The poor's place is *Malchut* when she is not in *Zivug* with ZA. This is because the poor has nothing of his own, except what he is given. The moon, *Malchut*, has no light of her own but what the sun, ZA, gives her.

23) The poor is as good as dead because that place caused him, since he is in a place of death. *Malchut* is the tree of knowledge of

340

good and evil. If one is rewarded, it is good and life. And if he is not rewarded, it is evil and death. This is why he is called "dead." And one who pities him gives him alms and makes the tree of life, called "righteousness," be over the tree of knowledge, which is the tree of death, as it is written, "But righteousness delivers from death."

It turns out that as one does below, reviving the poor, who is called "dead," precisely so he affects above, placing the tree of life over the tree of death. Happy is he for he is rewarded with making the Holy Name above, uniting her with ZA. For this reason, righteousness exceeds everything.

GIVING DONATION, MAASER [TITHING] AND HALLAH

VaYikra [The Lord Called]

119) Hunger comes to the world for the three sins of not giving "donation," "tithing," and *Hallah* [twist bread]. All these sins are only in the rich because their hearts are proud. They are absent in the poor. But what is the sentence? The Creator kills the poor and leaves the rich, for only the poor die of hunger, not the rich. Thus, the rich shall continue to sin before Him because they are not hurt. When the Creator wishes to avenge the wicked and obliterate them from the world, He gives them peace in this world and fulfills everything for them.

120) All the people in the world are not as close to the high King as those *Kelim* that He uses, which are, "A broken and a remorseful heart," and "The contrite and lowly of spirit." Those are the King's vessels, and when there is drought and hunger in the world, and the *Din* over the poor intensifies, they cry and yell before the King and the Creator brings them closer than any man, as it is written, "For He has not despised nor abhorred the lowliness of the poor." Then the Creator remembers why hunger has come to the world. Woe unto the wicked, who have caused it.

121) When the King awakens to watch over the world because of the sound of the cry of the poor, the Merciful one will save us from them and from their affront. Then it is written, "I will surely hear their cry." It writes hear twice [in Hebrew], once to watch over with their voice, and once to avenge them who caused it to them, as it is written, "That I will hear; for I am gracious, and My anger will be kindled." Hence, when there is hunger in the world, woe unto the wicked wealthy for the sound of the cry of the poor before the Creator.

MIXED MULTITUDE

THE MIXED MULTITUDE DETAIN ISRAEL IN EXILE MORE THAN ALL THE NATIONS

Pinhas

377) The mixed multitude are like the leaven in the dough, for they are mingled in Israel like leaven in dough. The nations of the world are similar to chaff. The mixed multitude detain Israel in exile more than the idol-worshipping nations, as the sages said, "Who detains? The leaven in the dough detains." This is so because the mixed multitude cling to Israel like leaven in dough, but the nations of the world are only like the chaff, which the wind carries.

STRAYING FROM THE INTERNALITY OF THE TORAH

Nasso [Take]

101) Elijah said to the loyal shepherd, "It is time to rise up and bring the complete redemption; speak of me in oath," meaning adjure me to hurry the redemption. "It is for you that I wish to rise, since the Creator has given me permission to appear to you in your prison, in your grave, and to do good to you, for you are desecrated by the sins of the people," since he is like a prisoner among them, as it is written, "And he is desecrated by our transgressions."

102) The loyal shepherd replied, "I swear upon you in the name of the Lord that you will not delay the redemption with all your capability, for I am afflicted. It is written about me, And he looked this way and that way, and saw that there was no man, to help me out of this affliction, this burial. It is said about me, 'And they made his grave with the wicked.' But they do not know

me; in their eyes I am considered among the mixed multitude and the wicked, like a dead dog that has reeked among them, for the wisdom of authors reeks among them in every city and in every place where Israel are scattered among them, among the kingdoms. And the mixed multitude have become the shepherds of Israel, who are the Creator's flock, of whom it was said, 'And you, My sheep, the sheep of My pasture, you are men.' And they are unable to do good with the disciples of the wise."

Moses, called "the loyal shepherd," is the Torah and the inner *Daat* [the *Sefira* but also knowledge], which will appear only in the complete redemption. Until then, it is said about him, "And he is desecrated by our transgressions," since the Torah, which is the loyal shepherd, has been desecrated and was emptied, for its internality has disappeared and we are left with only the externality. And I am regarded in their eyes as being among the wicked mixed multitude, like a dead dog that has reeked. They turn away from the internality of the Torah as one turns away from stench, of which it was said, "And the wisdom of the wise shall reek."

103) Men of valor and who fear sin wander from city to city and will not be pardoned, the mixed multitude ostracize them and in many places they are given only rations, so there will be no resurrection to their fall, not even temporary. And all the wise men, the brave, and them that fear sin are afflicted, poor, miserable, and are regarded as dogs. How are precious sons that are comparable to fine gold, valued as clay jars in public, and cannot find a place among them?

104) At the same time, the mixed multitude are wealthy, tranquil, joyous, sorrow-free, and without any grief at all. Thieves and bribers are judges and the heads of the people, for the earth is filled with violence because of them, and it is said about them, "Her adversaries have become her masters." The Loyal shepherd said to Elijah,

"I adjure you a second time, in the name of the Lord of hosts, the God of Israel, who dwells with the cherubim, that all these words will not fall out of your mouth, and you will say them before the Creator with all your might, to show their urgency."

BEAST AND MAN

Nasso [Take]

95)...Since the mixed multitude are the ignorant, which are darkness. And they are not called, "Israel," but slaves who are sold to Israel because they are as beasts.

96) And Israel are called, "men." But how do we know that there are beasts and men in Israel? It is written, "And you, My sheep, the sheep of My pasture, you are men." "And you, My sheep" are the ignorant who are good from the side of good. "You are men" are the disciples of the wise.

97) This text implies it, too, for it is written, "If My people heeded Me, Israel." Why does it say, "Israel," after it says, "My people"? It is that "My people" are the ignorant, and Israel are the disciples of the wise. And for them, it is said, "And the children of Israel were going out boldly."

98) As the Creator divided them at Mount Sinai, He will divide them in the last redemption. This is so because it is said about Israel, "And the children of Israel went up armed out of the land of Egypt." "Armed," from the side of the tree of life, ZA, which are fifty [spelled like "arms" in Hebrew] years of the *Yovel* [fifty years' anniversary], *Bina*, which ZA receives from *Bina*. It is said about them, "They shall come up to the mount." And among them was "the angel of God, who went before the camp of Israel." Also, it is they who were told, "And how I bore you on the wings of eagles," which are clouds of glory, "And brought you unto Myself," "And the children of Israel were going out boldly." Thus, He will bring

the disciples of the wise out with all this g99) As it was said about the ignorant from the side of the good, "And they stood at the foot of the mountain," so they will be in the last redemption—under the disciples of the wise, as a servant who walks by the feet of his master's horse. At the foot of the mountain they were told, "If you accept the law, good. If not, there will be your burial place." Similarly, they will be told in the last redemption, "If you take upon yourselves a disciple of the wise at the end of the exile, like a man who is riding a horse and his servant serves him, good. If not, there—in the exile—will be your burial."

FIVE KINDS OF MIXED MULTITUDE

Beresheet [Genesis]

224) There are five kinds of mixed multitude: Nephillim [fallen], Mighty, Anakim [giants], Rephaim [ghosts], and Amaleks. Because of them, the small Hey fell from her place, from Bina, since "God has made one corresponding the other." Thus, as there are five Behinot [discernments] KHB TM in holiness, they have their counterparts in the Klipot. And they are the five above-mentioned in the mixed multitude, whose acronym is Nega Ra [Hebrew: affliction or disease] or Oneg Ra [Hebrew: evil pleasure], since through the evil, pleasure is turned into affliction, and affliction becomes pleasure. And these are the five kinds of mixed multitude. They are mingled with Israel and cause them to sin. And for this reason, the small Hey falls from her place, from her mitigation place in the Bina.

Balaam and Balak were of the form of Amalek. This is because if you take the letters Ayin and Mem from the name, Balaam, and the letters Lamed and Kof from the name, Balak, the letters Bet, Bet, Lamed [which spell Babel in Hebrew] will remain, that is, Bet and Lamed from Balaam and Bet from Balak. It turns out that the two Klipot, Amalek and Babel, are implied in the names Balaam and Balak. By that, he tells us that Amalek is considered the *Keter* and *Rosh* [head] of the *Klipot*, like the *Klipa* of Babel, of which it was said, "Its head is made of fine gold," for had they not come from equal discernments, they would not have been able to cling to Balaam and Balak in a single bonding.

225) And they are the ones that remained of those of whom it was said concerning the flood, "And He blotted out every living thing." And those that remained from the *Klipa* of Amalek in the fourth exile, the exile in Edom, are heads in the world, with great force, since this *Klipa* is considered *Rosh* and *Keter* of the *Klipot*, and they become tools of destruction for Israel. It is said about them, in relation to the flood, "For the earth is filled with violence." These are the Amaleks. And this clarifies the first of the five kinds of mixed multitude, the Amaleks, which are the *Keter de* [of] *Klipot*.

226) It is said about the *Nephillim* [fallen] of the mixed multitude, "And the sons of God saw the daughters of men that they were beautiful." These are the second kind of mixed multitude, meaning the discernment of *Hochma de Klipot*. And they are from the *Nephillim* above, meaning those who extend from Uza and Aza'el, who were angels above, and the Creator dropped them from the heaven, hence their name, *Nephillim*. And the *Nephillim* of the mixture extend from them.

When the Creator wished to make man, He told the angels, "Let us make man in our image." The Creator wished to make him head of all the angels above, appointed over all the angels, and they would be subordinate to his governance, as it is said concerning Joseph, "Let him appoint overseers over the land."

227) For this reason, the angels wished to complain about him and said, "What is man, that You are mindful of him?" After all, he is destined to sin before You; hence, why do You degrade us to be under him? The Creator told them, "If you were below in

the earth, like man, you would sin more than him." Promptly, "And the sons of God saw the daughters of men that they were beautiful"; they lusted after them and the Creator dropped them down in chains.

228) And these sons of God are Uza and Aza'el, from which the souls of the second kind of mixed multitude extend. These are the *Nephillim*, since they had dropped themselves from holiness to lust after beautiful women. And this is also why the Creator dropped the mixed multitude from the next world, so they would have no share there, and gave them their reward in this world, as it is written, "And repays them that hate Him to their face." This explains the second kind of mixed multitude, called *Nephillim*, which are considered *Hochma de Klipot*.

229) The Mighty are the third kind of the mixed multitude that was mingled with Israel. It was said about them, "Those were the mighty men who were of old, men of renown," and they are drawn from the side of whom it was said, "Come, let us build us a city... and make us a name," meaning from the side of the generation of Babel.

This kind of mixed multitude build synagogues and seminaries and place within them a book of Torah with a crown on its head, corresponding to the verse, "A city, and a tower, with its top in heaven." They build synagogues and seminaries corresponding to, "A city," and place a book of Torah there corresponding to, "A tower," and a crown on its head corresponding to, "Its top in heaven." And they do not intend it for the Creator, but to make a name for themselves, as it is written, "And let us make us a name."

And the sons of the *Sitra Achra* overcome Israel, who were blessed with being like the dust of the earth, and rob them, and the work is ruined and destroyed, meaning the synagogues and seminaries that they made. It is said about them, "And the waters prevailed exceedingly upon the earth." In other words, the *Klipot* and the *Sitra Achra*, called "water," destroyed the land as they intensified. This explains the third kind of mixed multitude, the mighty, which correspond to *Bina de Klipa*.

230) *Rephaim* [ghosts] are the fourth kind of mixed multitude that was mingled with Israel. If they see a troubled time in Israel, they leave them and depart from them. And even if they have the strength to save them, they do not wish to save them; they neglect the Torah, and depart from it and from all who engage in the Torah. This means that they depart from the Torah and from Israel to do good to idol worshippers. And they will not rise at the revival of the dead. When the calling comes to Israel and they are salvaged from their affliction, it is said about them, "And You have wiped out all memory of them," since being an offspring of the darkness, they will necessarily be lost at the coming of the light to Israel. This explains the fourth kind of mixed multitude, the *Rephaim*, which correspond to ZA *de Klipa*.

231) *Anakim* [giants] are the fifth kind of mixed multitude. They disparage those of whom it was said, "And *Anakim* [Hebrew: necklaces, as well as giants] about your neck," meaning the Israel who keep the Torah. It is said about them, "*Rephaim* are regarded as *Anakim*, as well," since *Rephaim* and *Anakim* are equal to one another. They are the ones who revert the world back to being unformed and void.

And this is the meaning of the ruin of the Temple. It is said about it, "And the land was unformed and void," since the Temple is the essence of the world and the settlement of the world. This is why it is considered that the whole earth was unformed and void. And the two kinds of mixed multitude that were mingled with Israel caused the ruin of the Temple. And as soon as the light—the Creator—comes to Israel, they will be obliterated and lost from the world. But Israel's redemption does not depend on their obliteration, but only on the obliteration of Amalek, until they blot them out, for in it is the oath, meaning the words, "The hand upon the throne of the Lord."

IDOLATRY

Ki Tetze [If You Go Out]

39) These foreign maidservants are from the side of the potion of death, for they are opposite Divinity, Sam'el's *Nukva*, when the maidservant has become the queen, inheriting her mistress. Sam'el—who is another god—and his *Nukva*, were servants of the Creator, and then made themselves godliness. The Creator will remove them from the world and obliterate them.

40) If people made them godliness, and not of their own will, why were they punished with removal from the world? But when the generation of the flood and the generation of Babel made charms in them, offered them incense and bowed to them, by that power, that they were offering them incense and bowing to them, they would come down to them and do their wish. And they would speak in those forms that they had made, and thus became godliness and idol worship. And this is why the Creator was about to remove them and obliterate them from the world, meaning their statutes, which they worshipped, and from which they absorbed spirits and images.

41) And when there is the mixed multitude in the world, Sam'el and *Nukva* come down through these images to be materialized in them. Hence, the Creator will remove them from the world, as it is written, "And I will remove the spirit of impurity from the land." And should you say that there is no idolatry at the time of the last exile because people do not make charms in them, those who make charms there, in the mixed multitude, anger the Creator and His Divinity, and the Israel among them. And the mixed multitude succeed in them to keep what is written, "But repays those who hate Him to their faces, to destroy them."

RIGHTEOUS AND WICKED

THE RIGHTEOUS MUST BUY THE WICKED

Teruma [Donation]

38) "Raise a donation for Me from every man," from those who are called "men," who have overcome their inclination. "Whose heart moves him," meaning whom the Creator desires, as it is written, "To You my heart said." "The rock of my heart." "And a good heart." "And heart was merry." All were said about the Creator, meaning the Creator's heart, His will. Here, too, "Whose heart moves him" refers to the heart of the Creator. "From him shall you raise My donation," for there the Creator is present, for He is in it, and nowhere else.

39) How do we know that the Creator desires it and places His abode in it? When we see that a person wishes to chase and to exert after the Creator with his heart, his soul, and his will, we know for certain that Divinity is there. At that time, we must buy that person for the full price, bond with him, and learn from him. The first ones said about it, "And buy yourself a friend." One must buy him for the full price to be rewarded with the Divinity that is in him. Thus far one must chase a righteous man and buy him.

40) Just so, that righteous must chase after the wicked and buy him for the full price, to remove the filth from him and subdue the *Sitra Achra*, and make it, for it is considered for him as though he has created it. This is a praise by which the glory of the Creator rises more than on any other praise. Also, that rising is advantageous to all others because it causes the subjugation of the *Sitra Achra* and the elevation of the glory of the Creator. It is written about that in Aaron, "and he turned many back from iniquity," and it is written, "My covenant was with him."

41) Anyone who holds the hand of the wicked and implores him
to leave the bad way rises by three ascensions that no other man
has risen by before: he causes the subjugation of the *Sitra Achra*,
causes the Creator Himself to rise, and causes the entire world
to be sustained in its existence above and below. It is written
about that person, "My covenant with him was life and peace."
He is rewarded with seeing children to children, and is rewarded
with this world and with the next world. All the litigants will not
be able to sentence him in this world and in the next world; he
enters the twelve gates in the firmament and there is no one to
protest against him.

A RIGHTEOUS WHO SUFFERS
AND A WICKED WHO REJOICES

Mishpatim [Ordinances]

438) A righteous is judged by the good inclination. An evil one
is judged by the evil inclination. An intermediate, both judge
him. One who is from the tree of life, which extends from
ZA, is not judged at all, for he has no evil inclination. He is a
complete righteous. This is, "A righteous who is happy." And
there is no good except the Torah, as it is written, "For I give you
good doctrine; do not forsake My teaching." And a righteous
who is suffering is from the tree of knowledge of good and evil,
Malchut. He is called "righteous" because he is suffering, which
is the evil inclination. But because the good inclination governs
him, he is called "A righteous who is suffering," for he suffers
under its authority.

439) A wicked who is happy. The Torah is called "good." He is
called "evil" because he rose to being a *Rosh* in his evil inclination,
and the good is under his dominion, as a slave under his master.
And even though a wicked is crowning the righteous, and a
complete righteous can punish him, it is not good to punish the
righteous, too. This is so because since that good one is under

the feet of the wicked, he must not be punished, for perhaps he will repent and overcome his inclination, and the evil inclination will be dust under his feet.

ILLNESSES OF THE RIGHTEOUS

Pinhas

110) The people of the world are organs with one another. When the Creator wishes to give healing to the world, He strikes a righteous one among them with diseases and afflictions, and for him, He gives healing to all. How do we know it? It is written, "And he was wounded because of our transgressions, oppressed because of our iniquities ... and by his bruising we are healed." "His bruising" means bloodletting, as one lets out blood from an arm, for by that bruise we are healed; it is healing for us, to all the organs of the body.

111) He never strikes the righteous, except to heal a generation and to atone for their iniquities, for it is the most convenient for the *Sitra Achra* when the *Din* [judgment] rules over the righteous, for then he does not mind the world and does not notice them for all his delight from ruling over the righteous. And that righteous, who is tormented for the generation, is rewarded with high governance in this world and in the next world. And if there is a righteous who is happy, it is because the Creator is not concerned with atoning for the world.

112) If the two righteous—the one who is righteous and suffers, and the other who is righteous and happy—were not at the same time, it would be fine. This is because a righteous is happy because the Creator is not mindful of atoning for the world, and a righteous is suffering because the Creator is mindful of atoning for the world. However, there are two righteous at the same time, one with diseases and afflictions and the other with all the abundance in the world.

However, when one or two righteous are enough to atone for the generation, the Creator does not need to strike all of them, just as it is enough to let out blood from one arm to heal all the organs in the body. Here, too, one righteous is enough.

113) And if the disease has attacked all the organs, blood must be let out from both arms. Thus, if harsh iniquities have multiplied in the world, all the righteous are stricken to give healing to the entire generation. But when they are not so many, only one righteous is stricken and the rest of the righteous are at peace, since the world does not need for all of them to be stricken. And if the people are healed, the righteous are healed, as well.

Sometimes the righteous are afflicted all the days of their lives, to protect the generation when the iniquities are very harsh. When the righteous die, everything is healed and atoned.

THE KING'S LOVED ONE

Teruma [Donation]

86) Happy is the holy nation whose Master seeks them and calls upon them to bring them near Him.

87) At that time, the holy nation must come together and go to the assembly house, and all who are early conjoin with Divinity in a single bonding. The first one at the assembly house is happy, for he stands at the degree of righteous toward Divinity, as it is written, "And those who seek Me shall find Me." He rises to a high degree. We learned that when the Creator comes to the assembly house and does not find ten who are present there, He immediately becomes angry. And you say that that one who was early bonds with Divinity and is at the degree of righteous?

88) It is like a king who invited all the town's people to be with him on a certain day at a certain time. While the town's people were preparing themselves, there was one who arrived early at

that place. In the meantime, the king came there and found that man who was early. The king told him, "Mr. So-and-so, where are the town's people?" He replied to him, "My lord, I was early; they are coming after me at the request of the king." Then the king was pleased and he sat there with him and spoke to him, and he became the king's loved one. In the meantime, the rest of the people came and the king was pleased with them and sent them in peace. But if the town's people had not come, and that one did not come early to speak before the king and to show for them, and say that they are all coming, the king would have been angry at once.

89) Here, too, since one came early and was present at the assembly house, and Divinity came and found him, it is considered as though they are all there, for he is waiting for them there. Divinity promptly bonds with him and they sit in bonding and He comes to know him, and He places him at the degree of a righteous.

But if none had come and was there, it is written, "Why have I come and there was no one?" It does not say, "And there was not ten," but "And there was no one," meaning one person to bond with Me and to be with Me, as it is written, "A man of God," which means being at the degree of a righteous.

MIDDLE LINE

MAASE MERKAVA [THE ACT OF ASSEMBLING]

Pekudei [Accounts], 777

777) One who assembles a kind in its kind and knows how to connect what is connected, a palace in its palace, a degree in its degree, has a share in the next world. This is the wholeness of everything. And when the left is completed with the right, and the male in the female, as well as the palaces, all becomes one deed, a kind in its kind. What emerges from that perfection is called *Maase Merkava* [the act of assembling]. The word *Merkava* comes from the words *Markiv* [assembling] and *Murkav* [assembled].

LIGHT THAT APPEARED OUT OF THE DARKNESS

Tetzaveh [Command]

145) The Creator "Reveals the deep and secret things." He reveals all the deep, upper secrets. The middle line reveals the depths in the two lines of *Bina*. It reveals them because it knows what is in the darkness of the left, where the light of *Hochma* sinks for absence of *Hassadim*. And were it not for the darkness, the light would not appear later through the middle line.

BREAD AND WINE

VaEra [And I Appeared]

138) "Go then, eat your bread in happiness and drink your wine with a cheerful heart; for God has already approved your works." What did Solomon see that he said this verse?

139) All his words were with wisdom. "Go then, eat your bread in happiness" means that when a person goes in the ways of the

Creator, the Creator brings him closer and gives him peace and tranquility. Then the bread and wine that a man eats and drinks are with joy in the heart since the Creator desires his works.

140) Where is the wisdom in this verse?

141) Solomon warned people to crown the assembly of Israel, *Malchut*, with joy on the right side, meaning with light of *Hassadim*, which is bread. This is so because bread implies to the light of *Hassadim*. Afterwards he will be crowned with wine, left side, illumination of *Hochma* in the left of *Bina*, so that the faith of all, meaning *Malchut*, would be in complete joy on the right and on the left. And when she is between the two of them, all the blessings will be in the world, since this is the complete perfection of *Malchut*, that the illumination of the left, *Hochma*, will clothe in the light of *Hassadim* on the right, at which time both shine in her, which are bread and wine. And this is the meaning of the Creator wanting people's actions.

IMPORTANCE OF SALT

VaYechi [Jacob Lived]

666) "Neither shall you lack the salt of the covenant of your God." Why is salt so important? It is because it cleanses and perfumes the bitter, and makes it tasty. The salt of judgments in the *Masach de* [of] *Hirik*—on which the middle line emerges, which unites the right with the left—cleanses and perfumes the judgments of the left, which are bitter, with the *Hassadim* on the right. Had there not been salt, the middle line would not have been extended, and the world would not have been able to tolerate the bitterness, as it is written, "For when Thy judgments are in the earth, the inhabitants of the world learn righteousness." It is the law of *Tifferet*—the middle line from the *Chazeh* upwards—that the judgments in the *Masach* in it are called "salt." Justice is the harsh judgments in *Malchut*, and when

the law, which is salt, is to the earth, which is *Nukva*, then they "learn righteousness," and can tolerate the bitterness of justice. It is also written, "Righteousness and justice are the foundation of Thy throne," where righteousness is complemented through the justice, the salt.

667) Salt is a covenant, *Yesod*, middle line, from the *Chazeh* down, on which the world (*Nukva*) persists. It is written, "If My covenant for day and night stands not, I have not appointed the ordinances of heaven and earth." For this reason, because the middle line, which is *Yesod*, emerges on it, the salt is called "the covenant of your God." *Yesod* is called "covenant," and we call it the Sea of Salt [known in English as The Dead Sea], where the sea, which is the *Nukva*, is named after it, after the salt that sweetens it.

668) "For the Lord is righteous, He loves righteousness." This is the salt, which is *Yesod*, at sea, which is *Malchut*. Righteous is *Yesod*; righteousness is *Malchut*. And one who separates them brings death upon himself. This is why it is written, "Neither shall you lack the salt... from your meal-offering," so you will not separate the *Yesod*, which is salt, from the offering, which is the *Nukva*. One does not go without the other.

WAVES OF THE SEA

Noah

217) "You rule the swelling of the sea." When the sea jumps with its waves and the deep rise and fall, the Creator sends a thread of grace from the right side and pulls back its wheels, its anger subsides, and there is no one to attain it.

When the *Nukva* receives *Hochma*, she is called "sea." When the *Nukva* receives only from the left line, which is abundance of *Hochma* without *Hassadim*, the waves of the sea rise. This indicates disclosure, since it implies that the waters of *Hochma* rise, appear, and are attainable. However, the sea cannot receive *Hochma* without *Hassadim*, hence the waves fall down again, for they rise to be disclosed and promptly descend and vanish from attainment for lack of *Hassadim*.

This is why it is considered that the sea is angry, for it strains to raise its waters with great strength, and descends with great strength, as well, and so on and so forth incessantly. This continues until the middle line comes and extends the right line, which is *Hesed*, and clothes the *Hochma* on the left with *Hassadim* on the right. At that time the waves return to their place and the anger of the sea subsides, for now the *Hochma* and the *Hassadim* shine together in all their correction in the desired wholeness.

MANY WATERS CANNOT QUENCH THE LOVE

VaYechi [Jacob Lived]

735) "Its flashes are flashes of fire, the flame of the Lord." "The flame of the Lord" is a burning flame that emerges from the *Shofar* [a special horn], *Yesod Ima*, called *Yod-Hey*, which has awakened and burns. It is the left line of *Ima*, as it is written, "Let his left hand be under my head." This burns the flame of love of the assembly of Israel, Divinity, for the Creator.

736) For this reason, much water will not be able to quench the love, since when the right—water, *Hesed*—comes, it adds to the burning of the love and does not quench the flame of the left, as it is written, "And his right hand embrace me." This is so because during the illumination of *Hochma* in the left line of *Ima* to the *Nukva*, it is burning fire, as it is without *Hassadim*. And when the right line comes with its *Hassadim*, called "water," to quench the fire, it does not quench the illumination of *Hochma* by that. On the contrary, it adds and complements her illumination because it clothes the *Hochma* with *Hassadim*, and the *Hochma* shines in complete perfection.

739) In all the places, the male chases the *Nukva* and awakens the love toward her. But here it turns out that she awakens the love and chases him, as it is written, "Set me as a seal upon thy heart." Usually, however, it is not praised when the *Nukva* chases the male. Indeed, this must be an unclear matter, and a sublime thing, hidden in the treasures of the King.

A PRAYER THAT INCLUDES THREE LINES

VaYishlach [Jacob Sent]

45) A prayer of many rises before the Creator and the Creator crowns Himself with that prayer, since it rises in several ways. This is because one asks for *Hassadim*, the other for *Gevurot*, and a third for *Rachamim*. And it consists of several sides: the right side, the left, and the middle. This is so because *Hassadim* extend from the right side, *Gevurot* from the left side, and *Rachamim* from the middle side. And because it consists of several ways and sides, it becomes a crown over the head of the Righteous One That Lives Forever, *Yesod*, which imparts all the salvations to the *Nukva*, and from her to the whole public.

But a prayer of one does not comprise all the sides; it is only on one way. Either one asks for *Hassadim* or *Gevurot* or *Rachamim*. Hence, a prayer of one is not erected to be received like the prayer of many, as it does not include all three lines like the prayer of many.

DAVID AND BAT-SHEBA

Noah

315) Bat-Sheba belonged to King David since the day the world was created. Thus, why did the Creator first give her to Uriah the Hittite?

316) Such are the ways of the Creator. Although a woman is destined for a man to become his, another precedes him and

marries her before it is the time of the first. When his time came, the one who married her was rejected before the other one, who came later, and he departs from the world. And it is hard for the Creator to remove him from the world because of the other one before his time.

317) Why was Bat-Sheba first given to Uriah the Hittite? Go and see why the holy land was given to Canaan before Israel came, and then you will find all is one. Both Bat-Sheba and the land of Israel are the *Nukva*. The beginning of the construction of the *Nukva* is in *Mochin* of illumination of the left, and then she is built with *Mochin de Panim* [anterior *Mochin*] from all three lines.

Uriah is the *Mochin* of *Hochma* without *Hassadim*, which is the illumination of the left, and King David is the *Mochin de Panim* from the three lines. Hence, even though Bat-Sheba was David's mate, to be able to receive the *Mochin de Panim* from David, she had to first marry Uriah, to receive from him the *Mochin de Achoraim* [posterior *Mochin*] from the illumination of the left, since she cannot receive *Mochin de Panim* before she receives the *Mochin de Achoraim*, which are the *Mochin* of the illumination of the left.

WHEN A WOMAN INSEMINATES AND BEARS A MALE CHILD

Ki Tazria [When a Woman Inseminates]

25) Everyone comes as male and female, included together, and then divide and come separately into the male and separately into the female. But "She delivers a male child" means that the male and female are included together from the right side, which is considered male.

If she delivered a female it would mean that the female and male are included together from the left side, which is considered a female. Then the left side would be ruling over the right side, and the male on the right would yield and not dominate. In that state, such a male, who emerged from the *Nukva*, *Malchut*, from her left side, all his ways are as a female, hence he would be called "female." But a male that emerges from the right side of *Malchut* is the dominant, and the female that emerges with it surrenders, since the left side is not dominant. Hence, it is written about it, "She delivers a male child."

THE SOUND OF THE ROLLING WHEEL

VaYechi [Jacob Lived]

507) The sound of the rolling wheel rolls from below upwards. Hidden *Merkavot* [structures/chariots] go and roll. The sound of melodies rises and falls, wanders and roams the world; the sound of the *Shofar* [ram's horn] stretches through the depth of the degrees and orbits around the wheel.

The *Mochin* come out in three places one at a time. They are called "the three points—*Holam*, *Shuruk*, *Hirik*," and they are the three lines—right, left, and middle. Also, they shine by rolling in three places, in which they walk and roll one at a time. Hence, their mode of illumination is called "rolling."

These three points are included in one another, hence there are three points in the *Holam*—the right line, three points in the *Shuruk*—the left line, and three points in the *Hirik*—the middle line. It follows that there is rolling in each of the three lines. Here *The Zohar* speaks of the three lines in *Hirik*, the middle line, which is ZA, which is called "Voice." This is why it refers to them as "three voices."

The sound of the wheel rolls from below upwards. This means that the rolling is from the right line to the left line. Yet, the illumination of the left is only from below upwards, which is why it was said, "Rolling from below upwards." However, before the left line connects with the right, its illuminations are shut, for it cannot shine without *Hassadim*. Afterwards, the left line rolls to the right line and the sound of melodies rises and falls, meaning the abundance of pleasantness and *Hassadim* that appears from the right line and shines from above downwards, too. This is why it was said, "Walks and wanders in the world."

Subsequently, it rolls from the right line to the middle line. ZA is the middle line, called "the voice of the *Shofar*." It extends and comes out on the *Masach de Hirik*, which is *Dinim*, at the depth of the *Dinim*, and it is the essence that completes and discloses the illumination of the three lines, and mainly what orbits around the wheel, uniting the three lines in one another.

THE MORNING DEER

Pinhas

691) "As the deer longs for the water brooks, so my soul longs for You, O God." Although there are masculine and feminine forms [in the Hebrew], it is all one, since "Deer" is read in masculine form and it is read in feminine form. It is written, "As the deer longs," where "longs" is in feminine form. It does not say "long" in masculine form, since it is all one—the *Malchut*. However, in the first state, when she is with *Zeir Anpin*, the two great lights, she is called "a deer," and in the second state, after she has been diminished, she is called "a deer."

692) The morning deer is one merciful animal, the *Malchut*, of which there are none so merciful among all the animals in the world. When she is in a hurry and needs food for herself and for all the animals, which are all the hosts, BYA (*Beria, Yetzira, Assiya*), she goes far away to a far away road, and comes carrying food. She does not wish to eat until she comes and returns to her place, so that the rest of the animals will gather to her and she will dispense to them from that food. And when she comes, all the

other animals gather to her and she stands in the middle, giving to each and everyone. And the sign is, "She rises while it is still night and gives prey to her household." And from what she gives to them, she is satiated as if she has eaten more than all of them.

693) And when the morning comes, which is called "dawn," the pangs of exile shall come to her, and this is why she is called "the morning deer," after the darkness in the morning. At that time she suffers pangs as one who is in labor, as it is written, "As the expectant approaches the time of labor, she writhes and cries out in her pangs."

694) She dispenses to them when the morning should come, while it is still night, and the darkness departs before the light, as it is written, "She rises while it is still night and gives prey to her household." When the morning has risen, they are all satiated with her food.

695) At that time, a voice in the middle of the firmament awakens, calls out loud and says, "Those who are near, go into your places. Those who are far, go out. Each will gather unto his proper place." When the sun shines, each gathers to his place, and she goes by the day, appears by night, and dispenses food in the morning. This is why she is called "the morning deer."

696) Afterwards, she prevails as a mighty one and goes, and she is called "a buck," a masculine name. She walks 60 parsas [parasangs, approx 2.5 miles from the place from which she left, goes into the mountain of darkness, and walks inside the mountain of darkness. One slant serpent smells after her feet and walks at her feet, and she rises from there to the mountain of light. When she has arrived there, the Creator brings her a serpent and leaves. They fight each other and she is saved, and from there she takes food and returns to her place at midnight. And from midnight onward she begins to dispense until the

morning dawn rises. When the morning rises she goes and she is not seen.

697) When the world needs rains, all the other animals gather to her and she rises to the top of a high mountain and covers her head between her knees and yells one yell. The Creator hears her voice and fills with mercy over the world, and she comes down from the top of the mountain and runs, hides herself, and all the other animals run after her but cannot find her, as it is written, "As the deer longs for the water brooks," those water brooks that have gone dry, and the world is thirsty for water, then she longs.

698) When she is impregnated, she becomes blocked. When it is time for her to deliver, she yells and raises her voices, voice after voice, up to seventy voices, as the number of the words in "The Lord will answer you on a day of plight," which is a poem of that impregnated one. And the Creator hears her and brings her salvation to her. Then, one large serpent comes out of the mountains of darkness and comes among the mountains, his mouth licking in the dust. He reaches that buck and comes and bites her in that place two times.

699) In the first time, blood comes out of her and the serpent licks; and in the second time, water comes out, and all those animals in the mountains drink. Then she opens and delivers. Your sign is "And struck the rock twice with his rod," and it is written, "And the congregation and their beasts drank."

700) At that time when the Creator pities her for the deed of that serpent, it is written, "The voice of the Lord makes the deer to calve and strips the forests bare." "The voice of the Lord makes the deer to calve" are the pangs and the pains to evoke those seventy voices. Promptly, "And strips the forests bare," to evoke a serpent and to disclose that animal, to walk among them in the Creator's hall, which is the *Malchut*. All those multitudes

in *BYA* start and say, "Glory," meaning "Blessed is the glory of the Creator from His place," which is the *Malchut*, who is called "the glory of the Lord."

Here he explains to us a profound matter in regard to *Malchut*...

You already know that *Zeir Anpin* is the governance of the day, right, the governance of *Hassadim*. *Malchut* is the governance of the night, left, the governance of *Hochma* on the left. Hence, during the day, when *Hochma* cannot govern, time is pressing for *Malchut* and she does not have her food—the light of *Hochma* on the left. Later in the day, there is no disclosure of light of *Hochma*—her's and her armies' food, which extend from it—and she must extend her food because *Hochma* is dispensed only with *Dinim*. And as long as she is not clothed in *Hassadim* in a *Zivug* of the middle line, harsh *Dinim* extend from her and these *Dinim* appear through her appearance. They are regarded as far and as a far away road.

It is written, "His sister stood at a distance." "His sister" implies *Hochma*. Also, "I said, 'I will be wise,' but it was far from me." This is done right at the beginning of the night, hence at that time, the darkness spreads over the land, since the illumination of *Hochma* on the left without right is darkness. However, then her food, which is illumination of *Hochma*, is extended, and then she brings and takes the food, the *Hochma* of the left.

But then, when she extends the *Hochma*, she freezes from all the *Dinim* in the *Hochma* without *Hassadim*. This means that she cannot give anything, since *Malchut* does not wish to be in a left without a right, at the place of the elicitation of *Hochma*, which is a far away road, until she returns to her place in the middle line of *Zeir Anpin*, where the left unites with the right, for this is her perpetual place, between the two arms of the king.

Why must she return to her place? It is because before she arrives at her place in the middle line, her lights freeze in her and she cannot give anything to the rest of the animals, to her armies, which extend from her. But when she comes to her place, all the animals gather to her and she bestows upon them from the light of *Hochma*. She stands in a *Zivug* with the middle line, her lights open, and she can dispense to anyone. Also, reception of illumination is called "rising," as it is written, "She rises while it is still night," for then she receives *Hochma*, called "rising," "And gives prey to her household," meaning she gives to all her armies.

RABBI SHIMON BAR YOCHAI
[RASHBI]

DWELLING IN THE CAVE

Introduction of The Book of Zohar

187) Rabbi Pinhas, son of Yair, saw two birds coming and flying over the sea. He raised his voice and said, "Birds, birds, since you fly over the sea, have you seen the place where Yochai is?" He waited a little, then said, "Birds, birds, go and tell me." They flew away into the sea and departed.

Rabbi Shimon fled from the kingship, which ordered that he should be killed. He and his son hid in a cave, and they did not know his whereabouts. This is why Rabbi Pinhas, son of Yair, went to look for him in the islands of the sea.

188) Before he went out to the ship, the birds came and one of them held a letter in her beak. It said, "Rabbi Shimon Bar Yochai has come out of the cave with his son, Rabbi Elazar." Rabbi Pinhas went to him and found that he had changed. His body was filled with holes and sores from sitting in the cave. He wept with him and said, "Woe that I have seen you so." Rabbi Shimon told him, "Happy I am that you have seen me so, for had you not seen me so, I would not be so."

...For all the years that he had to dwell in a cave, he had to sit there inside the sand to cover his nakedness and engage in Torah, and his flesh rusted because of it. He wept over him and said, "Woe unto me that I have seen you so." Rabbi Shimon told him, "Happy I am that you have seen me so, for had you not seen me so, I would not be so," meaning I would not have been rewarded with the revelations of the secrets of the Torah, for he was awarded all the great sublimity of his wisdom during those 13 years of hiding in the cave.

OWNER OF THE CANDLES

Yitro [Jethro]

411) "For this is your life." One who is rewarded with the Torah and does not part from it is rewarded with two lives: one in this world and one in the next world. It is written, "Your life" in plural form [in Hebrew], which are two. Anyone who parts from it, it is as though he parted from life. And one who parts from Rabbi Shimon, it is as though he parted from everything.

412) ...Woe unto a generation from which Rabbi Shimon departs, since when we stand before Rabbi Shimon, the fountains of the heart open to all directions and everything becomes revealed. And when we part from him, we know nothing and all the fountains close.

413) It is written, "And He took of the Spirit who was upon him and placed Him upon the seventy elders." It is like that candle from which several candles are lit, while it remains whole, with nothing subtracted from it due to the lighting of candles from it. So is Rabbi Shimon Bar Yochai, owner of the candles: he shines for all and the light does not depart from him, and he remains complete.

THE BOOK OF ZOHAR—NOAH'S ARK

BeHaalotcha [When You Mount the Candles]

88) "And the wise shall shine as the brightness of the firmament" are the authors of the Kabbalah. They are the ones who exert in this brightness, called *The Book of Zohar*, which is like Noah's ark, gathering two from a town, and seven kingdoms, and sometimes one from a town and two from a family, in whom the words, "Every son that is born you shall cast into the river" come true. The Torah is called "a son." The newborn is the attained. "Into the river" means the light of Torah. "Cast" is like "You will study it" [it's an anagram in Hebrew], where you study each insight

that is born in you by the light of Torah and by its soul. This is the light of this *Book of Zohar*, and it is all because of you.

THE CREATOR SENTENCES
AND THE RIGHTEOUS REVOKES

VaYikra [The Lord Called]

240) There was no decree that was sentenced on the world from above that Rabbi Shimon did not revoke, as it is written, "The Rock of Israel spoke to me: 'Ruler over men shall be the righteous; a righteous rules the fear of God.'" The Creator rules over man. Who rules over the Creator? The righteous rules, for the Creator sentences and the righteous revokes.

241) Such was Rabbi Shimon Bar-Yochai. One day he was sitting at the door of the gate to the city of Lod. He raised his eyes and saw that the sun was shining. He blocked its light three times. Thus, the light was darkened and black and green were seen in the sun. He said to Rabbi Elazar, his son, "Follow me, my son, and we will see; a decree must have been declared above and the Creator wishes to inform me." Indeed, that thing which was sentenced hangs above for thirty days and the Creator does not act before He alerts the righteous, as it is written, "For the Lord God will do nothing, but He reveals His counsel unto His servants the prophets."

242) While they were walking in that vineyard, they saw a serpent that came with its mouth open, blazing in the dust of the earth. Rabbi Shimon was disturbed and his hands struck the serpent's head. The serpent went silent and lowered its mouth, and Rabbi Shimon saw its tongue dangling. He told it, "Serpent, serpent, go and tell that high serpent, which incites and slanders, that Rabbi Shimon Bar-Yochai is in the world." The serpent put its head into a hole in the ground and Rabbi Shimon said, "I declare that as the lower serpent returned to the hole in the ground, the upper serpent will return to the hole of the great deep."

243) Rabbi Shimon whispered a prayer. While they were praying, they heard a voice saying, "The sentences have ceased; return to your places. The strikes of the saboteurs are gone from the world because Rabbi Shimon Bar-Yochai cancelled them. Happy are you Rabbi Shimon that your Master wishes for your best more than for all the people in the world." It is written about Moses, "And Moses besought," meaning that he was sickened [in Hebrew, "besought" can also mean "be sick"]. But you, Rabbi Shimon, sentence, and the Creator keeps; He sentences and you revoke.

244) In the meantime, he saw that the sun had shone and that black was removed. Rabbi Shimon said, "It must be that the world has been perfumed." He went into his house and interpreted, "For the Lord is righteous, He loves righteousness; the upright shall behold His face." What is "His face"? "For the Lord is righteous, He loves righteousness" because "The upright shall behold His face," meaning the high faces of the people of the world, for they need to ask of the Creator for mercy for everything they need.

245) What is, "The upright shall behold His face"? These are the ancient days, the *Sefirot* of *Atik*, the hidden of all that are hidden, the *Keter*. And the days of the world are the *Sefirot* of ZA, which are called "His face." They see each other in an upright way what they should see, meaning the *Panim* [face] of ZA sees the *Panim* of *Atik*, and the *Panim* of *Atik* sees the *Panim* of ZA in an upright way, without turning right or left.

246) When the Creator watches over the world and sees that the acts of people below are upright, *Atik*, which is *Keter*, appears in ZA, *Tifferet*, and all those *Panim* of ZA look at the hidden *Panim* of *Atik*. Then, all are blessed because they look at each other in an upright way, in the middle line, which leans neither to the right nor to the left. It is written about that, "The upright shall behold His face," meaning that the faces of *Atik* and ZA look at each other in an upright way, in the middle line. And then they are

all blessed and water each other until all the worlds are blessed and all the worlds are as one. At that time, it is considered that "The Lord is one and His name One."

BEGINNING OF THE IDRA ZUTA

Haazinu [Give Ear]

26) Rabbi Shimon said, "It is a good time now and I would like to come to the next world without shame. Thus, I wish to disclose before Divinity sacred things that I have not disclosed thus far, lest it will be said that I departed from the world deficient. Thus far, they have been hidden in my heart to enter with them into the next world.

27) "This is how I am arranging you: Rabbi Aba will write, Rabbi Elazar will learn orally, and the rest of the friends will speak in their hearts." Rabbi Aba rose behind his shoulders. Rabbi Elazar, his son, sat before him and Rabbi Shimon told him, "Arise, my son, for another will sit in this place." Rabbi Elazar arose.

28) Rabbi Shimon cloaked in his garment and sat. He started and said, "The dead do not praise the Lord, nor do any who go down to Dumah." Indeed, "The dead do not praise the Lord," for they are called "dead," since the Creator is called "living," and He is among those who are called "living," the righteous ones, and not among those who are called "dead," the wicked ones. And the end of the verse proves, as it is written, "Nor do any who go down to Dumah," meaning all those who go down to Angel Dumah, who will remain in Hell. But not so are those who are called "living." They are the righteous ones and the Creator wants to honor...

31) Rabbi Shimon started and said, "I am my beloved's, and his desire is for me." all the days that I have been tied to this world, I have been tied to the Creator with one knot. For this reason, now, "And his desire is for me," for He and all His camp have

come to joyfully hear hidden words and the praise of Holy *Atik*, the most hidden of all that are hidden, the most secluded and separated from all. But he is not separated, for everything clings to him and he clings to everything; he is everything.

THE DEPARTURE OF RABBI SHIMON BAR YOCHAI

Idra Zuta, *Haazinu* [Give Ear]

196) Rabbi Aba said, "The Holy Light did not complete saying life before his words abated. And I wrote, and thought that I would write some more, but I did not hear. I did not raise my head, for the light was great and I could not look. In the meantime, I was shaken; I heard a voice calling and saying, 'Length of days and years of life.' Then I heard another voice, 'He asked life of You.'"

197) The whole of that day, the fire did not stop from the house, but there was none to reach him. They could not, since the light and the fire surrounded him. That whole day, I was fallen on the earth and cried bitterly. Once the fire went, I saw the Holy Light, the holy of holies, departed from the world, cloaked and lying on his right side, and his face was smiling.

198) Rabbi Elazar, his son, arose, took his hands, and kissed them. And I licked the dust under his feet. The friends wished to cry but could not speak. The friends began to cry, and Rabbi Elazar, his son, fell three times and could not open his mouth. Afterwards, he started and said, "My father, my father, they were three and they have become one again." That is, there were three great ones in the land—Rabbi Elazar, his father, Rashbi, and his grandfather, Rabbi Pinhas, son of Yair—and now Rabbi Elazar remained orphaned from is grandfather and from his father, Rashbi. He remained alone in the world. Now that this great tree has left. Under it, the animals of the field would stroll, in its branches, the birds of the sky would dwell, and nourishments for all were in it. Now the animals migrated and the birds of the trees that sat on its branches settle in the holes of the great sea.

And the friends, instead of the nourishment that they received from it, they drink blood.

199) Rabbi Hiya rose to his feet and said, "Thus far the Holy Light was watching over us. Now it is the time to toil only for his glory."

Rabbi Elazar and Rabbi Aba rose and took him from his place onto a bed that was made as a ladder, to raise him to his bed. Who saw the confusion of the friends? And the whole house was smelling of good fragrances. They raised him to his bed and only Rabbi Elazar and Rabbi Aba served him.

200) Strikers and men with shields came from the village Tzippori, and wished to bury him in their place. They came to take him by force and by war. The children of Meron drove them away and yelled at them in hordes, for they did not want him buried there, but that he would be buried in their place. When the bed was out of the house, it rose in the air and fire was flaming before it. They heard a voice, "Come in, come and gather for the celebration of Rabbi Shimon, may peace come and they will rest in peace."

201) When he entered the cave they heard a voice inside the cave. That man was quaking the land, irritating from *Malchut*, several slanderers in the firmament are quieted on this day for you. This is Rabbi Shimon Bar Yochai, whose Master praises every day. Happy is he above and below. Several high treasures are kept for him. It was said about him, "And you, go to the end and rest and rise again for your fate at the end of the right."

DESIRE

DESIRE REVEALS SUBLIME SECRETS

New *Zohar, Beresheet* [Genesis]

110) Happy are those who look into their will, matters of high secrets, to walk in the path of truth, to be rewarded in this world and to shine for them for the next world. It is written about them, "And they that are wise shall shine as the brightness of the firmament; and they that turn the many to righteousness as the stars forever and ever." Happy are they in this world and in the next world.

Those who adhere to the Creator in truth, their will guides them to walk in their work as is established above in the upper worlds, as it is written, "And Abram went as the Lord commanded him." Hence, when they later look into their will, they know the high secrets, for they are looking at the tilts in their desires and know how the high secrets are determined above.

THEY WHO GOVERN THE WILL OF THEIR HEARTS

VaYera [The Lord Appeared]

239) "And these are the nations which the Lord left, to test Israel by them." I was looking at that eternal world, and the world stood only on those righteous who reign over their hearts' desire. It is said, "He appointed it in Joseph for a testimony." Why was Joseph rewarded with that virtue and kingship? For he had conquered his inclination. This is because we learned that all who reign over their inclination, the kingdom of heaven awaits them.

THE TOWER OF BABEL AND COMMON WILL

Noah

384) "And the Lord said, 'Behold, they are one people, and they all have the same language.'" "And it came to pass when they journeyed from the east." "From the east means from the ancient one of the world." "That they found" means that they found a finding from the secrets of the wisdom of the first ones, the generation of the flood, who were shaken there. In this wisdom that they found, they tried to do the work that they did to defy the Creator. Also, they would utter with their mouths swears to the high ministers. And they did the work—the construction of the city and the tower.

385) "They are one people, and they all have the same language." And because they are all of the same heart and same will, and speak the holy tongue, "And now nothing which they purpose to do will be impossible for them," and there is no one who can prevent their actions. "But," said the Creator, "What I shall do is I shall confuse the degrees above and their tongue below, and then their work will be arrested."

386) Because they were of one will and one heart, and spoke the holy tongue, it is written, "Nothing which they purpose to do will be impossible for them," and the upper Din [judgment] cannot rule over them, we, or the friends who are engaging in Torah. And we, who are of one heart and one will, it is several times more so: nothing which we purpose to do will be impossible for us.

PEACE

HER WAYS ARE PLEASANT
AND ALL HER PATHS ARE PEACE

VaEra [And I Appeared]

183) "Her ways are ways of pleasantness, and all her paths are peace." "Her ways are ways of pleasantness" are the ways of the Torah. Anyone who walks in the ways of Torah, the Creator brings upon him the pleasantness of Divinity, so it would never leave him. "And all her paths are peace" are the paths of the Torah, since all the paths of the Torah are peace—peace for him above, peace for him below, peace for him in this world, and peace for him in the next world.

ONE WHO DISPUTES WITH PEACE

Korah

6) The world stands only on peace. When the Creator created the world, it could not exist until He came and established peace on them, the Sabbath, which is the peace of upper and lower. Then the world persisted. Hence, one who disagrees with peace will be lost from the world.

IF THEY ARE AT PEACE,
JUDGMENT DOES NOT RULE OVER THEM

Miketz [At the End]

168) "Thus says the Lord, though they are at full strength and likewise many, Even so, they will be cut off and pass away." When the whole people has peace in it, and no dispute is among them, the Creator has pity on them and the judgment does not govern them. And even though they are idol worshippers, if they are at

peace, judgment does not rule over them, as it is written, "Joined idols," idol worshipping, "Ephraim let him alone." This means that even if one is serving idols, meaning idol worshipping, if they are nonetheless united, "Let him alone."

CLOSENESS OF RIGHTEOUS INCREASES PEACE IN THE WORLD

VaYigash [Then Judah Approached]

61) Happy are the righteous, whose closeness to each other brings peace to the world because they know how to unite the unification and to make nearness, to increase peace in the world. As long as Joseph and Judah were not close to one another, there was no peace. When Joseph and Judah drew close together, peace increased in the world and joy was added above and below while Joseph and Judah were brought closer. All the tribes were together with Joseph, and that closeness increased peace in the world, as it is written, "Then Judah approached him."

HE WHO WALKS ON THE PATH OF TRUTH

Miketz [At the End]

186) Rabbi Abba was sitting at the gate of the city of Lod. He saw a man coming and sitting on a protrusion that bulged at the side of the mountain. He was weary from the road and he sat and slept there. At that time, he saw a serpent approaching him, and a varmint came out and killed the serpent.

When the man woke, he saw the serpent dead in front of him. The man rose and the protrusion he had been sitting on was torn off the mountain and fell to the valley below it. But the man was saved. Had he been late standing up by even a minute, he would have fallen to the valley along with the protrusion and he would have been killed.

187) Rabbi Abba came to him and told him: "Tell me, what do you do?" for the Creator brought you these two miracles, saved you from the serpent and from the protrusion that fell. And that was not for nothing.

188) He told him. "Through my whole life, never has anyone done evil to me that I did not make peace with him and forgave him. Moreover, if I could not make peace with him, I did not go to my bed before I forgave him and all those who afflicted me, and I did not hold any grudge the whole day for that evil which he had done to me. And I do not suffice for that, but even more, from that day forth, I have tried to do them good."

189) The deeds of this one are greater than Joseph's, for with Joseph, the wrong doers were his brothers, and he certainly should have pitied them because of the brotherhood. But what this one did, when he did this with all the people, is greater than Joseph. He is worthy of the Creator bringing him a miracle over a miracle.

190) "He who walks in integrity walks securely" is a man who walks in the ways of the Torah. "Walks securely" means that the damagers of the world will not be able to harm him. "But he who perverts his ways will be found out." Who will be found out? One who has strayed from the path of truth, and seeks to collect from his friend, who wishes to pay him evil for evil, and breaches "Thou shall not take vengeance, nor bear any grudge." "Will be found out" means that it will be apparent to the eyes of all the litigants, that they will not lose the image of that person, so as to bring him to the place where they will avenge him, an eye for an eye. This is why it is written, "Will be found out."

191) One who walks in the path of truth, the Creator covers him, so he will not be found out and will not be recognized by the litigants. "But he who perverts his ways will be found out," and will be recognized by them. Happy are those people who walk in the path of truth. They walk safely in the world and they are not afraid, neither in this world nor in the next world.

JOY

SERVE THE LORD WITH GLADNESS

VaYikra [The Lord Called]

109) "Serve the Lord with gladness." Any work that a person wishes to do for the Creator should be done with gladness, willingly, so that his work will be whole.

HIGHER JOY

Tetzaveh [Command]

94) "Serve the Lord with gladness," since man's joy draws another joy, the higher one.

A WHOLE PLACE, A PLACE OF JOY

VaYechi [Jacob Lived]

116) "And the spirit of Jacob their father revived." This means that in the beginning, his spirit was dead. He also did not intend to continue and receive another spirit, since the upper spirit is not present in an empty place. Divinity is present only in a whole place, and not in a deficient place, or a flawed place, or a place of sadness, but in a proper place—a place of joy. For this reason, all those years when Joseph was separated from his father and Jacob was sad, Divinity was not on him.

117) "Serve the Lord with gladness; come before Him with singing." There is no service of the Creator unless out of joy. Divinity is not present in sadness, as it is written, "'And now bring me a player.' And it came to pass that when the player played." It writes "Play" three times, to evoke the spirit from the source of wholeness, ZA, which includes three lines, which is the complete spirit. The threefold "play" corresponds to his three lines.

THE REASON FOR THE JOY OF THE HEART

VaEra [And I Appeared]

139) "Go then, eat your bread in happiness" means that when a person goes in the ways of the Creator, the Creator brings him closer and gives him peace and tranquility. Then the bread and wine that you eat and drink are with joy of the heart because the Creator is pleased with his deeds.

THE REWARD OF ONE
WHO DELIGHTS THE CREATOR

Pinhas

2) Anyone who engages in Torah in this world is rewarded with several gates being opened to him, several lights to that world. Hence, when he passes away from this world, the Torah walks before him and goes to all the gate-keepers, declares and says, "Open the gates and let the gentile righteous in, set up a chair for so and so, the King's servant," for there is no joy to the Creator except in one who engages in the Torah.

THE KING HAS BROUGHT ME TO HIS CHAMBERS

Aharei Mot [After the Death]

50) "The king has brought me to his chambers." If the King brings me to His chambers, "We will rejoice in you and be glad," Me and all My hosts. All the hosts, when the Assembly of Israel is glad and blessed, everyone is glad. At that time there is no Din [judgment] in the world. This is why it is written, "Let the heavens be glad, and let the earth rejoice."

TORAH

ALL THE GOOD

Chayei Sarah [The Life of Sarah]

219) "Open my eyes, that I may see wonders from Your law." How foolish are people, for they do not know and do not consider engaging in the Torah. But the Torah is the whole of life, and every freedom and every goodness in this world and in the next world. Life in this world is to be rewarded with all their days in this world, as it is written, "The number of thy days I will fulfill." And he will be rewarded with long days in the next world, for it is the perfect life, a life of joy, life without sadness, life that is life—freedom in this world and liberation from everything. Freedom from the Angel of Death

220) ...the Torah is freedom from the angel of death, so he cannot control him.

Certainly, if Adam were to cling to the tree of life, which is the Torah, he would not cause death to himself or to the whole world. But because he left the tree of life, which is the Torah, and ate from the tree of knowledge, he caused death to himself and to the world. For this reason, the Creator gave the Torah to Israel.

It is written, "*Harut* [carved] on the tables; do not pronounce it *Harut*, but rather *Herut* [freedom]," for then they were liberated from the angel of death. Had Israel not sinned with the calf and not departed the tree of life, which is the Torah, they would not cause death to return to the world to begin with.

And the Creator said, "I said, 'You are gods, and all of you are sons of the Most High,'" meaning upon the reception of the Torah. And since you damaged yourselves, meaning sinned, you will indeed die as humans. Hence, that evil serpent that darkened the world cannot govern anyone who engages in the Torah.

UPPER LIFE

VaYishlach [And Jacob Sent]

46) "Happy is the man that fears always; but he that hardens his heart shall fall into evil." Happy are Israel, for the Creator desires them and gave them the true law, to be rewarded by it with everlasting life. The Creator draws the upper life upon anyone who engages in Torah, and brings him to the life of the next world, as it is written, "For He is your life, and the length of your days." And it is written, "And through this thing ye shall prolong your days," because she is life in this world and life in the next world.

THE WORLD WAS CREATED WITH THE TORAH

Teruma [Donation]

635) When the Creator created the world, He looked in the Torah and created the world. The world was created with the Torah, as it is written, "And I was beside Him an Amon [apprentice]." Do not pronounce it, Amon, but Oman [craftsman], for the Torah is the craftsmanship of the world...

639) It is written in the Torah, "In the beginning God created the heaven and the earth." He looked in this word and created the heaven. It is written in the Torah, "And God said, 'Let there be light.'" He looked in this word and created the light. And so it was with each and every word that is written in the Torah: the Creator looked, and did that thing. This is why it is written, "And I was beside Him an Oman [craftsman]," as the whole world was created.

640) When the world was created, not a thing existed before there was the desire to create man, so he will engage in Torah, and for that, the world existed. Now, anyone who looks in the

Torah and engages in it, seemingly sustains the entire world. The Creator looked in the Torah and created the world; man looks in the Torah and sustains the world. It follows that the deed and the keeping of the entire world is the Torah. For this reason, happy is he who engages in the Torah, for he sustains the world.

ONE WHO ENGAGES IN TORAH SUSTAINS THE WORLD

Toldot [Generations]

3) Anyone who engages in Torah sustains the world and sustains each and every operation in the world in its proper way. Also, there is not an organ in a man's body that does not have a corresponding creation in the world.

This is so because as man's body divides into organs and they all stand degree over degree, established one atop the other and are all one body, similarly, the world, meaning all creations in the world are many organs standing one atop the other, and they are all one body. And when they are all corrected they will actually be one body. And everything, man and the world, will be like the Torah because the whole of Torah is organs and joints standing one atop the other. And when the world is corrected they will become one body.

STUDYING FOR THE CREATOR

Lech Lecha [Go Forth]

282) When Rabbi Abba came from Babel, he declared, "Whomever wishes for wealth and whomever wishes for long days in the next world will engage in the Torah!" The whole world gathered unto him to engage in the Torah.

A bachelor, a man vacant of a woman, was in his neighborhood. One day, he came to him and told him, "I want to learn Torah so as to have wealth." Rabbi Abba told him, "You will certainly be rewarded with wealth through the Torah." He sat, and engaged in the Torah.

283) In time, he said, "Rabbi, where is the wealth?" Rabbi Abba replied, "It means that you are not studying for the Creator," and he walked into his room to consider what to do about him. He heard a voice saying, "Do not punish him, for he will be a great man." He returned to him and told him, "Sit, my son, sit, and I will give you wealth."

284) In the meantime, a man walked in holding a golden vessel. He took it out so it would be seen, and its shine radiated in the house. He said, "Rabbi, I want to be rewarded with the Torah. I myself have not been privileged with understanding the Torah, and I ask that someone will engage for me. I have great wealth, which my father had left for me." While he was seated at his desk, he set up thirteen cups of gold on it. "I want to be rewarded with the Mitzva [good deed] of studying the Torah, and in return, I will give wealth."

285) He said to that man, who did not have a wife, "You engage in Torah, and this man will give you wealth." The man gave him that gold cup. Rabbi Abba said about him, "Gold or glass cannot equal it, nor can it be exchanged for articles of fine gold." He sat and engaged in Torah, and that man was giving him wealth.

286) In time, the beauty of Torah came within him. One day, he was sitting and crying. His rabbi found him crying and asked him, "Why are you crying?" He replied, "And what am I neglecting for this wealth—the life of the next world! I do not want to study for the man any longer; I want to be rewarded with

the Torah for myself." Rabbi Abba said, "Now it means that he is already studying for the Creator."

287) He called upon that man and told him, "Take your wealth and give it to orphans and poor, and I will give you a greater share in the Torah, in everything we learn." He gave him back the gold cup. There is no better reward in the world than one who engages in Torah. And there is no need for anything in return for it, as it is written, "Gold or glass cannot equal it, nor can it be exchanged for articles of fine gold."

TORAH THAT DOES NOT RISE UP

VaYechi [Jacob Lived]

293) "What advantage does man have in all his work, which he does under the sun?" The toil of Torah, too, means to toil under the sun. The toil of Torah is different; it is above the sun, from the upper ones. Thus, so is the toil of Torah. It is said about it, "What advantage does man have in all his work, which he does under the sun?" whether he toils in Torah for people or for his own honor. It is about that that the verse says, "Under the sun," since this Torah does not rise, and even if one lived a thousand years, on the day he departs from the world, it will seem to him as though he lived only one day.

WORDS OF TORAH REQUIRE INTENTION

Noah

275) It is written, "Prepare to meet your God, O Israel," and it is written, "Be silent and listen, O Israel," for words of Torah require intention, and must be corrected in the body and will as one.

276) ...Words of Torah require correction of the body and correction of the heart.

SUBLIME SECRETS THAT APPEAR FOR A MOMENT AND DISAPPEAR ONCE MORE

Toldot [Generations]

4) The Torah holds all the hidden, sublime, and unattainable secrets. The Torah holds all the sublime, revealed, and unrevealed matters, that is, that for their profoundness, they appear to the eye of the one who observes them and soon after disappear. Then they briefly reappear and disappear, and so on and so forth before those who scrutinize them. The Torah holds all the things that are above in the Upper World and that are below. And everything in this world and everything in the next world is in the Torah, and there is no one to observe and to know them.

AWAKEN THE LOVE

Mishpatim [Ordinances]

99) A loved one, comely and beautiful, hides in her palace. She has a lover, of whom people do not know, but he is hiding. That lover, for the love that he loves her, always passes by the gate to her house and raises his eyes to every direction. She knows that her lover is always surrounding the gate to her house. She opens a little door in her palace and shows her face to her lover, and immediately covers herself again. All those who were with the lover did not see and did not look, only the lover alone, whose heart and soul cling after her. And he knows that for the love that she loves him, she appears to him for a moment, to evoke the love for him.

So is a word of Torah: she appears only for her lover. The Torah knows that that wise-of-heart surrounds the gate to her house each day. What did she do? She showed her face to him from within the palace and hinted him a hint, then promptly returned to her place and hid. All those from there neither knew nor looked, but he alone, and his heart and soul follow her. Hence, the Torah appears and disappears, and walks with love toward the one who loves her, to awaken the love with him.

THE TORAH DOES NOT TELL LITERAL STORIES

BeHaalotcha [When You Mount]

58) Woe unto one who says that the Torah comes to tell literal tales and the uneducated words of such as Esau and Laban. If this is so, even today we can turn the words of an uneducated person into a law, and even nicer than theirs. And if the Torah indicates to mundane matters, even the rulers of the world have among them better things, so let us follow them and turn them into a law in the same way. However, all the words of the Torah have the uppermost meaning.

59) The upper world and the lower world are judged the same. Israel below correspond to the high angels above. It is written of the high angels, "Who makes winds His messengers," and when they come down, they clothe in dresses of this world. Had they not clothed in dresses such as in this world, they would not be able to stand in this world, and the world would not tolerate them. And if this is so with angels, it is all the more so with the law that created the angels and all the worlds, and they exist for it. Moreover, when it came down to this world, the world could not tolerate it if it had not clothed in these mundane clothes, which are the tales and words of the uneducated.

60) Hence, this story in the Torah is a clothing of the Torah. And one who considers this clothing as the actual Torah and nothing else, damned will be his spirit, and he will have no share in the next world. This is the reason why David said, "Open my eyes, that I may behold wondrous things out of Your law," that is, gaze upon what lies beneath the clothing of the Torah.

61) There is an openly visible clothing, and when fools see a person dressed handsomely, whose dress seems elegant, they look no further and judge him by his elegant clothes. They regard the clothes as the man's body and regard the man's body as his soul.

62) Such is the Torah. It has a body, which is the Mitzvot of the Torah, which are called "the bodies of the Torah." This body clothes in dresses, which are mundane stories, and the fools in the world consider only that clothing, which is the story of the Torah. They do not know more and do not consider what exists underneath that clothing.

Those who know more do not consider the clothing, but the body under that clothing. But the sages, the servants of the High King, those who stood on Mount Sinai, consider only the soul in the Torah, which is the essence of it all, the actual law. In the future, they will gaze upon the soul within the soul of the Torah.

63) This is also how it is above. There is Levush [clothing], Guf [body], Neshama [soul], and Neshama to Neshama. The heavens and their hosts are the Levush, and the assembly of Israel is Malchut—the Guf that receives the Neshama, which is the Tifferet [glory] of Israel, ZA. Hence, Malchut is the Guf to the Neshama, for ZA clothes in her like a soul in the body. The Neshama is Tifferet, Israel, the actual law, the soul of the Torah, upon which the sages gaze.

And Neshama to Neshama is Atika Kadisha [the Holy, Ancient One], upon whom they will gaze in the future. All are intertwined: Atika Kadisha clothes in ZA, ZA clothes in Malchut, and Malchut in the worlds BYA and all their hosts.

64) Woe unto the wicked ones who say that the Torah is nothing more than fables and consider only the clothing. Happy are the righteous who consider the Torah as they should. As wine sits only in a jar, the Torah dwells only in that clothing. Hence, one needs to regard what is found under the clothing, which is why all these tales are dresses.

TO WHOM DOES THE TORAH SEEM EMPTY

VaYetze [Jacob Went Out]

341) Woe unto the wicked of the world who do not know and do not look at words of Torah. And when they do look at it, because there is no wisdom in them, the words of Torah seem to them as though they were empty and useless words. It is all because they are devoid of knowledge and wisdom, since all the words in the Torah are sublime and precious words, and each and every word that is written there is more precious than pearls, and no object can compare to it.

342) When all the fools whose heart is blocked see the words of Torah, not only do they not know, but they even say that the words are spoiled, useless words, woe unto them. When the Creator seeks them out for the disgrace of the Torah, they will be punished with a punishment fit for one who rebels against one's Master.

343) It is written in the Torah, "For it is no vain thing." And if it is vain, it is only vain for you, since the Torah is filled with every good stone and precious gem, from all the abundance in the world.

344) King Solomon said, "If you are wise, you are wise for yourself." This is so because when one grows wise in the Torah, it is to his benefit, not for the Torah, since he cannot add even a single letter to the Torah. "And if you scorn, you alone shall bear it," for nothing shall be subtracted from the praise of Torah because of that. His scorn is his alone and he will remain in it, to annihilate him from this world and from the next world.

A HEALING FOR ALL THE WORLD'S TROUBLES

VaYechi [Jacob Lived]

317) The people of the world will shout but no one will watch over them. Their heads will search in every direction for some salvation but they will not return with any cure for their plight. But I have found them one remedy in the world: Where they engage in Torah, and a book of Torah that is unflawed is among them, when they take it out, the upper ones and lower ones will awaken. And it is all the more so if the Holy Name is written in it properly.

WRITTEN TORAH AND ORAL TORAH

New Zohar, Toldot [Generations]

13) All the upper fathers who are gripped above—Abraham, Isaac, Jacob, Moses, Aaron, and Joseph—are all implied in the written Torah, the Torah of HaVaYaH. This is because they are the six edges of Zeir Anpin, who is called HaVaYaH, and about whom it is written, "The law of the Lord [HaVaYaH]." Hence, they are all written Torah.

David, who is gripped outside of them, is the oral Torah, Malchut, and is implied in words of reception, meaning in the writings. This is the reason why Malchut is called "reception," since she receives light from the written Torah, who is called Tzadik [righteous], Yesod, and it is called Joseph, and it is called "all."

TORAH – NIGHT STUDY

THREAD OF HESED [MERCY/GRACE]

Miketz [At the End]

33) ...When a person engages in Torah at night, a thread of mercy extends upon him during the day, as it is written, "By day the Lord will command His mercy, and in the night His song shall be with me."

GREAT LOVE AT NIGHT

Aharei Mot [After the Death]

217) "My spirit within me seeks You," to cling to you at night with great love. Man needs to rise each night because of the love of the Creator to engage in His work until the morning rises, and draw upon him a thread of *Hesed* [mercy/grace]. Happy is the man who loves the Creator with this love. And those true righteous, who love the Creator in this way, the world exists for them, and they govern all the harsh decrees above and below.

THEY WHO RISE FROM THEIR BED
TO ENGAGE IN TORAH

VaYikra [The Lord Called]

379) "When the morning stars sang together, and all the sons of God shouted for joy." When the Creator comes to entertain with the righteous in the Garden of Eden, all things, meaning degrees in the lower world, *Malchut*, and all the upper ones and lower ones awaken toward Him. And all the trees, meaning degrees, in the Garden of Eden begin to praise before Him, as it is written, "Then shall all the trees of the wood sing for joy before the Lord, for He has come." And even the birds in the land all utter praise before Him.

At that time, a flame comes out and strikes the wings of the rooster, who calls and praises the holy King. He calls upon people to exert in Torah, in praising their Master, and in His work. Happy are those who rise from their bed to engage in Torah.

380) When the morning comes, the doors on the south, meaning *Hesed*, open and the gates of healing come out to the world. And Eastern wind, ZA, awakens and *Rachamim* are present. And all those stars and signs, meaning degrees, which are appointed under the governance of that morning, which is *Yesod* that shines *Hassadim*, they all begin to praise and to sing for the High King. It is written about that, "When the morning stars sang together, and all the sons of God shouted for joy."

But what do the sons of God, who are *Din*, want here, summoning a shout on this morning, which is the time of *Hesed*? After all, all the *Dinim* are removed when the *Hesed* awakens in the world. However, "And all the sons of God shouted for joy" means that the authority of the harsh *Dinim* has been broken, their strength has been shattered, since "Shout" means that they broke, as it is written, "The earth is broken, broken down."

GIFTS FOR MEMBERS OF THE PALACE

Beshalach [When Pharaoh Sent]

46) The Creator and all the righteous in the Garden of Eden, all listen to His voice. It is written, "You who sit in the gardens, friends listen to your voice; let me hear it." "You who sit in the gardens" is the assembly of Israel, *Malchut*. At night, she praises the Creator with the praise of the Torah. Happy is he who partakes with her in praising the Creator in the praise of the Torah.

47) When the morning comes, the assembly of Israel, *Malchut*, comes and plays with the Creator, and He gives her the scepter of *Hesed* [grace/mercy]. But not only to her, but to her and to all

those who partake with her. One who engages in Torah at night, the Creator draws to him a thread of *Hesed* during the day. This is why *Malchut* is called "The morning star," for she praises the Creator at night with the praise of the Torah.

48) When the morning should rise, the light darkens and grows black, and the blackness is present. Then a woman clings to her Husband, which is the third watch, when a woman tells with her husband, meaning ZON, to tell with Him, and she comes to His palace.

49) Afterwards, when the sun should set, the night shines and comes and takes the sun. Then, all the gates close, donkeys bray, and dogs bark. When half the night is through, the King begins to rise and the queen, *Malchut*, begins to sing. The King, ZA, comes and knocks on the palace's gate and says, "Open for me, my sister, my wife." And then He plays with the souls of the righteous.

50) Happy is he who has awakened at that time with words of Torah. For this reason, all the children of the queen's palace must rise at that time and praise the King. All praise before Him, and the praise rises from this world, which is far from Him, and this is more favorable to the Creator than anything.

51) When the night departs and the morning comes and dawns, the King and queen are in joy, in *Zivug*, and He gives her presents, as well as to all the dwellers of the palace. Happy is he who is numbered among the dwellers of the palace.

SIXTY BREATHS

VaYigash [Then Judah Approached]

34) King David would sleep as a horse; he slept little. Thus, how did he rise at midnight? After all, this measure of sixty breaths of the horse's sleep is little and he would not rise even at a third of the night.

35) However, when the night came, he would sit with all the great ones of his house and he would sentence judgments and engage in words of Torah. This means that he did not go to sleep in the beginning of the night, but close to midnight. Afterwards, he would sleep his sleep until midnight, rise at midnight, awaken, and engage in the work of his Master, in song and in praise.

36) King David lives and exists forever and ever. King David kept himself all his life from tasting the taste of death, since sleep is one part of sixty of death. And David, because of his place, which is "alive," slept only sixty breaths, since he lived only through sixty breaths, minus one, and from there on, man tastes the taste of death and the side of the spirit of impurity governs him.

37) This is why King David kept himself from tasting the taste of death and from being governed by the side of the other spirit. This is because sixty breaths minus one means that the life above—up to sixty breaths—are sixty high breaths, and life depends on them. And from there down it is death.

38) This is why King David was measuring the night until midnight, so he would remain alive and the taste of death would not govern him. And when half the night was through, David would exist in his place, in his degree, living and existing, since he had woken up from his sleep and sang and praised. This is so because when he awoke at midnight and the holy *Keter*—the *Nukva*, awakened—it must not find David connected to another place, the place of death.

39) When half the night was through and the upper holiness awakened, if a person who sleeps in his bed does not rise from his sleep to observe the glory of his Master, by that he connects to death and clings to another place, to the *Sitra Achra*. This is why King David would always rise at midnight to observe the glory of his Master, living in a living, and he would not sleep in slumber to the point of tasting the taste of death. This is the

reason why he would sleep as a horse, sixty breaths, but not in completeness, for they lacked one.

Sleeping means shutting of the eyes, meaning the *Mochin*. This is as one who is lying mindlessly with his eyes shut. Its root extends from the domination of the illumination of the left line, *Hochma*, when it is in dispute with the right line, *Hassadim*, where because the *Hochma* cannot shine without *Hassadim*, the *Mochin* are blocked out.

Awakening from sleep extends from the middle line, since the state of sleep continues until the ascent of the middle line with the *Masach de Hirik* in it. This is the point of *Man'ula* [lock], which diminishes the left line and includes it in the right, when the *Hochma* in the left is included in the *Hassadim* in the right. At that time, the *Mochin* open and the *Hochma* can shine.

TORAH THAT IS STUDIED TOGETHER IS PURER

VaYikra [The Lord Called]

394) Torah that is studied at night is purer than Torah that is studied during the day, since the purity of the written Torah is in the oral Torah, in *Malchut*, which is called "night." The oral Torah, *Malchut*, governs at night and awakens more than at daytime, and when *Malchut* governs, she is the purity in the Torah.

CHILDREN OF FAITH—THOSE WHO KNOW HOW TO UNITE THE HOLY NAME

VaYikra [The Lord Called]

200) "Bless the Lord, all you servants of the Lord." This is a praise for all those with faith. Who are those with faith? They are the ones who engage in Torah and know how to unite the Holy Name properly. And the praise of those with faith is that they stand at midnight to engage in Torah and adhere to the assembly of Israel, *Malchut*, to praise the Creator with words of Torah.

201) When one rises at midnight to engage in Torah, a Northern wind—meaning illumination of the left—awakens at midnight, which is the deer and *Malchut*, and stands and praises the Creator, ZA. And when she stands, several thousands and several tens of thousands stand with her in their existence, and they all begin to praise the holy King.

202) The Creator listens to he who was rewarded and rose at midnight to engage in Torah...And all that multitude above and those who praise their Master in song keep silent for the praises of those who engage in Torah. They declare and say, "Bless the Lord, all servants of the Lord." In other words, you who engage in Torah, bless the Lord. You—praise the holy King; you—crown the King.

203) And the deer, *Malchut*, is crowned in that man. She rises before the King and says, "See in what son I have come to You, in what son I have awakened toward You." And who are those that all their merit is before the King? It is they who stand in the house of the Creator in the nights. They are the ones who are called "servants of the Creator"; they are the ones who are worthy of blessing the King and whose blessing is a blessing, as it is written, "Lift up your hands to the sanctuary, and bless the Lord." You, who merit the holy King being blessed by you, the blessing through you is a blessing.

CORRECTION

WHATEVER YOU FIND THAT YOU HAVE THE POWER TO DO, DO

Pinhas

134) "Whatever you find that you have the power to do, do." How good it is for a person to exert to do his Master's will while the candle is lit and is present over his head, since the light of the candle is a power that is over him. It is written about it, "Let the power of the Lord grow." This is the power of the Creator that is present over the head of the righteous and all those who engage in their Master's will, who is Divinity.

INTERMEDIATE

Bo [Come unto Pharaoh]

211) "One should always consider oneself as though the whole world depends on him," meaning he should consider himself and the whole world as intermediate. And if he keeps one commandment, he sentences himself and the whole world to a scale of merit. And if he commits one transgression, he sentences himself and the whole world to a scale of sin.

SUPPORT FROM THE CREATOR

VaYetze [Jacob Went Out]

350) King David always attached himself to the Creator. He had no concern for any other thing in the world, but to adhere to Him with his soul and will, as it is written, "My soul clings to You." And since he always clung to the Creator, He supported him and did not leave him, as it is written, "Your right supported me." We learn from it that when one comes to cling to the Creator, the Creator holds him and does not leave him.

THE AWAKENING OF THE UPPER ONE

Lech Lecha [Go Forth]

231) The awakening of the upper one is only through the awakening of the lower one because the awakening of the upper one depends on the craving of the lower one.

WHEN ONE COMES TO PURIFY

Lech Lecha [Go Forth]

268) It is written, "I am my beloved's, and his desire is for me." In the beginning, "I am my beloved's," and afterwards, "And his desire is for me." "I am my beloved's" is to first set up a place for him with an awakening from below, and then, "And his desire is for me."

269) Divinity is not present with the wicked. When a person comes to purify and bring himself closer to the Creator, Divinity is over him. It is written about it, "I am my beloved's," first, and then, "And his desire is for me," since when one comes to purify, he is purified.

ONE WHO SANCTIFIES IS SANCTIFIED

VaYikra [The Lord Called]

423) Happy are the righteous, for they have a high share in the Creator, in the holy share, in the King's sanctities, since they sanctify themselves in the sanctities of their Master. And anyone who sanctifies, the Creator sanctifies him, as it is written, "Sanctify yourselves therefore, and be holy." A person who sanctifies himself from below is sanctified from above. And when one sanctifies with the sanctity of his Master, his is clothed with a holy soul, which is the inheritance of the Creator and the assembly of Israel, for the soul is an offspring of ZON. And

then he inherits everything. These are the ones who are called, "children of the Creator," as it is written, "You are the children of the Lord your God."

BUILDING OF THE TEMPLE

Noah

323) "The house, while it was being built, was built of a perfect stone carried." "The house, while it was being built" means it was being built by itself. But did Solomon and all the craftsmen who were there not build it?

324) Indeed, so it is, as it is written, "The lamp shall be made of one piece." If it is one piece, which means that the craftsmen were beating the bar with a sledge-hammer, then what is, "Shall be made"? It means it was made by itself. Of course, everything at the Temple was made by itself, by token and a miracle. When the craftsmen began to work, the work taught the craftsmen who to do it, which they did not know how to do prior to beginning it.

325) What is the reason? It is because the blessing of the Creator was on them. This is why it is written, "While it was being built," for it was built by itself, since it taught the craftsmen the learning, how to begin to do it, and the registration of that work would literally be going out of their eyes, and they would look at that registration and work until the entire house was built.

MAKING THE SANCTUARY

Pekudei [Accounts]

15) When the Creator said unto Moses, "Make the Tabernacle," Moses was bewildered; he did not know what to do until the Creator vividly showed him, as it is written, "And see and make them after their pattern, which is being shown to you in the mountain." "In their pattern" means that the Creator showed Moses everything in

its higher, spiritual shape, and each of the spiritual shapes above was making its shape similar to the fictitious shape that was made below, on earth. This is how Moses knew.

16) "Which is being shown to you in the mountain." The mirror that does not shine, *Malchut* was showing him within her all the manners and forms that are being done below.

17) It is written, "Which is being shown to you." "You" is the mirror that does not shine, *Malchut*, which showed him within her all these forms. And Moses saw each of them in its corrected form, as one who sees within a crystal lamp, within a mirror that shows all the forms.

And when Moses gazed upon them, he found them perplexing, since there, in *Malchut*, everything stood in its spiritual form, but each form equalized its shape to the fictitious shape in this world, in the Tabernacle. It turns out that two forms were apparent: the spiritual one and the fictitious one. This is why Moses was bewildered; he did not know which of them to grasp. The Creator told him, "You with your signs, and I with Mine," that Moses would perceive the fictitious signs in every thing and the Creator perceives the spiritual signs of every thing, and then the spiritual form is placed over the fictitious form. Then Moses was settled in all the work of the Tabernacle.

THE DONKEY DRIVER

Teruma [Donation]

536) Rabbi Yosi and Rabbi Hiya were walking along the way and a donkey driver was leading the donkeys behind them. Rabbi Yosi said to Rabbi Hiya, "We should engage and exert in words of Torah because the Creator is walking ahead of us, hence it is time to make corrections for Him, so He will be with us on this way." A donkey driver stings the donkeys with a piece of wood to make them walk faster.

537) Rabbi Hiya started and said, "It is time to do for the Lord; they have broken Your law." Anytime when the Torah exists in the world and people engage in it, the Creator is seemingly happy with His works, there is joy in all the worlds, and heaven and earth maintain their existence. Moreover, the Creator gathers His entire household and tells them, "See the holy people that I have in the land, the Torah is crowned because of them, see My works, of whom you have said, 'What is man, that I should remember him?'" And they, when they see their Master's joy, they promptly start and say, "And who is as Your people, as Israel, one nation in the land."

538) And when Israel idle away from the Torah, His might seemingly fades, as it is written, "You neglected the Rock who begot you," and then it is written, "And all the host of heaven stand." Hence, it is time to do for the Lord. Those righteous that remained should muster their strength and do good deeds so that the Creator will be strengthened with the righteous and with His camps and armies, since they have broken Your law and the people do not engage in it properly.

539) The donkey driver, who was leading the donkeys behind them, told them, "Please, I would like to know one question." Rabbi Yosi replied, "Certainly, the road is set before us, ask your question." He said, "This verse, had it said, 'It should be done' or 'It was done,' I would say so. What is 'Time'? And also, it is written, 'To do for the Lord.' It should have said, 'Before the Lord.' What is 'To do for the Lord'?" Rabbi Yosi said, "The road is set before us in several ways: One, that we were two and now we are three, for Divinity has been included with us. One, that I thought you were as a dry tree, while you are as fresh as an olive. And one, that you asked very well, and since you have begun to speak, do speak."

540) He started and said, "Time to do for the Lord," since there is a time and there is a time—a time to love and a time

to hate. A time above, faith, *Malchut*, is called 'Time.' This is called 'A time of good will,' and it means that man must always love the Creator, as it is written, 'And you shall love the Lord your God.' About that, the time to love, it is a time, meaning that one must love.

541) "And there is another time, which is another god, which one must hate and not follow him with his heart. Hence, it is a time to hate. And this is why it is written, 'Tell your brother Aaron that he shall not enter at any time into the holy place.'

542) "When Israel engage in Torah and in the *Mitzvot* [commandments] of the Torah, at that time the holy faith, *Malchut*, is corrected in her corrections and is fully adorned as it should be. And when Israel do not engage in Torah, at that time it is seemingly not corrected and is incomplete, and not in the light. Then it is time to do for the Lord.

543) "What is 'To do for the Lord'? It is written, 'That God has created to do.' What is 'To do'? It means that bodies of demons remained, which were not done because the day has been sanctified, and they remained to do because they are spirits without bodies. Here, too, it is time to do, the time remained without correction and without wholeness because they have broken Your law, for Israel have been idling away from words of Torah, for that time is so, either ascending or descending for Israel. If they engage in Torah, it ascends. If they idle away from the Torah, it descends."

544) Rabbi Yosi said, "It is indeed beneath you to lead the donkeys behind us. Happy is this road, for we have been rewarded with hearing this. Happy is the generation that Rabbi Shimon is inside it, that wisdom is found even among the mountains." Rabbi Yosi and Rabbi Hiya came down from their donkeys and the three of them walked along the way.

BY WHAT ONE ASSUMES IN ONE'S HEART

VaYera [The Lord Appeared]

153) "Her husband is known in the gates" is the Creator, who is known and attained by what each assumes in his heart, to the extent that he can attain by the spirit of the wisdom. Thus, according to that which one assumes in one's heart, He is known in his heart. This is why it is written, "Known in the gates," in those measures [the same word as "gates" in Hebrew] that each assumes in his heart. But it should be properly known that there is no one who can attain and know Him.

154) "Her husband is known in the gates." What are gates? It is written, "Lift up your heads, O gates." By these gates, which are high degrees, by them is the Creator known. Were it not for these gates, they would not be able to attain in Him.

CORRECTION IS ONLY IN THIS WORLD

Korah

31) One should not say, "When I come into that world, I will beg for mercy of the King, and will repent before Him." Rather, it is written about that, "There is no deed or contemplation or knowledge or wisdom" once a person departs this world. If one wishes for the Holy King to shine for him in that world and give him a share in the next world, he should engage in including his deeds in the right in this world, and that all his actions will be for the Creator.

248 ORGANS OF THE SOUL

Shoftim [Judges]

8) Happy is he who grips to the tree of life, ZA, with his body and with his organs, which is a candle. Each and every branch is

a candle of Mitzva, in his 248 Mitzvot, which correspond to the 248 organs, a candle of Mitzva for each organ.

9) When both of them, the tree of life and the candle of Mitzva, meaning ZA and Malchut, grip the same person, the words, "And he looked, and, behold, the bush burned with fire, and the bush was not consumed," come true, referring to man. And SAM and the serpent and all his appointees, which are thorns, grip to the man's body and burn, while the branches of the bush, its fruits, and the leaves do not burn. This is what the Creator showed Moses.

365 TENDONS OF THE SOUL

Pekudei [Accounts]

151) Explaining the correction of Yesod of the Malchut, which was done by the effect of ZA. There are 365 tendons under the influence of the hoses—white, black, red, included in one another, and they have become one color. These tendons are reticulated in seventeen nets, and each net is called "tendons." They are webbed in one another and descend at the end of the abyss, the Yesod in Malchut, called "abyss." Under these, two nets stand in a mirror of iron and two other nets in a mirror of copper.

Tendons are illumination of Hochma on the left of Bina, which extends to Malchut. They are called tendons because they are from Bina, since KHB is called Mocha, Atzamot, Gidin.

A GOAT FOR AZAZEL

Emor [speak]

236) "And Aaron shall cast lots for the two goats." This is an honor for Azazel because have you seen that a servant casts lots equally with his master? Usually, a servant receives what his master gives, but because on that day, Sam'el was ready to gossip

about Israel, to prevent him from having something to say, he is given a share in it.

238) And not only that, each time the slanderer is ready and is given permission, it should be given something to deal with, and leave Israel alone.

REBUKE OUT OF LOVE

Ki Tazria [When a Woman Delivers]

72) How do we know that? It is written, "Better is open rebuke than love that is hidden," which means that open rebuke is better. And if the rebuke is out of love, it is hidden from people. Similarly, one who rebukes one's friend with love must hide his words from people so his friend will not be shamed by them. And if his words are open before people, they are not with love.

73) So is the Creator. When He rebukes a person, He rebukes him with love in everything. First, He strikes him in his body, from within. If he repents, good. If not, He strikes him under his clothes. And these are called "Pangs of love." If he repents, good. If not, He strikes him openly in his face, in front of everyone, so people will look at him and know that he is a sinner and is not loved by his Master.

A YEAR—A CYCLE OF CORRECTION

Emor [Speak]

193) When this *Shofar* [festive horn] awakens and people repent from their iniquities, they must draw from below by the sound of a *Shofar*, and that sound rises up. At that time, another *Shofar* awakens above, meaning *Bina*, *Rachamim* [mercies] awaken, and the *Din* [judgment] departs...

Every *Rosh Hashanah* [Hebrew New Year's Eve], the world returns to its beginning, as it was on the fourth day of creation, when *Malchut* was diminished. This is so because *Malchut* is called "a year," and the twelve months of the year are the order of her corrections from her beginning to the end of correction. If the year is completed and its correction is not completed, she is given for us to correct on the next year, and we need to start over from initiation, as she was on the fourth day of creation. And so it is every single year until the end of correction.

PRAYEA PRAYER FOR THE POOR

Yitro [Jethro]

414) "A Prayer for the poor, when he is cloaked, and pours out his complaint before the Lord." All the prayers of Israel are prayers, and a prayer for the poor is the highest because it rises up to the King's throne and crowns His head, and the Creator is praised indeed in that prayer. For this reason, a prayer for the poor is called "a prayer."

415) "When he is cloaked." This cloaking is not cloaking of clothes, since he has no clothes. Rather, it is written here "When he is cloaked," and it is written there, "Who are cloaked in hunger." Here, too, "When he is cloaked" is in hunger. "And pours out his complaint before the Lord" means that he will cry out before his Master. It is convenient for him before the Creator because the world exists in Him when there are no other sustainers of the world in the world. Woe unto one that that poor cries out about him to his Master, since the poor is the closest to the King, as it is written, "And it shall come to pass that when he cries out to Me, I will hear him, for I am gracious."

416) And as for the rest of the people in the world, at times He hears them, at times He does not hear, since the abode of the Creator is in those broken *Kelim* [vessels], as it is written, "And

the oppressed and the low-spirited." And it is written, "The Lord is near to the broken-hearted." "A broken and an oppressed heart, O God, You will not despise."

GATES OF TEARS

Pekudei [Accounts]

489) Above the palace door, there is another door, which the Creator dug out of *Dinim* [judgments] of *Miftacha* [key], which is "A well that the ministers have dug." It opens three times a day, meaning that three lines illuminate in it, and it does not close, and stands open for those who repent, who have shed tears in their prayer before their Master.

And all the gates and the doors close until they enter the domain, except for these gates, which are called "gates of tears." They are open and need no permission, since the first gate is "Sin crouches at the door," and there the *Malchut* of *Man'ula* [lock] is present, ten thousand. In that discernment, repentance does not help, for it is the quality of judgment. However, the Creator dug a second door above it, from the *Miftacha*, which is *Malchut* that is mitigated in *Bina*, and there repentance helps.

490) When this prayer in tears rises through these gates, that *Ofan*, who is an angel from *Malchut*, comes. He is called *Ofan*, and he stands over six hundred big animals, and his name is Yerachmiel. He takes the prayer in tears, the prayer enters and is sanctified above, and the tears remain here. And they are written in a door that the Creator dug.

The prayer in tears raises MAN for correction of the key, to raise *Malchut* to *Bina*; hence, the prayer is accepted and the tears remain carved on the door, where they cause the mitigation of *Malchut* in *Bina*. *Dema* [tearing] comes from the word mixing, for it mixes and mingles *Malchut* in *Bina*.

PRAYER OF MANY

VaYechi [Jacob Lived]

514) Indeed, all the prayers in the world, meaning prayers of many, are prayers. But a solitary prayer does not enter before the Holy King, unless with great force. This is so because before the prayer enters to be crowned in its place, the Creator watches it, observes it, and observes the sins and merits of that person, which He does not do with a prayer of many, where several of the prayers are not from righteous, and they all enter before the Creator and He does not notice their iniquities.

515) "He has regarded the prayer of the destitute." He turns the prayer and examines it from all sides, and considers with which desire the prayer was made, who is the person who prayed that prayer, and what are his deeds. Hence, one should pray one's prayer in the collective, since He does not despise their prayer, even though they are not all with intent and the will of heart, as it is written, "He has regarded the prayer of the destitute." Thus, He only observes the prayer of an individual, but with a prayer of many, He does not despise their prayer, even though they are unworthy.

516) "He has regarded the prayer of the destitute" means that He accepts his prayer, but it is an individual who is mingled with many. Hence, his prayer is as a prayer of many. And who is an individual who is mingled with many? It is Jacob, for he contains both sides—right and left, Abraham and Isaac, and he calls out to his sons and prays his prayer for them.

And what is the prayer that is fully granted above? It is a prayer that the children of Israel will not perish in the exile. This is because every prayer in favor of Divinity is received in full. And when Israel are in exile, Divinity is with them. This is why the prayer is regarded as being in favor of Divinity and is accepted in full.

I DWELL AMONG MY OWN PEOPLE

VaYetze [Jacob Went Out]

284) Wherever a person prays his prayer, he should incorporate himself in the public, in the manifold public, as it is written about Shunammite when Elisha told her, "Would you be spoken for to the king or to the captain of the army?" "Would you be spoken for to the king," since that day was the festival of the first day of the year, and the day when *Malchut* of the firmament rules and sentences the world. At that time, the Creator is called "The king of the sentence," and this is why he told her, "Would you be spoken for to the king," since he called the Creator "King."

285) And she said, "I dwell among my own people." In other words, she said, "I have no wish to be mentioned above, but to put my head among the masses and not leave the public." Similarly, man should be included in the public and not stand out as unique, so the slanderers will not look at him and mention his sins.

QUANTITY AND QUALITY

Teruma [Donation]

694) When the Creator comes to the house of gathering and the whole people come together, pray, thank, and praise the Creator, it is the glory of the King, for the Creator is established with beauty and correction to rise up to *Aba* and *Ima*.

695) When the Creator comes to the house of gathering early and the people did not come to pray and to praise the Creator, the whole of the governance above and all those upper appointees and camps break from that elevation of theirs, which they correct in the corrections of the King, the Creator.

696) The reason why they break from their elevation is that when Israel below establish their prayers and litanies, and praise the

high King, all those upper camps praise and become corrected in the sacred correction, since all the upper camps are friends with Israel below, to praise the Creator together so that the rising of the Creator will be above and below at the same time.

697) And when the angels come to be friends with Israel, to praise the Creator together, and Israel below do not come to establish their prayers and litanies, and to praise their Master, all the holy camps in the upper government break from their corrections. It is so because they do not rise in an ascension, since they cannot praise their Master because the praises of the Creator must be above and below together, upper and lower at the same time. This is why it was said, "Deficiency of thinness," and not "Deficient of a king," as it concerns only the camps of angels, not the King Himself.

698) And even though not many came to the house of gathering, but only ten, the upper camps come into these ten, to be friends with them and to praise the Creator, since all the King's corrections are in ten. Hence, ten are enough, if they are not more.

FURTHER READING

To help you determine which book you would like to read next, we have divided the books into six categories—Beginners, Intermediate, Advanced, Good for All, Textbooks, and For Children. The first three categories are divided by the level of prior knowledge readers are required to have in order to easily relate to the book. The Beginners Category requires no prior knowledge. The Intermediate Category requires reading one or two beginners' books first; and the Advanced level requires one or two books of each of the previous categories. The fourth category, Good for All, includes books you can always enjoy, whether you are a complete novice or well versed in Kabbalah.

The fifth category—Textbooks—includes translations of authentic source materials from earlier Kabbalists, such as the Ari, Rav Yehuda Ashlag (Baal HaSulam) and his son and successor, Rav Baruch Ashlag (the Rabash). As its name implies, the sixth category—For Children—includes books that are suitable for children ages 3 and above. Those are not Kabbalah books per se, but are rather inspired by the teaching and convey the Kabbalistic message of love and unity.

Additional material that has not yet been published can be found at www.kabbalah.info. All materials on this site, including e-versions of published books, can be downloaded free of charge directly from the store at www.kabbalahbooks.info.

BEGINNERS

A Guide to the Hidden Wisdom of Kabbalah

A Guide to the Hidden Wisdom of Kabbalah is a light and reader-friendly guide to beginners in Kabbalah, covering everything from the history of Kabbalah to how this wisdom can help resolve the world crisis.

The book is set up in three parts: Part 1 covers the history, facts, and fallacies about Kabbalah, and introduces its key concepts. Part 2 tells you all about the spiritual worlds and other neat stuff like the meaning of letters and the power of music. Part 3 covers the implementation of Kabbalah at a time of world crisis.

Kabbalah Revealed

This is the most clearly written, reader-friendly guide to making sense of the surrounding world. Each of its six chapters focuses on a different aspect of the wisdom of Kabbalah, illuminating its teachings and explaining them using various examples from our day-to-day lives.

The first three chapters in *Kabbalah Revealed* explain why the world is in a state of crisis, how our growing desires promote progress as well as alienation, and why the biggest deterrent to achieving positive change is rooted in our own spirits. Chapters Four through Six offer a prescription for positive change. In these chapters, we learn how we can use our spirits to build a personally peaceful life in harmony with all of Creation.

Wondrous Wisdom

This book offers an initial course on Kabbalah. Like all the books presented here, *Wondrous Wisdom* is based solely on authentic teachings passed down from Kabbalist teacher to student over thousands of years. At the heart of the book is a sequence of lessons revealing the nature of Kabbalah's wisdom and explaining how to attain it. For every person questioning "Who am I really?" and "Why am I on this planet?" this book is a must.

Awakening to Kabbalah

A distinctive, personal, and awe-filled introduction to an ancient wisdom tradition. In this book, Rav Laitman offers a deeper understanding of the fundamental teachings of Kabbalah, and how you can use its wisdom to clarify your relationship with others and the world around you.

Using language both scientific and poetic, he probes the most profound questions of spirituality and existence. This provocative, unique guide will inspire and invigorate you to see beyond the world as it is and the limitations of your everyday life, become closer to the Creator, and reach new depths of the soul.

Kabbalah, Science, and the Meaning of Life

Science explains the mechanisms that sustain life; Kabbalah explains why life exists. In *Kabbalah, Science, and the Meaning of Life*, Rav Laitman combines science and spirituality in a captivating dialogue that reveals life's meaning.

For thousands of years Kabbalists have been writing that the world is a single entity divided into separate beings. Today the cutting-edge science of quantum physics states a very similar idea: that at the most fundamental level of matter, we are all literally one.

Science proves that reality is affected by the observer who examines it; and so does Kabbalah. But Kabbalah makes an even bolder statement: even the Creator, the Maker of reality, is within the observer. In other words, God is inside of us; He doesn't exist anywhere else. When we pass away, so does He.

These earthshaking concepts and more are eloquently introduced so that even readers new to Kabbalah or science will easily understand them. Therefore, if you're just a little curious about why you are here, what life means, and what you can do to enjoy it more, this book is for you.

From Chaos to Harmony

Many researchers and scientists agree that the ego is the reason behind the perilous state our world is in today. Laitman's groundbreaking book not only demonstrates that egoism has been the basis for all suffering throughout human history, but also shows how we can turn our plight to pleasure.

The book contains a clear analysis of the human soul and its problems, and provides a "roadmap" of what we need to do to once again be happy. *From Chaos to Harmony* explains how we can rise to a new level of existence on personal, social, national, and international levels.

Kabbalah for Beginners

Kabbalah for Beginners is a book for all those seeking answers to life's essential questions. We all want to know why we are here, why there is pain, and how we can make life more enjoyable. The four parts of this book provide us with reliable answers to these questions, as well as clear explanations of the gist of Kabbalah and its practical implementations.

Part One discusses the discovery of the wisdom of Kabbalah, and how it was developed, and finally concealed until our time. Part Two introduces the gist of the wisdom of Kabbalah, using ten easy drawings to help us understand the structure of the spiritual worlds, and how they relate to our world. Part Three reveals Kabbalistic concepts that are largely unknown to the public, and Part Four elaborates on practical means you and I can take, to make our lives better and more enjoyable for us and for our children.

INTERMEDIATE

The Kabbalah Experience

The depth of the wisdom revealed in the questions and answers within this book will inspire readers to reflect and contemplate. This is not a book to race through, but rather one that should be read thoughtfully and carefully. With this approach, readers will begin to experience a growing sense of enlightenment while simply absorbing the answers to the questions every Kabbalah student asks along the way.

The Kabbalah Experience is a guide from the past to the future, revealing situations that all students of Kabbalah will experience at some point along their journeys. For those who cherish every moment in life, this book offers unparalleled insights into the timeless wisdom of Kabbalah.

The Path of Kabbalah

This unique book combines beginners' material with more advanced concepts and teachings. If you have read a book or two of Laitman's, you will find this book very easy to relate to.

While touching upon basic concepts such as perception of reality and Freedom of Choice, *The Path of Kabbalah* goes deeper and expands beyond the scope of beginners' books. The structure of the worlds, for example, is explained in greater detail here than in the "pure" beginners' books. Also described is the spiritual root of mundane matters such as the Hebrew calendar and the holidays.

ADVANCED

The Science of Kabbalah

Kabbalist and scientist Rav Michael Laitman, PhD, designed this book to introduce readers to the special language and terminology of the authentic wisdom of Kabbalah. Here, Rav Laitman reveals authentic Kabbalah in a manner both rational and mature. Readers are gradually led to understand the logical design of the Universe and the life that exists in it.

The Science of Kabbalah, a revolutionary work unmatched in its clarity, depth, and appeal to the intellect, will enable readers to approach the more technical works of Baal HaSulam (Rabbi Yehuda Ashlag), such as *The Study of the Ten Sefirot* and *The Book of Zohar*. Readers of this book will enjoy the satisfying answers to the riddles of life that only authentic Kabbalah provides. Travel through the pages and prepare for an astonishing journey into the Upper Worlds.

Introduction to the Book of Zohar

This volume, along with *The Science of Kabbalah*, is a required preparation for those who wish to understand the hidden message of *The Book of Zohar*. Among the many helpful topics dealt with in this text is an introduction to the "language of roots and branches," without which the stories in *The Zohar* are mere fable and legend. *Introduction to the Book of Zohar* will provide readers with the necessary tools to understand authentic Kabbalah as it was originally meant to be—as a means to attain the Upper Worlds.

The Book of Zohar:
Annotations to the Ashlag commentary

The Book of Zohar (*The Book of Radiance*) is an age-old source of wisdom and the basis for all Kabbalistic literature. Since its appearance nearly 2,000 years ago, it has been the primary, and often only, source used by Kabbalists.

For centuries, Kabbalah was hidden from the public, which was deemed not yet ready to receive it. However, our generation has been designated by Kabbalists as the first generation that *is* ready to grasp the concepts in *The Zohar*. Now we can put these principles into practice in our lives.

Written in a unique and metaphorical language, *The Book of Zohar* enriches our understanding of reality and widens our worldview. Although the text deals with one subject only—how to relate to the Creator—it approaches it from different angles. This allows each of us to find the particular phrase or word that will carry us into the depths of this profound and timeless wisdom.

GOOD FOR ALL

The Point in the Heart

The Point in the Heart; a Source of Delight for My Soul is a unique collection of excerpts from a man whose wisdom has earned him devoted students in North America and the world over. Michael Laitman is a scientist, a Kabbalist, and a great thinker who presents ancient wisdom in a compelling style.

This book does not profess to teach Kabbalah, but rather gently introduces ideas from the teaching. *The Point in the Heart* is a window to a new perception. As the author himself testifies to the wisdom of Kabbalah, "It is a science of emotion, a science of pleasure. You are welcome to open and to taste."

Attaining the Worlds Beyond

From the introduction to *Attaining the Worlds Beyond*: "...Not feeling well on the Jewish New Year's Eve of September 1991, my teacher called me to his bedside and handed me his notebook, saying, 'Take it and learn from it.' The following morning, he perished in my arms, leaving me and many of his other disciples without guidance in this world.

"He used to say, 'I want to teach you to turn to the Creator, rather than to me, because He is the only strength, the only Source of all that exists, the only one who can really help you, and He awaits your prayers for help. When you seek help in your search for freedom from the bondage of this world, help in elevating yourself above this world, help in finding the self, and help in determining your purpose in life, you must turn to the Creator, who sends you all those aspirations in order to compel you to turn to Him.'"

Attaining the Worlds Beyond holds within it the content of that notebook, as well as other inspiring texts. This book reaches out to all those seekers who want to find a logical, reliable way to understand the world's phenomena. This fascinating introduction to the wisdom of Kabbalah will enlighten the mind, invigorate the heart, and move readers to the depths of their souls.

Bail Yourself Out

In *Bail Yourself Out: how you can emerge strong from the world crisis*, Laitman introduces several extraordinary concepts that weave into a complete solution: 1) The crisis is essentially not financial, but *psychological*: People have stopped trusting each other, and where there is no trust there is no trade, but only war, isolation, and pain. 2) This mistrust is a result of a *natural process* that's been evolving for millennia and is culminating today. 3) To resolve the crisis, we must first *understand* the process that created the alienation. 4) The first, and most important, step to understanding the crisis is to *inform* people about this natural process through books, such as *Bail Yourself Out*, TV, cinema, and any other means of communication. 5) With this information, we will "*revamp*" our relationships and build them on trust, collaboration, and most importantly, care. This mending process will guarantee that we and our families will prosper in a world of plenty.

Basic Concepts in Kabbalah

This is a book to help readers cultivate an *approach to the concepts* of Kabbalah, to spiritual objects, and to spiritual terms. By reading and re-reading in this book, one develops internal observations, senses, and approaches that did not previously exist within. These newly acquired observations are like sensors that "feel" the space around us that is hidden from our ordinary senses.

Hence, *Basic Concepts in Kabbalah* is intended to foster the contemplation of spiritual terms. Once we are integrated with these terms, we can begin to see, with our inner vision, the unveiling of the spiritual structure that surrounds us, almost as if a mist has been lifted.

This book is not aimed at the study of facts. Instead, it is a book for those who wish to awaken the deepest and subtlest sensations they can possess.

Children of Tomorrow: Guidelines for Raising Happy Children in the 21st Century

Children of Tomorrow is a new beginning for you and your children. Imagine being able to hit the reboot button and get it right this time. No hassle, no stress, and best of all—no guessing.

The big revelation is that raising kids is all about games and play, relating to them as small grownups, and making all major decisions together. You will be surprised to discover how teaching kids about positive things like friendship and caring for others automatically spills into other areas of our lives through the day.

Open any page and you will find thought-provoking quotes about every aspect of children's lives: parent-children relations, friendships and conflicts, and a clear picture of how schools should be designed and function. This book offers a fresh perspective on how to raise our children, with the goal being the happiness of all children everywhere.

The Wise Heart:
Tales and allegories by three contemporary sages

"Our inner work is to tune our hearts and our senses to perceive the spiritual world," says Michael Laitman in the poem Spiritual Wave. The Wise Heart is a lovingly crafted anthology comprised of tales and allegories by Kabbalist Dr. Michael Laitman, his mentor, Rav Baruch Ashlag (Rabash), and Rabash's father and mentor, Rav Yehuda Ashlag, author of the acclaimed *Sulam* (Ladder) commentary on *The Book of Zohar*.

Kabbalah students and enthusiasts in Kabbalah often wonder what the spiritual world actually feels like to a Kabbalist. The allegories in this delicate compilation provide a glimpse into those feelings.

The poems herein are excerpts from letters and lessons given by these three spiritual giants to their students through the years. They offer surprising and often amusing depictions of human nature, with a loving and tender touch that is truly unique to Kabbalists. Indeed, *The Wise Heart* is a gift of wisdom and delight for any wisdom seeking heart.

TEXTBOOKS

Shamati

Rav Michael Laitman's words on the book: Among all the texts and notes that were used by my teacher, Rav Baruch Shalom Halevi Ashlag (the Rabash), there was one special notebook he always carried. This notebook contained the transcripts of his conversations with his father, Rav Yehuda Leib Halevi Ashlag (Baal HaSulam), author of the *Sulam* (Ladder) commentary on *The Book of Zohar*, *The Study of the Ten Sefirot* (a commentary on the texts of the Kabbalist, Ari), and of many other works on Kabbalah.

Not feeling well on the Jewish New Year's Eve of September 1991, the Rabash summoned me to his bedside and handed me a notebook, whose cover contained only one word, *Shamati* (I Heard). As he handed the notebook, he said, "Take it and learn from it." The following morning, my teacher perished in my arms, leaving me and many of his other disciples without guidance in this world.

Committed to Rabash's legacy to disseminate the wisdom of Kabbalah, I published the notebook just as it was written, thus retaining the text's transforming powers. Among all the books of Kabbalah, *Shamati* is a unique and compelling creation.

Kabbalah for the Student

Kabbalah for the Student offers authentic texts by Rav Yehuda Ashlag, author of the *Sulam* (Ladder) commentary on *The Book of Zohar*, his son and successor, Rav Baruch Ashlag, as well as other great Kabbalists. It also offers illustrations that accurately depict the evolution of the Upper Worlds as Kabbalists experience them. The book also contains several explanatory essays that help us understand the texts within.

In *Kabbalah for the Student*, Rav Michael Laitman, PhD, Rav Baruch Ashlag's personal assistant and prime student, compiled all the texts a Kabbalah student would need in order to attain the spiritual worlds. In his daily lessons, Rav Laitman bases his teaching on these inspiring texts, thus helping novices and veterans alike to better understand the spiritual path we undertake on our fascinating journey to the Higher Realms.

Rabash—the Social Writings

Rav Baruch Shalom HaLevi Ashlag (Rabash) played a remarkable role in the history of Kabbalah. He provided us with the necessary final link connecting the wisdom of Kabbalah to our human experience. His father and teacher was the great Kabbalist, Rav Yehuda Leib HaLevi Ashlag, known as Baal HaSulam for his *Sulam* (Ladder) commentary on *The Book of Zohar*. Yet, if not for the essays of Rabash, his father's efforts to disclose the wisdom of Kabbalah to all would have been in vain. Without those essays, few would be able to achieve the spiritual attainment that Baal HaSulam so desperately wanted us to obtain.

The writings in this book aren't just for reading. They are more like an experiential user's guide. It is very important to work with them in order to see what they truly contain. The reader should try to put them into practice by living out the emotions Rabash so masterfully describes. He always advised his students to summarize the articles, to work with the texts, and those who attempt it discover that it always yields new insights. Thus, readers are advised to work with the texts, summarize them, translate them, and implement them in the group. Those who do so will discover the power in the writings of Rabash.

Gems of Wisdom:
Words of the great Kabbalists from all generations

Through the millennia, Kabbalists have bequeathed us with numerous writings. In their compositions, they have laid out a structured method that can lead, step by step, unto a world of eternity and wholeness.

Gems of wisdom is a collection of selected excerpts from the writings of the greatest Kabbalists from all generations, with particular emphasis on the writings of Rav Yehuda Leib HaLevi Ashlag (Baal HaSulam), author of the *Sulam* [Ladder] commentary of *The Book of Zohar*.

The sections have been arranged by topics, to provide the broadest view possible on each topic. This book is a useful guide to any person desiring spiritual advancement.

FOR CHILDREN

Together Forever

On the surface, *Together Forever* is a children's story. But like all good children's stories, it transcends boundaries of age, culture, and upbringing.

In *Together Forever*, the author tells us that if we are patient and endure the trials we encounter along our life's path, we will become stronger, braver, and wiser. Instead of growing weaker, we will learn to create our own magic and our own wonders as only a magician canIn this warm, tender tale, Michael Laitman shares with children and parents alike some of the gems and charms of the spiritual world. The wisdom of Kabbalah is filled with spellbinding stories. *Together Forever* is yet another gift from this ageless source of wisdom, whose lessons make our lives richer, easier, and far more fulfilling.

Miracles Can Happen

"Miracles Can Happen," Princes Peony," and "Mary and the Paints" are only three of ten beautiful stories for children ages 3-10. Written especially for children, these short tales convey a single message of love, unity, and care for all beings. The unique illustrations were carefully crafted to contribute to the overall message of the book, and a child who's heard or read any story in this collection is guaranteed to go to sleep smiling.

The Baobab that Opened Its Heart: And Other Nature Tales for Children

The Baobab that Opened Its Heart is a collection of stories for children, but not just for them. The stories in this collection were written with the love of nature, of people, and specifically with children in mind. They all share the desire to tell nature's tale of unity, connectedness, and love.

Kabbalah teaches that love is nature's guiding force, the reason for creation. The stories in this book convey it in the unique way that Kabbalah engenders in its students. The variety of authors and diversity of styles allows each reader to find the story that they like most.

ABOUT BNEI BARUCH

Bnei Baruch is an international group of Kabbalists who share the wisdom of Kabbalah with the entire world. The study materials (in over 30 languages) are authentic Kabbalah texts that were passed down from generation to generation.

HISTORY AND ORIGIN

In 1991, following the passing of his teacher, Rav Baruch Shalom HaLevi Ashlag (The Rabash), Michael Laitman, Professor of Ontology and the Theory of Knowledge, PhD in Philosophy and Kabbalah, and MSc in Medical Bio-Cybernetics, established a Kabbalah study group called "Bnei Baruch." He called it Bnei Baruch (Sons of Baruch) to commemorate his mentor, whose side he never left in the final twelve years of his life, from 1979 to 1991. Dr. Laitman had been Ashlag's prime student and personal assistant, and is recognized as the successor to Rabash's teaching method.

The Rabash was the firstborn son and successor of Rav Yehuda Leib HaLevi Ashlag, the greatest Kabbalist of the 20th century. Rav Ashlag authored the most authoritative and comprehensive commentary on *The Book of Zohar*, titled *The Sulam* (Ladder) *Commentary*. He was the first to reveal the complete method for spiritual ascent, and thus was known as Baal HaSulam (Owner of the Ladder).

Bnei Baruch bases its entire study method on the path paved by these two great spiritual leaders.

THE STUDY METHOD

The unique study method developed by Baal HaSulam and his son, the Rabash, is taught and applied on a daily basis by Bnei Baruch. This method relies on authentic Kabbalah sources such as *The Book of Zohar*, by Rabbi Shimon Bar-Yochai, *The Tree of Life*, by the Ari, and *The Study of the Ten Sefirot*, by Baal HaSulam.

While the study relies on authentic Kabbalah sources, it is carried out in simple language and uses a scientific, contemporary approach. The unique combination of an academic study method and personal experiences broadens the students' perspective and awards them a new perception of the reality they live in. Those on the spiritual path are thus given the necessary tools to study themselves and their surrounding reality.

Bnei Baruch is a diverse movement of tens of thousands of students worldwide. Students can choose their own paths and intensity of their studies according to their unique conditions and abilities.

THE MESSAGE

The essence of the message disseminated by Bnei Baruch is universal: unity of the people, unity of nations and love of man.

For millennia, Kabbalists have been teaching that love of man should be the foundation of all human relations. This love prevailed in the days of Abraham, Moses, and the group of Kabbalists that they established. If we make room for these seasoned, yet contemporary values, we will discover that we possess the power to put differences aside and unite.

The wisdom of Kabbalah, hidden for millennia, has been waiting for the time when we would be sufficiently developed and ready to implement its message. Now, it is emerging as a solution that can unite diverse factions everywhere, enabling us, as individuals and as a society, to meet today's challenges.

ACTIVITIES

Bnei Baruch was established on the premise that "only by expansion of the wisdom of Kabbalah to the public can we be awarded complete redemption" (Baal HaSulam). Therefore, Bnei Baruch offers a variety of ways for people to explore and discover the purpose of their lives, providing careful guidance for beginners and advanced students alike.

Internet

Bnei Baruch's international website, www.kab.info, presents the authentic wisdom of Kabbalah using essays, books, and original texts. It is by far the most expansive source of authentic Kabbalah material on the Internet, containing a unique, extensive library for readers to thoroughly explore the wisdom of Kabbalah. Additionally, the media archive, www.kabbalahmedia.info, contains thousands of media items, downloadable books, and a vast reservoir of texts, video and audio files in many languages.

Bnei Baruch's online Kabbalah Education Center offers free Kabbalah courses for beginners, initiating students into this profound body of knowledge in the comfort of their own homes.

Dr. Laitman's daily lessons are also aired live on www.kab.tv, along with complementary texts and diagrams.

All these services are provided free of charge.

Television

In Israel, Bnei Baruch established its own channel, no. 66 on both cable and satellite, which broadcasts 24/7 Kabbalah TV. The channel is also aired on the Internet at www.kab.tv. All broadcasts on the channel are free of charge. Programs are adapted for all levels, from complete beginners to the most advanced.

Conferences

Twice a year, students gather for a weekend of study and socializing at conferences in various locations in the U.S., as well as an annual convention in Israel. These gatherings provide a great setting for meeting like-minded people, for bonding, and for expanding one's understanding of the wisdom.

Kabbalah Books

Bnei Baruch publishes authentic books, written by Baal HaSulam, his son, the Rabash, as well as books by Dr. Michael Laitman. The books of Rav Ashlag and Rabash are essential for complete understanding of the teachings of authentic Kabbalah, explained in Laitman's lessons.

Dr. Laitman writes his books in a clear, contemporary style based on the key concepts of Baal HaSulam. These books are a vital link between today's readers and the original texts. All the books are available for sale, as well as for free download.

Paper

Kabbalah Today is a free paper produced and disseminated by Bnei Baruch in many languages, including English, Hebrew, Spanish, and Russian. It is apolitical, non-commercial, and written in a clear, contemporary style. The purpose of *Kabbalah Today* is to expose the vast knowledge hidden in the wisdom of Kabbalah at no cost and in a clear, engaging style for readers everywhere.

Kabbalah Lessons

As Kabbalists have been doing for centuries, Laitman gives a daily lesson. The lessons are given in Hebrew and are simultaneously interpreted into seven languages—English, Russian, Spanish, French, German, Italian, and Turkish—by skilled and experienced interpreters. As with everything else, the live broadcast is free of charge.

FUNDING

Bnei Baruch is a non-profit organization for teaching and sharing the wisdom of Kabbalah. To maintain its independence and purity of intentions, Bnei Baruch is not supported, funded, or otherwise tied to any government or political organization.

Since the bulk of its activity is provided free of charge, the prime sources of funding for the group's activities are donations and tithing—contributed by students on a voluntary basis—and Dr. Laitman's books, which are sold at cost.

HOW TO CONTACT BNEI BARUCH

1057 Steeles Avenue West, Suite 532
Toronto, ON, M2R 3X1
Canada

Bnei Baruch USA,
2009 85th street, #51,
Brooklyn, New York, 11214
USA

E-mail: info@kabbalah.info
Web site: www.kabbalah.info

Toll free in USA and Canada:
1-866-LAITMAN
Fax: 1-905 886 9697